More Windows 7 for Seniors

Studio Visual Steps

More Windows 7 for Seniors

Get more out of your computer!

Visual Steps™

www.visualsteps.nl

This book has been written using the Visual Steps™ method.
Cover design by Studio Willemien Haagsma bNO

© 2010 Visual Steps
Edited by Rilana Groot, Jolanda Ligthart, and Mara Kok
Translated by Irene Venditti, *i-write* translation services and Chris Hollingsworth, *1ˢᵗ Resources*.
Editor in chief: Ria Beentjes

First printing: September 2010
ISBN 978 90 5905 346 5

Do you have questions or suggestions?
E-mail: info@visualsteps.com

Would you like more information?
www.visualsteps.com

Website for this book:
www.visualsteps.com/morewin7
Here you can register your book.

Register your book
We will keep you aware of any important changes that are necessary to you as a user of the book. You can also take advantage of our periodic newsletter informing you of our product releases, company news, tips & tricks, special offers, free guides, etcetera.

Table of Contents

Foreword   13
Visual Steps Newsletter   13
Introduction to Visual Steps™   14
What You Will Need   15
Prior Computer Experience   15
How to Use This Book   16
The Screenshots   17
Website   18
Test Your Knowledge   18
For Teachers   18

1. Adapting Your Work Environment   19
   1.1 The Desktop   20
   1.2 Creating Shortcuts   21
   1.3 Moving Icons   23
   1.4 Enabling the *Auto Arrange Icons* Option   25
   1.5 Change the Shortcut's Icon   27
   1.6 Deleting an Icon   29
   1.7 Taskbar Settings   30
   1.8 Shortcuts on the Taskbar   34
   1.9 Pinning a Program To the Taskbar   34
   1.10 Unpinning a Program From the Taskbar   36
   1.11 Modifying the System Tray   36
   1.12 Modifying the Start Menu   42
   1.13 Using Gadgets   44
 1.14 Exercises   48
 1.15 Background Information   49
 1.16 Tips   50

2. Setting Up Windows   53
   2.1 The *Control Panel*   54
   2.2 Setting the Date and Time   55
   2.3 The *Ease of Access Center*   56
   2.4 Setting Default Programs   59
   2.5 Associating a File Type With a Program   62
   2.6 Setting the AutoPlay Options for CDs, DVDs and
      Other Multimedia   65
 2.7 Exercises   68
 2.8 Background Information   69

2.9 Tips   70

3. User Accounts   71
3.1 Types of User Accounts   72
3.2 Change Your Name   72
3.3 Select a Different Picture   75
3.4 Creating a New User Account   77
3.5 Deleting a User Account   78
3.6 Setting a Password for a User Account   80
3.7 Changing a Password   84
3.8 Creating a Password Reset Disk   85
3.9 Using the *Guest Account*   92
3.10 Quickly Switch Between Users   93
3.11 *User Account Control*   97
3.12 *Parental Controls*   99
3.13 Deleting a Password   102
3.14 Exercises   104
3.15 Background Information   105

4. Your Computer   107
4.1 What Is Inside Your Computer?   108
4.2 The Hard Disk Properties   109
4.3 Gigabyte, Megabyte, Kilobyte   110
4.4 Your DVD drive   111
4.5 Removable Media   114
4.6 View Your Computer's Components   116
4.7 View Your Computer's Performance   117
4.8 Practice Files   118
4.9 Various File Types   120
4.10 File Properties   121
4.11 How to Open a File   122
4.12 Exercises   125
4.13 Background Information   127
4.14 Tips   128

5. Photos, Music and Videos   129
5.1 The *Pictures* Library   130
5.2 Viewing a Photo In the Preview Pane   132
5.3 *Windows Photo Viewer*   133
5.4 Zoomen In and Zooming Out   135
5.5 Viewing a Slide Show   138
5.6 Using Tags   140
5.7 Rating Photos   143
5.8 Arranging Photos   144

5.9 Printing Photos   148
5.10 Sending Photos by E-mail   151
5.11 Sharing Photos With Other Users   154
5.12 Connecting Your Digital Camera To the Computer   157
5.13 Importing Photos From Your Digital Camera   160
5.14 Opening *Windows Media Player*   165
5.15 Playing a Music CD   167
5.16 Playing Tracks In A Random Order   172
5.17 Repeat   172
5.18 Playing a Video File   174
5.19 Playing a DVD   178
5.20 Exercises   184
5.21 Background Information   187
5.22 Tips   189

6. Burning Files to a CD, DVD or Blu-ray Disc   **191**
6.1 What Will You Need?   192
6.2 Choose Between Two Formats   193
6.3 Formatting a Disc   194
6.4 Creating a Data Disc   196
6.5 Burning a Data Disc   199
6.6 Adding Data To a *Live File System* Disc   200
6.7 Deleting data from a *Live File System* Disc   202
6.8 Erasing a *Live File System* rewritable Disc   204
6.9 The *Mastered* File system   206
6.10 Adding Files to a Queue   208
6.11 Removing Files From the Queue   212
6.12 Burn Files in a Queue to Disc   212
6.13 Viewing the Contents of a Disc With *Windows Explorer*   214
6.14 Burn a *Windows DVD*   215
6.15 Exercises   223
6.16 Background Information   225
6.17 Tips   230

7. Interesting Programs and Handy Features in Windows 7   **235**
7.1 *Sticky Notes*   236
7.2 *Snipping Tool*   237
7.3 *Calculator*   239
7.4 Jump Lists   244
7.5 *Aero Peek*   247
7.6 *Aero Shake*   249
7.7 Use *Aero Snap* to Quickly Maximize Windows   251
7.8 Align Windows With *Aero Snap*   252

7.9 *Aero Flip 3D*   254
7.10 Games   255
7.11 Exercises   259
7.12 Background Information   262

8. Windows Explorer, Libraries and Folder Windows   263
8.1 Opening a Library   264
8.2 Creating a New Library   267
8.3 Select the Properties for a Library   268
8.4 Adding Folder Locations To a Library   269
8.5 Using the Search Box   276
8.6 Using a Search Filter   278
8.7 Search Outside the Library   281
8.8 Filtering Search Results With Column Headers   283
8.9 Saving a Search Operation   285
8.10 Execute a Saved Search Operation   286
8.11 Deleting a File From a Library   287
8.12 Deleting a Folder From a Library   289
8.13 Deleting a Library   291
8.14 Exercises   292
8.15 Background Information   294

9. System Management and Computer Maintenance   295
9.1 Uninstall a Program   296
9.2 Install a Program   298
9.3 Installing *Adobe Reader*   299
9.4 Open *Adobe Reader*   302
9.5 Opening a PDF File   303
9.6 Install the *Visual Steps Alarm* Gadget   308
9.7 Cleaning Up Your Hard Drive   313
9.8 Defragmenting Your Hard Drive   317
9.9 Frequently Occurring Problems   320
9.10 Troubleshooters   323
9.11 *System Restore Tool*   325
9.12 Creating Restore Points   326
9.13 Restoring the System   328
9.14 Exercises   331
9.15 Background Information   332

10. Bonus Online Chapters and Extra Information   333
10.1 Opening the Bonus Online Chapters   334
10.2 Visual Steps Website and Newsletter   337

Appendices

Appendix A. Download Practice Files   339
Appendix B. How Do I Do That Again?   343
Appendix C. Index   354

Bonus Online Chapters

At the website accompanied to this book, you will find more bonus chapters. In *Chapter 10 Bonus Online Chapters and Extra Information* you can read how to open these chapters.

11. Word Processing with WordPad
11.1 Selecting Text
11.2 Lists
11.3 Never an Empty List
11.4 Applying Bullet Style in Advance
11.5 Paragraph Formatting
11.6 Indenting Paragraphs
11.7 Hanging Indentation
11.8 Indenting the First Line
11.9 Undoing the Indentation
11.10 Right Indentation
11.11 Tables
11.12 Tab Stops
11.13 Removing a Tab Stop
11.14 Selecting All
11.15 Paper Orientation
11.16 Exercises
11.17 Background Information

12. Special Editing Operations in Paint
12.1 Opening a Photo
12.2 The *Free-form Selection* Tool
12.3 Copying the Selection
12.4 Making the Selection Smaller
12.5 Making a Transparent Selection
12.6 Moving a Selection
12.7 Adding Shapes To a Photo
12.8 Colors and Effects
12.9 Adding Text To a Photo
12.10 Formatting Text
12.11 Enlarging and Moving

12.12 Saving a File

12.13 Exercises

Foreword

This book is suitable for every computer user who possesses some basic computer skills. If you already have worked through the beginners manual **Windows 7 for SENIORS** (ISBN 978 90 5905 126 3), you will have acquired these skills.

This book will take you much further. You will learn all there is to know about computer safety, creating user accounts, burning CDs and DVDs, and setting (grand)parental controls. All important issues will be dealt with, in order to let you work safely and without any problems.
You will learn how to organize your photo collection, and view your photos with *Windows Photo Viewer*; furthermore, you will learn how to use *Windows Media Player* to play music CDs and movies.
You can work through this hands-on book in your own time, without extra help. Just place the book next to your computer and execute all the operations, step by step. The detailed instructions and lots of screenshots will tell you exactly what to do.

I wish you lots of fun exploring your computer.

Yvette Huijsman
Studio Visual Steps

P.S.
Feel free to send us your questions and suggestions.
The e-mail address is: info@visualsteps.com

Visual Steps Newsletter

All Visual Steps books follow the same methodology: clear and concise step-by-step instructions with screen shots to demonstrate each task.
A complete list of all our books can be found on our website **www.visualsteps.com**
You can also sign up to receive our **free Visual Steps Newsletter**.

In this Newsletter you will receive periodic information by e-mail regarding:
- the latest titles and previously released books;
- special offers, supplemental chapters, tips and free informative booklets.

Also, our Newsletter subscribers may download any of the documents listed on the web pages **www.visualsteps.com/info_downloads** and **www.visualsteps.com/tips**

When you subscribe to our Newsletter you can be assured that we will never use your e-mail address for any purpose other than sending you the information as previously described. We will not share this address with any third-party. Each Newsletter also contains a one-click link to unsubscribe.

Introduction to Visual Steps™

The Visual Steps handbooks and manuals are the best instructional materials available for learning how to work with computers and computer programs. Nowhere else will you find better support for getting to know the computer, the Internet, *Windows* or related software.

Properties of the Visual Steps books:
- **Comprehensible contents**
  Addresses the needs of the beginner or intermediate computer user for a manual written in simple, straight-forward English.
- **Clear structure**
  Precise, easy to follow instructions. The material is broken down into small enough segments to allow for easy absorption.
- **Screen shots of every step**
  Quickly compare what you see on your own computer screen with the screen shots in the book. Pointers and tips guide you when new windows are opened so you always know what to do next.
- **Get started right away**
  All you have to do is switch on your computer, place the book next to your keyboard, and begin at once.

In short, I believe these manuals will be excellent guides for you.

dr. H. van der Meij
Faculty of Applied Education, Department of Instruction Technology, University of Twente, the Netherlands

What You Will Need

In order to work through this book, you will need a number of things on your computer:

The primary requirement for working with this book is having one of the US versions of *Windows 7* installed on your computer:
- *Windows 7 Starter*
- *Windows 7 Home Premium*
- *Windows 7 Professional*
- *Windows 7 Ultimate/Enterprise*

 Network and Internet

A functioning Internet connection is needed for downloading the Bonus Online Chapters (Chapters 11, and 12).
For the settings for your Internet connection, please see the software and information supplied by your Internet Service Provider.

Other necessities, for instance blank, writable CDs or DVDs, are mentioned in the applicable chapters.

Prior Computer Experience

If you want to use this book, you will need some basic computer skills. If you do not have these skills, it is a good idea to read the following book first:

Windows 7 for Seniors
ISBN 978 90 5905 126 3

What You Will Learn
When you finish this book, you will have the skills to:
• work independently with your computer
• write a letter using your computer
• adjust your computer settings so you can work with it most comfortably

For more information, visit
www.visualsteps.com/windows7

How to Use This Book

This book has been written using the Visual Steps™ method. You can work through this book independently at your own pace.

In this Visual Steps™ book, you will see various icons. This is what they mean:

Techniques
These icons indicate an action to be carried out:

 The mouse icon means you should do something with the mouse.

 The keyboard icon means you should type something on the keyboard.

 The hand icon means you should do something else, for example insert a CD-ROM in the computer. It is also used to remind you of something you have learned before.

In addition to these icons, in some areas of this book *extra assistance* is provided to help you successfully work through each chapter.

Help
These icons indicate that extra help is available:

 The arrow icon warns you about something.

 The bandage icon will help you if something has gone wrong.

 Have you forgotten how to do something? The number next to the footsteps tells you where to look it up at the end of the book in the appendix *How Do I Do That Again?*

In separate boxes you will find tips or additional, background information.

Extra information
Information boxes are denoted by these icons:

 The book icon gives you extra background information that you can read at your convenience. This extra information is not necessary for working through the book.

 The light bulb icon indicates an extra tip for using the program.

The Screen Shots

The screen shots in this book were made on a computer running *Windows 7 Ultimate*. The screen shots used in this book indicate which button, folder, file or hyperlink you need to click on your computer screen. In the instruction text (in **bold** letters) you will see a small image of the item you need to click. The black line will point you to the right place on your screen.

The small screen shots that are printed in this book are not meant to be completely legible all the time. This is not necessary, as you will see these images on your own computer screen in real size and fully legible.

Here you see an example of an instruction text and a screen shot. The black line indicates where to find this item on your own computer screen:

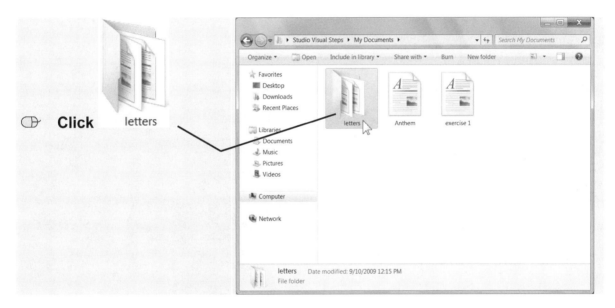

Sometimes the screen shot shows only a portion of a window. Here is an example:

It really will **not be necessary** for you to read all the information in the screen shots in this book. Always use the screen shots in combination with the image you see on your own computer screen.

Website

On the website that accompanies this book, **www.visualsteps.com/morewin7** you will find some Bonus Online Chapters, practice files and more information about the book. This website will also keep you informed of any errata, recent updates or other changes you need to be aware of, as a user of the book.
Please, also take a look at our website **www.visualsteps.com** from time to time to read about new books and other handy information such as informative tips and booklets.

Test Your Knowledge

Have you finished reading this book? Then test your knowledge with the *More Windows 7* test. Visit the website: **www.ccforseniors.com**

This multiple-choice test will show you how good your knowledge of *Windows 7* is. If you pass the test, you will receive your *free Computer Certificate* by e-mail.

For Teachers

This book is designed as a self-study guide. It is also well suited for use in a group or a classroom setting. For this purpose, we offer a free teacher's manual containing information about how to prepare for the course (including didactic teaching methods) and testing materials. You can download this teacher's manual (PDF file) from the website which accompanies this book: **www.visualsteps.com/morewin7**

1. Adapting Your Work Environment

Windows 7 allows you the ability to adjust many of the settings according to your own preferences. In the bonus chapters of the book **Windows 7 for Seniors** (ISBN 978 90 5905 126 3) you learned how to set a different background for your desktop and how to select a different screensaver. But you can do much more.

Windows 7 is packed with all sorts of useful functions which will help you work faster. Such as placing shortcuts on your desktop for frequently used programs. By double-clicking the icon, your program will start right away. You can also place these shortcuts on the taskbar. Then you just need one click to open the program.

Furthermore, you can choose to lock the taskbar to keep it permanently in view, or hide it while you are using a program. You can also personalize and adorn your desktop with all sorts of nifty gadgets. These are tiny programs that execute specific tasks.

This chapter shows you step-by-step how to adapt your work environment.

In this chapter you will learn how to:

- put shortcuts on the desktop;
- organize, move and delete the icons on the desktop;
- lock the taskbar;
- add shortcuts to the taskbar and how to remove them when desired;
- modify the system tray on the taskbar;
- add programs to the Start menu;
- place gadgets on the desktop.

 Please note!

Depending on your computer's settings and the Windows 7 edition you are using, the windows on your computer may look slightly different from the screenshots in this book. However, this will make no difference to the procedures and operations you are going to learn.

1.1 The Desktop

The *Windows 7* desktop is the first screen you see when you start up your computer and enter the password for your user account (if required).

☞ **Start up the computer**

☞ **If necessary, turn the monitor on**

☞ **If necessary, enter the password for your user account**

Now you will see the desktop, which contains one or more icons:

At the bottom of the desktop you will see the taskbar:

The desktop on your computer may look different. This depends on the settings you have selected for your computer.

1.2 Creating Shortcuts

If you frequently use specific programs, it is very useful to create shortcuts for these programs and place them on your desktop. You can then open the programs faster. In *Windows 7* these shortcuts take the shape of icons: these are tiny pictures.

If you want to create a shortcut to a program, you first need to look it up in the program list of the Start menu. To illustrate how to do this, you can create a shortcut to the program *WordPad*. You will find *WordPad* in the *Accessories* folder:

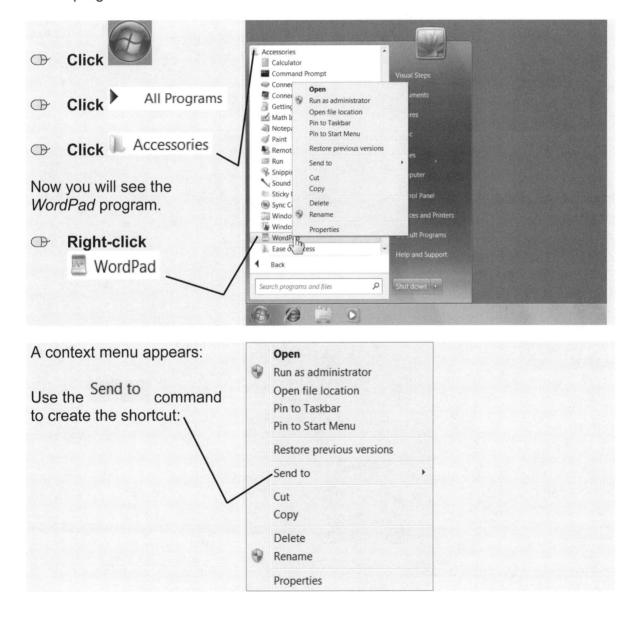

☞ **Click** [Start button]

☞ **Click** ▶ All Programs

☞ **Click** 📁 Accessories

Now you will see the *WordPad* program.

☞ **Right-click**
📝 WordPad

A context menu appears:

Use the Send to command to create the shortcut:

Open
Run as administrator
Open file location
Pin to Taskbar
Pin to Start Menu

Restore previous versions

Send to ▶

Cut
Copy

Delete
Rename

Properties

⏻ **Click** Send to

A submenu appears:

⏻ **Click**
 Desktop (create shortcut)

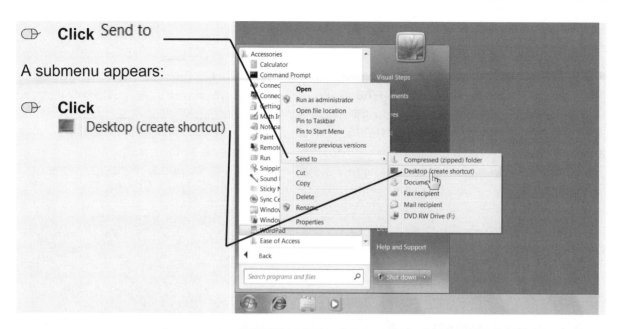

⏻ **Click an empty section of your desktop**

Now the Start menu will disappear and the *WordPad* shortcut will appear somewhere on the desktop: ——

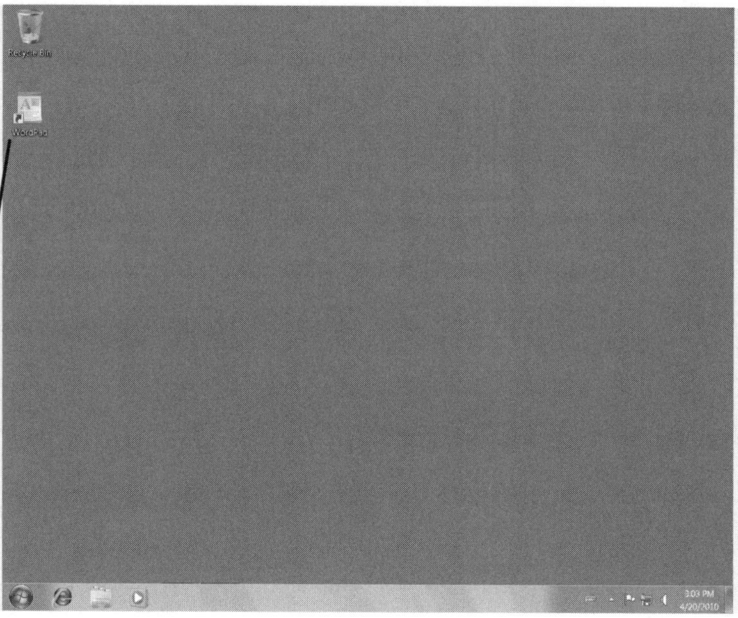

The shortcut is shaped like an

icon .

The little arrow at the bottom left of the icon indicates that this is a shortcut.

In the same way you can add other frequently used programs to your desktop. By double-clicking a shortcut's icon you can start the program right away.

1.3 Moving Icons

If your desktop contains a large number of icons, it may look a bit chaotic. You can tidy up your desktop by dragging the icons to different positions. You first need to make sure the *Auto arrange icons* option is disabled. If this option is not disabled, you will not be able to move the icons where you want.

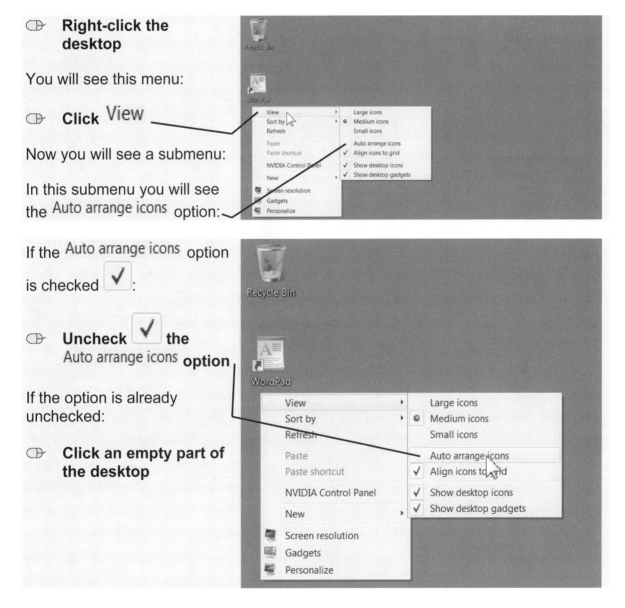

☞ **Right-click the desktop**

You will see this menu:

☞ **Click** View

Now you will see a submenu:

In this submenu you will see the Auto arrange icons option:

If the Auto arrange icons option is checked ✓:

☞ **Uncheck** ✓ **the** Auto arrange icons **option**

If the option is already unchecked:

☞ **Click an empty part of the desktop**

Now the *Auto arrange icons* option has been disabled. This means you can freely move the icons anywhere you want to on the desktop.

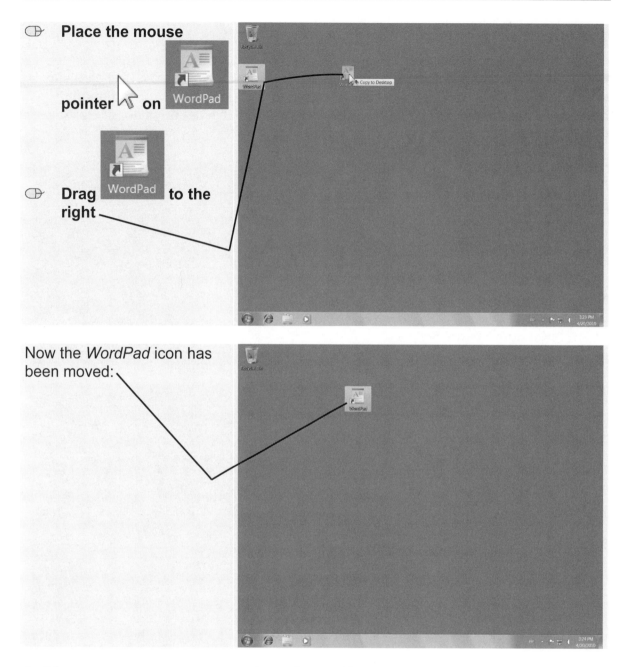

☞ **Place the mouse**

pointer on

☞ **Drag** WordPad **to the right**

Now the *WordPad* icon has been moved:

In this way, you can arrange your icons in specific positions on your desktop and locate them more easily.

1.4 Enabling the Auto Arrange Icons Option

If you prefer to position all your icons in organized rows and columns, you can let *Windows* do that for you with the auto arrange option. Here is how you do that:

Right-click an empty area somewhere on the desktop

A context menu appears:

Click View

In the submenu:

Click Auto arrange icons

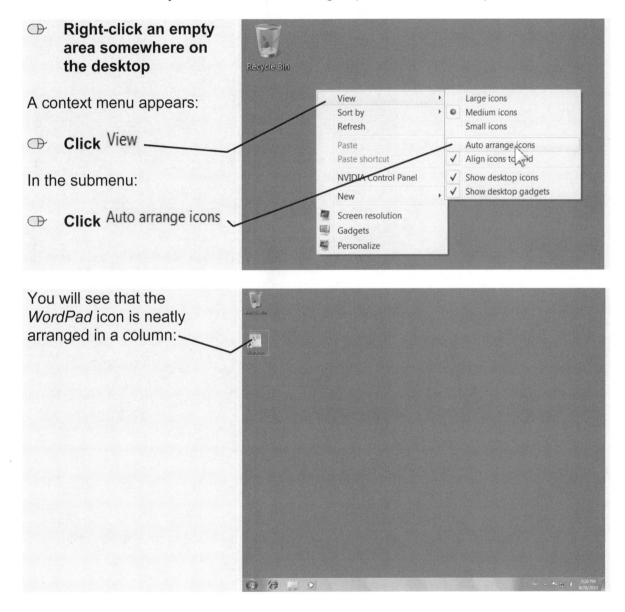

You will see that the *WordPad* icon is neatly arranged in a column:

If you use this option your icons will always be lined up in rows and columns, even if you move them. Just give it a try:

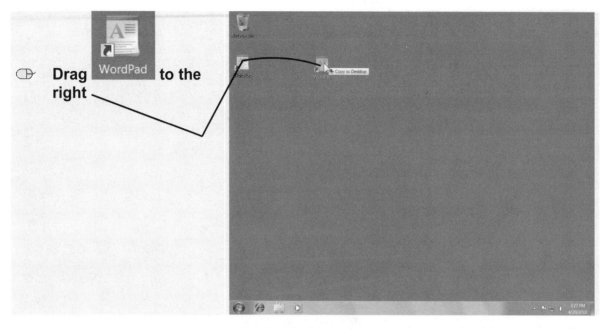

⊕ **Drag** WordPad **to the right**

You will see that the *WordPad* icon automatically reverts to its original position:

 Tip

Drag to a different row
If you have enabled the *Auto arrange icons* option, you will still be able to drag an icon to a different row or column. The other icons will adjust themselves accordingly.

 Tip

Drag into a folder

You can also place folders [folder icon] on your desktop. If you do have folders on your desktop, be careful not to drag an icon into one of them. The icon will seem to have disappeared, but in fact is now located in the folder.

1.5 Change the Shortcut's Icon

Did you know that you can change the icon's picture for a specific shortcut? This comes in handy when you have icons that look a lot alike.

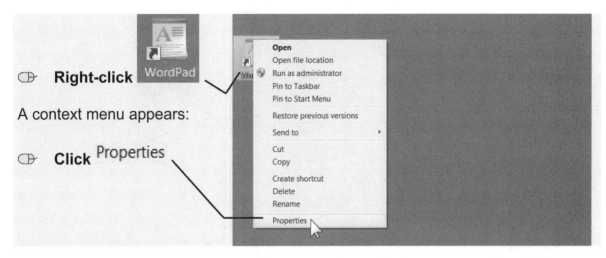

Right-click

A context menu appears:

Click Properties

Now you will see the *WordPad Properties* window:

Click

Change Icon...

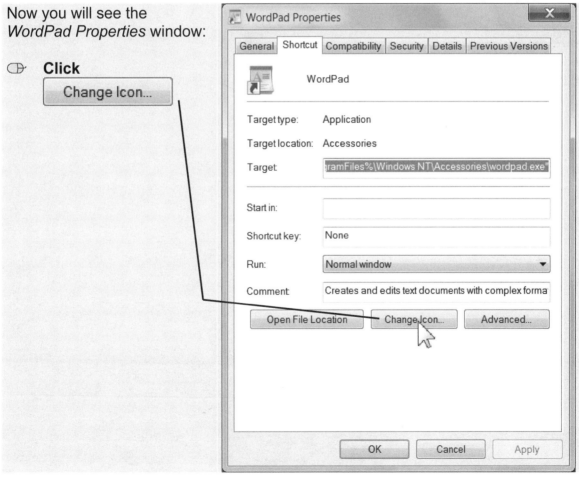

You will see a window
containing various icons:

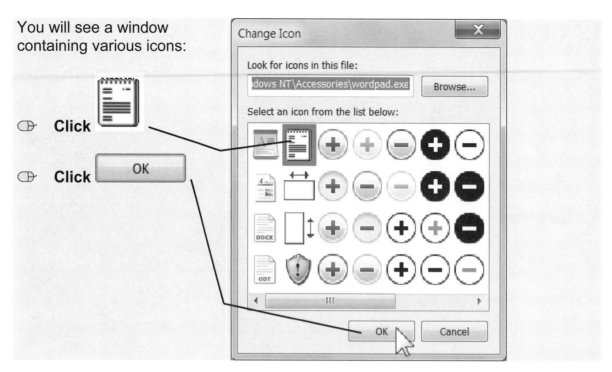

⊕ **Click**

⊕ **Click** [OK]

You will return to the
Properties window:

At the bottom of the window:

⊕ **Click** [OK]

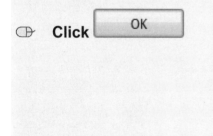

The icon's picture has
changed:

1.6 Deleting an Icon

You can remove an icon from the desktop very easily:

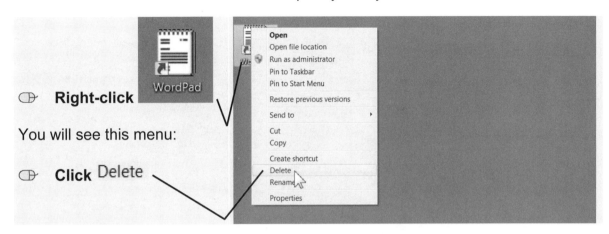

⊕ **Right-click**

You will see this menu:

⊕ **Click** Delete

Windows will ask you if you are sure you want to move the shortcut to the *Recycle Bin*:

⊕ **Click** Yes

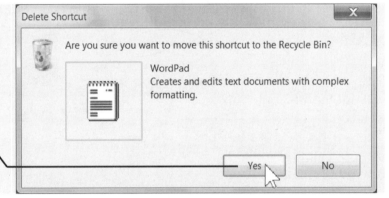

The *WordPad* icon has been moved to the *Recycle Bin*:

If your *Recycle Bin* was empty, you will now see that there is something in it:

1.7 Taskbar Settings

You can also modify a number of taskbar properties. First you need to display these properties:

☞ **Right-click an empty part of the taskbar**

You will see this menu:

☞ **Click** Properties

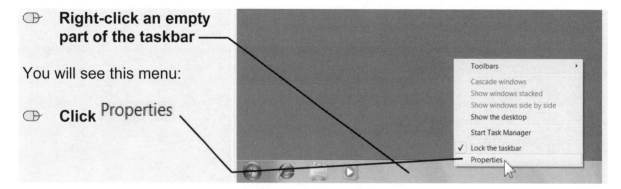

The *Taskbar and Start Menu Properties* window will appear. The *Taskbar* tab is active. You can modify a number of settings and change the appearance of the taskbar:

The Lock the taskbar setting will put the taskbar in a fixed position:
This will prevent the taskbar from accidentally being moved or minimized.

By default, this option is disabled. If this option on your computer is disabled:

☞ **Check the box** ✓ **next to** Lock the taskbar

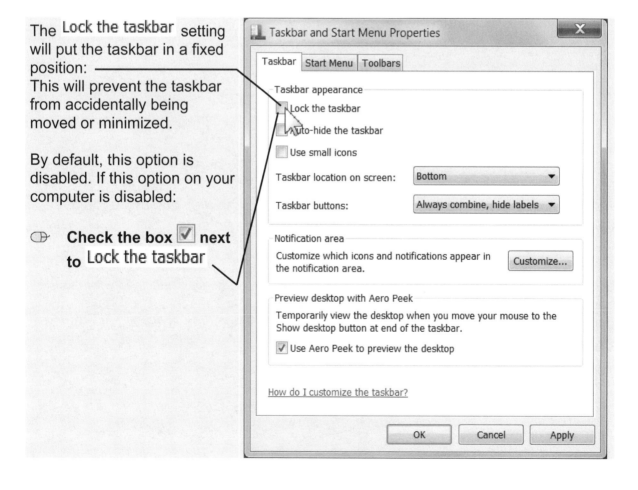

If you check the box ☑ next to Auto-hide the taskbar, the taskbar will disappear:

In this case the taskbar will only appear if you place the mouse pointer ⊾ on the taskbar's usual spot.

If you check the box ☑ next to Use small icons, the icons on the taskbar will become much smaller:
This way, the taskbar will be able to store more icons.

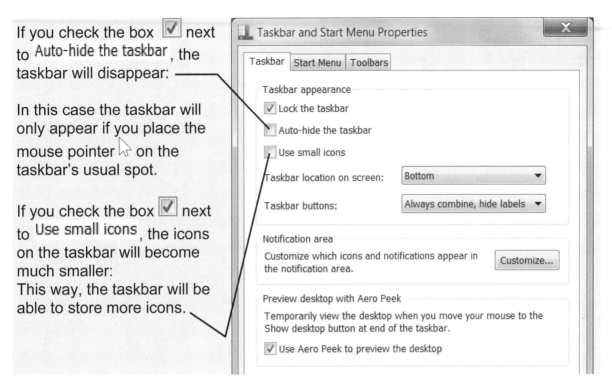

A taskbar button is an icon that represents the programs or files you have opened. These buttons are displayed on the taskbar.

If the option Auto-hide the taskbar is not checked ☑ the taskbar will always be displayed, even if you have maximized a program window. This option is useful because it enables you to switch between program windows by clicking the buttons on the taskbar.

The option Taskbar location on screen: Bottom ▼ lets you decide where to position the taskbar on your screen: to the left, to the right, at the top or at the bottom.

The option Taskbar buttons: Always combine, hide labels ▼ lets you change the appearance of the taskbar buttons. *Combine* means that similar taskbar buttons will be piled on top of each other when the taskbar is full. For instance, if you have opened *WordPad* twice in order to edit two different documents, the taskbar buttons for these two documents will be displayed as a single button: . To the right of the button you will still see a small part of the second button.

If you do not want to combine similar buttons, select the Never combine ▼ option.

Tip

Labels on taskbar buttons

Would you like to be able to more easily identify the programs and files you have opened? You can add labels to your taskbar buttons. Here is how to do that:

☞ **Click** `Always combine, hide labels ▼`

☞ **Click** `Combine when taskbar is full`

☞ **Click** `Apply`

Now the taskbar buttons will become larger and you can read the text on these buttons. In *Windows* this text is called a *label*.

In this example, three programs are opened. That is to say, the *Taskbar and Start Menu Properties* window, the *Calculator* window and the *WordPad* window:

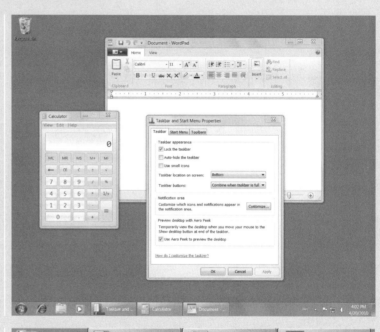

The taskbar will look like this: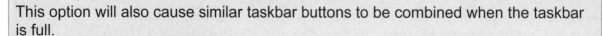

This option will also cause similar taskbar buttons to be combined when the taskbar is full.

If you want to save these settings:

☞ **Click** `OK`

If you do not want to apply these settings:

☞ **Click** `Cancel`

If necessary change your computer's settings according to this example

Click OK

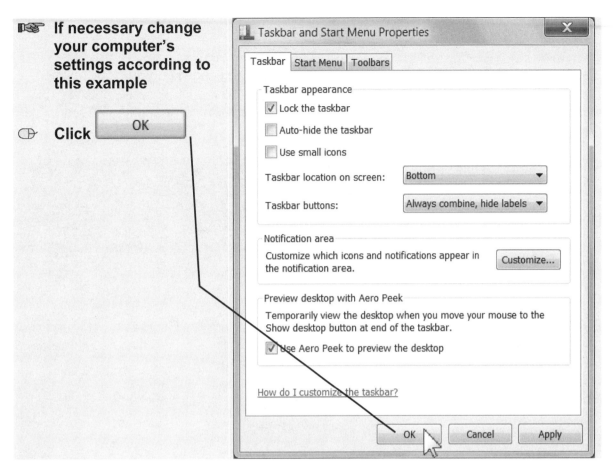

Taskbar and Start Menu Properties

| Taskbar | Start Menu | Toolbars |

Taskbar appearance

☑ Lock the taskbar

☐ Auto-hide the taskbar

☐ Use small icons

Taskbar location on screen: Bottom ▼

Taskbar buttons: Always combine, hide labels ▼

Notification area

Customize which icons and notifications appear in the notification area.   Customize...

Preview desktop with Aero Peek

Temporarily view the desktop when you move your mouse to the Show desktop button at end of the taskbar.

☑ Use Aero Peek to preview the desktop

How do I customize the taskbar?

OK   Cancel   Apply

💡 Tip

Additional options

The other options in this window will be discussed later in the book.
In the *section 1.11 Modifying the System Tray,* you will learn more about adjusting the system tray. *Aero Peek* will be discussed in *Chapter 7 Interesting Programs and Handy Features in Windows 7.*

If you have followed the instructions from above, the taskbar on your computer should reflect the same settings as described in this book.

1.8 Shortcuts on the Taskbar

The taskbar contains more than just the buttons for the programs you have opened. By default, you also see three additional buttons next to the Start menu button. These buttons can be used to open their specific programs very quickly. These *shortcuts* have been *pinned* to the taskbar:

Taskbar button of the open
WordPad program: ———

Default shortcuts: ——

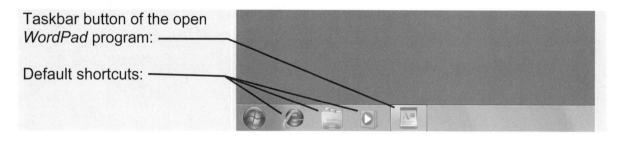

By default, the shortcuts to *Internet Explorer* , *Windows Explorer* , and

Windows Media Player have been pinned to the taskbar.

You can add or remove buttons to the taskbar yourself, to suit your needs.

1.9 Pinning a Program To the Taskbar

If you use *WordPad* often, it is useful to add a shortcut to that program to your taskbar. Then you just need to click the *WordPad* button once to open the program.

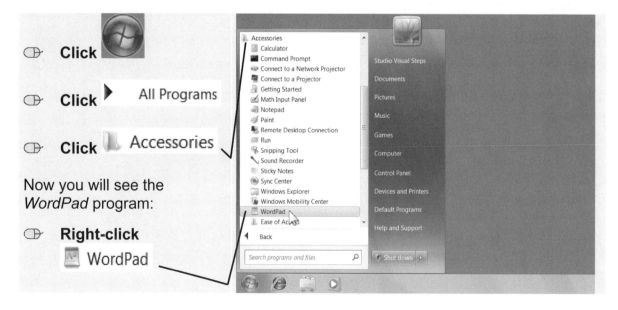

Click

Click ▶ All Programs

Click ▌ Accessories

Now you will see the
WordPad program:

Right-click
  ▓ WordPad

You will see this menu:

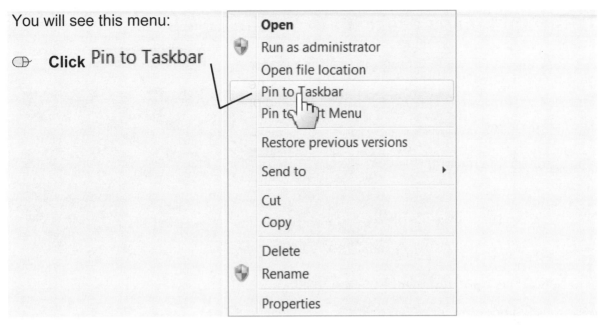

⊕ **Click** Pin to Taskbar

The *WordPad* icon has been pinned to the taskbar:

💡 **Tip**

Copy a shortcut from the desktop to the taskbar

If you want to use a desktop-shortcut on the taskbar, you can also drag this shortcut to the taskbar:

You will need to release the mouse button as soon as you see the

Pin to Taskbar text appear next to the mouse pointer.

Now the shortcut will be copied. The shortcut will still be displayed on the desktop as well.

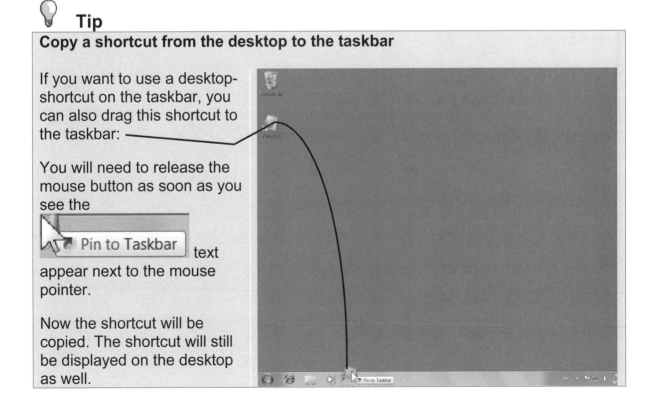

1.10 Unpinning a Program From the Taskbar

It is very easy to remove a program from the taskbar:

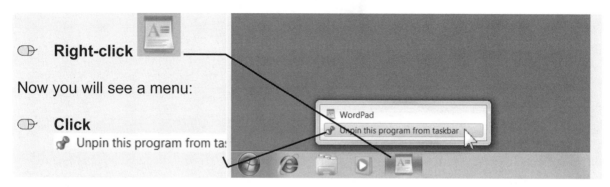

☞ **Right-click**

Now you will see a menu:

☞ **Click**
    📌 Unpin this program from ta:

The button has been removed from the taskbar.

1.11 Modifying the System Tray

The *system tray* is located on the right side of the *Windows* taskbar. The system tray contains the icons for several shortcuts and additional information about your system.

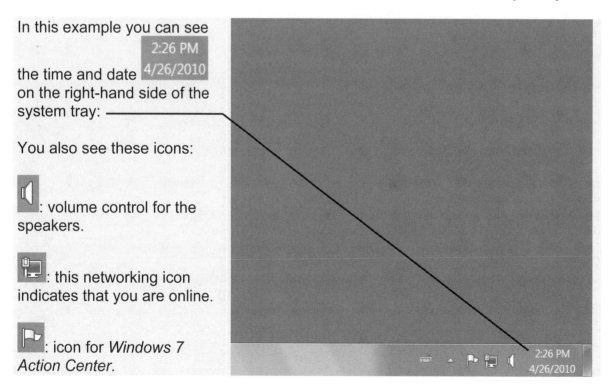

In this example you can see

the time and date
on the right-hand side of the
system tray: ──────

You also see these icons:

🔊 : volume control for the speakers.

🖧 : this networking icon indicates that you are online.

🚩 : icon for *Windows 7 Action Center.*

There are still more icons, but these are hidden. This is how to display the hidden icons:

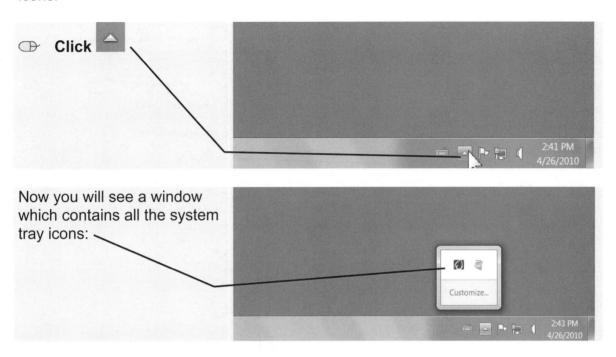

Click ⏏

Now you will see a window which contains all the system tray icons:

Your own computer will display different icons. The exact number of additional icons depends on the particular programs installed on your computer.
You can decide which icons are to be displayed in your system tray:

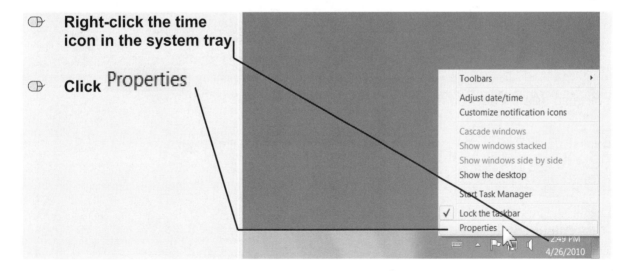

Right-click the time icon in the system tray

Click Properties

Now you will see the properties of the system tray. Here you can select which icons you want to display. For instance, you can choose to hide the time icon in the system tray:

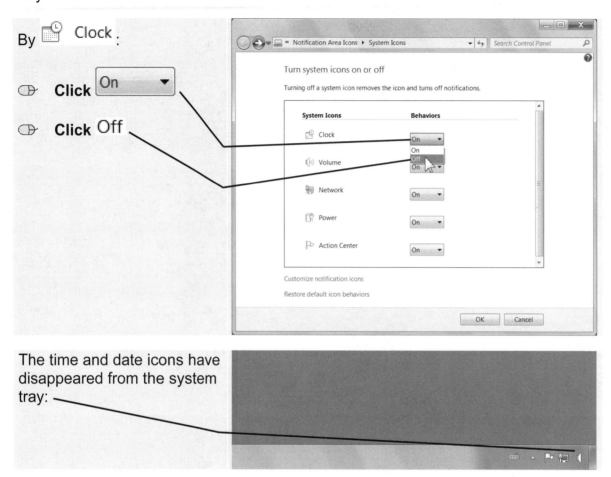

By 🗓 Clock .

☞ **Click** On ▼

☞ **Click** Off

The time and date icons have disappeared from the system tray:

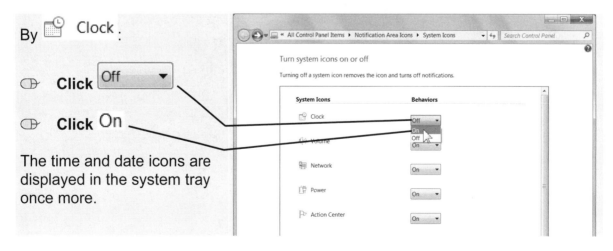

Here is how to restore the time and date icons to the system tray:

By 🗓 Clock .

☞ **Click** Off ▼

☞ **Click** On

The time and date icons are displayed in the system tray once more.

The 📓 Power system icon will only be displayed in the system tray if you are using a laptop computer.

The system tray displays icons for various system operations, such as time, volume control, and network settings. Other icons may appear in the system tray as well, indicating a program is running or additional information is available. These icons are either displayed in a different color or a small pop-up window appears occasionally. This window might contain a notification concerning the status of your antivirus software, for example.

By default this information is hidden, but you can choose for yourself which type of information you want to have displayed in your system tray:

☞ **Click**
   Customize notification icons

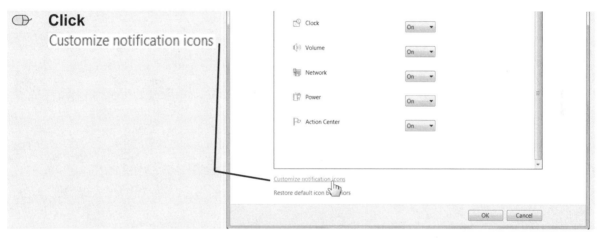

In this window you can select which icons or notifications you want to display in the system tray:

☞ **Drag the scroll bar downwards**

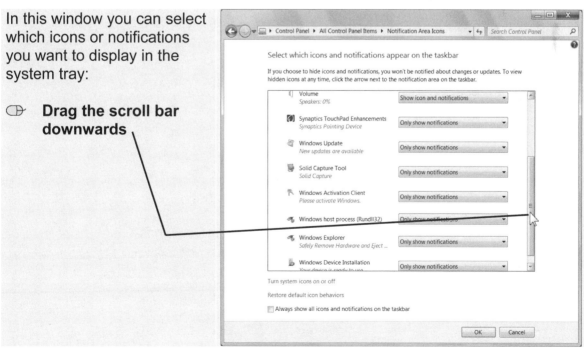

Please note!

The number of icons shown depends upon the programs installed on your computer. You will most likely see different icons than the ones shown here in this screenshot.

Each program offers you three options:

- Only show notifications: the program icon will not be displayed in the system tray, but you will only see the notifications for this program.
- Show icon and notifications: the program icon will be displayed in the system tray, as well as the notifications.
- Hide icon and notifications: both the program icon and the notifications remain hidden.

 Tip

New programs or devices
When you are installing a new program or device, an icon is often added to the system tray automatically. By clicking this icon you can directly access the new program or device.

If you select Only show notifications for such a new program or device, the icon will disappear. You will only see the notifications for these new programs or devices.

For this exercise, you do not need to change anything in this window:

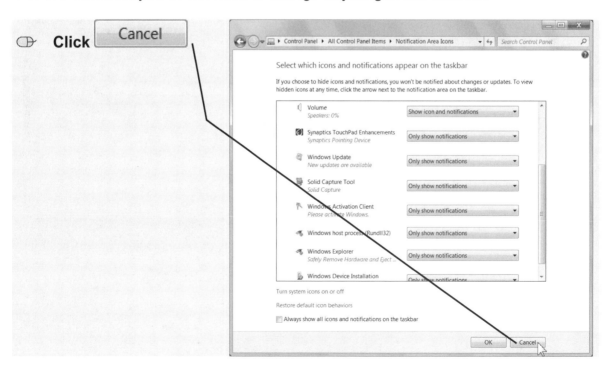

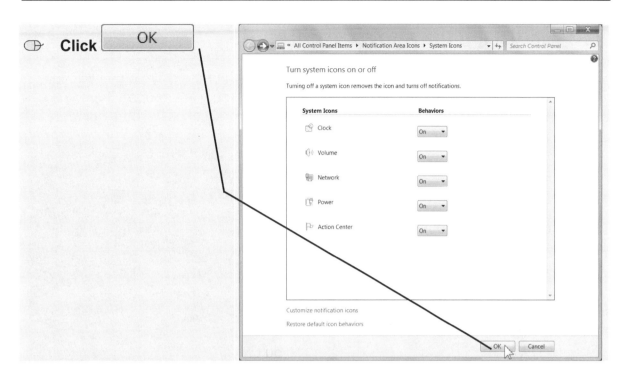

Click [OK]

The system tray is now displaying the default system icons. By clicking these icons you can quickly access the corresponding program, for instance the time settings on your computer:

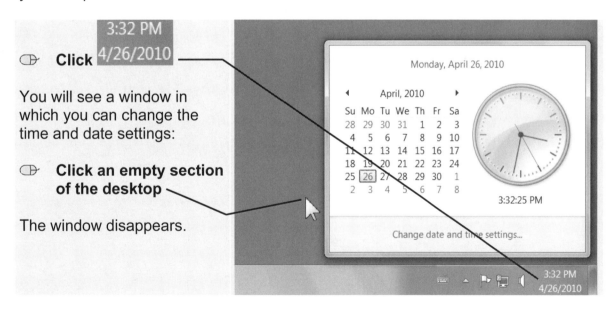

Click 3:32 PM 4/26/2010

You will see a window in which you can change the time and date settings:

Click an empty section of the desktop

The window disappears.

From time to time, other information is displayed in the system tray.

For example, when you execute a print command, you will see a printer icon   .

1.12 Modifying the Start Menu

You can add the programs you use the most to your Start menu. Then you will not need to look them up in the full program list each time you want to open them. You can practice doing this with the *WordPad* program. This action is called *pinning*:

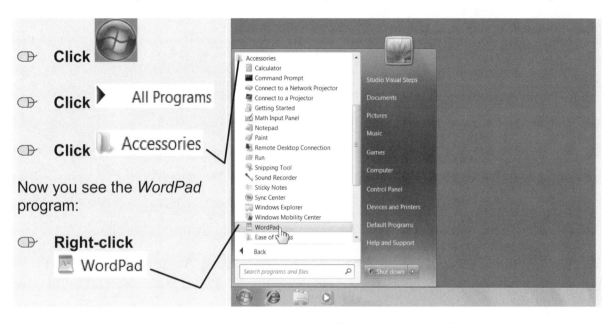

⊕ **Click**

⊕ **Click** ▶ **All Programs**

⊕ **Click** ⿴ **Accessories**

Now you see the *WordPad* program:

⊕ **Right-click**
    ⿴ **WordPad**

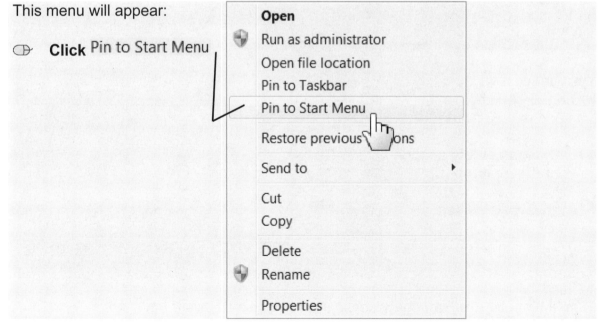

This menu will appear:

⊕ **Click** Pin to Start Menu

At the top of the Start menu you will see a thin horizontal line. All programs shown above this line are *pinned* to the Start menu and will always be displayed.

Click twice

Here you see the horizontal line:

WordPad is currently shown above the line.

The programs underneath the line may vary. Here you will see the programs you have opened most recently.

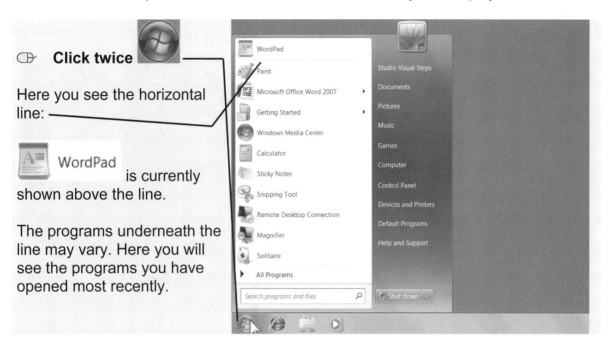

You can also *unpin* a program from the Start menu:

Right-click WordPad

Click Unpin from Start Menu

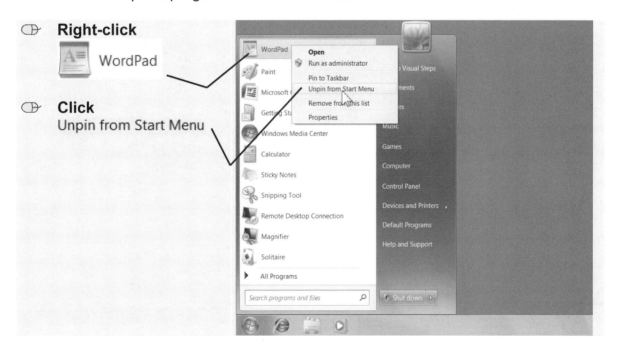

Now *WordPad* is no longer displayed above the horizontal line in the Start menu. You see how easy it is to customize the Start menu and allow the icons for your favorite programs to be shown at all times.

1.13 Using Gadgets

You can adapt your *Windows 7* work environment even further by using *gadgets*. Gadgets are small programs on your desktop that execute specific tasks.

☞ **Right-click an empty section on the desktop**

You will see a menu:

☞ **Click ⬛ Gadgets**

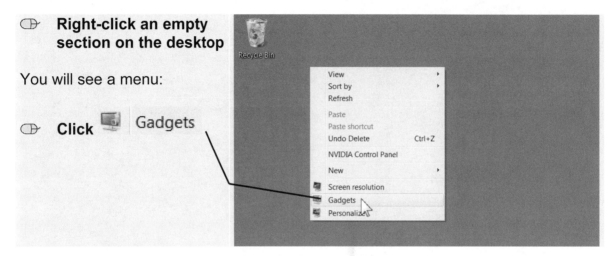

In this window you will see the default gadgets that are included in the *Windows 7* operating system:

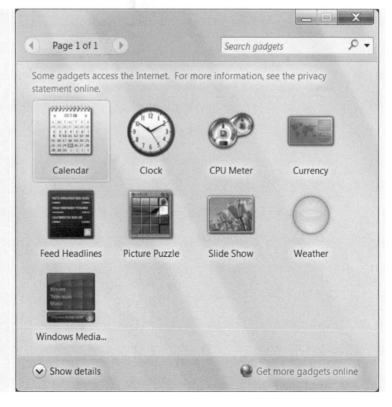

For example, this is how you add a clock to your desktop:

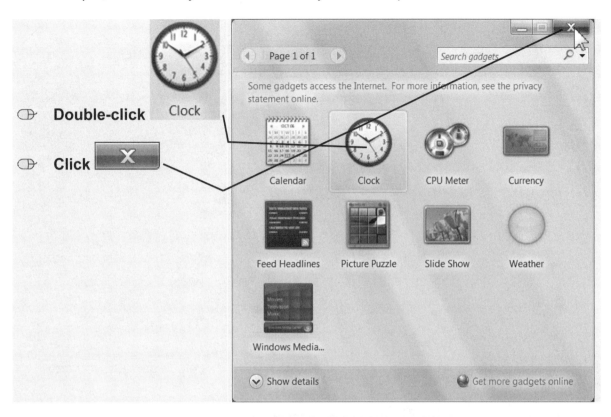

Now you will see that the clock icon has been placed on your desktop:

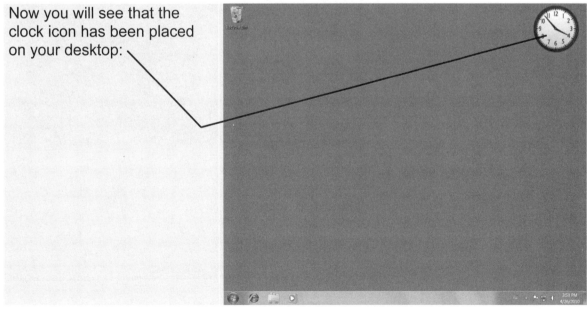

You can drag the gadgets around the desktop and position them wherever you like. Give it a try:

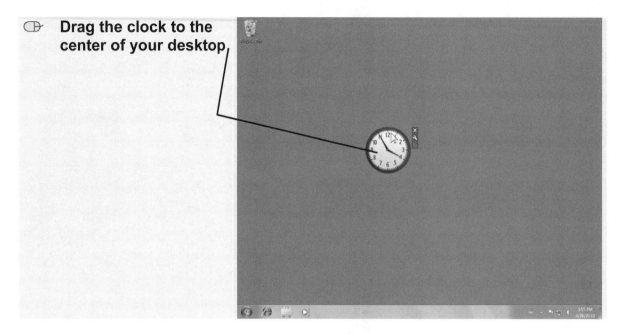

⊕ **Drag the clock to the center of your desktop**

Some gadgets offer various options. For instance, with this clock gadget, you can select different kinds of clocks. Here is how to do that:

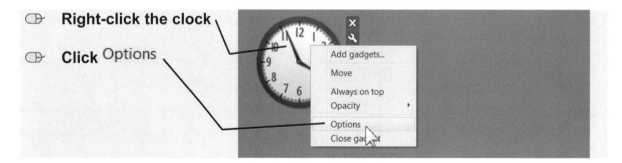

⊕ **Right-click the clock**

⊕ **Click** Options

The *Clock* window will be opened:

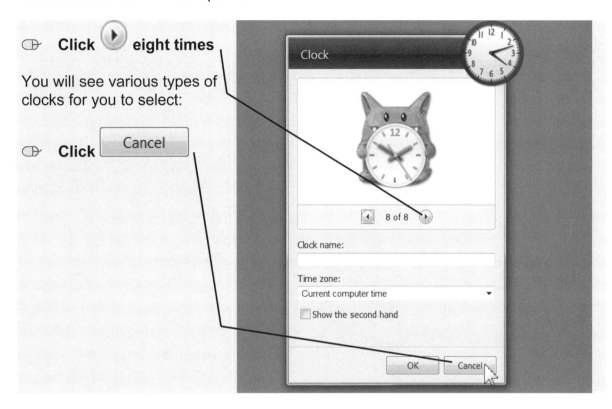

☞ **Click** ▶ **eight times**

You will see various types of clocks for you to select:

☞ **Click** Cancel

You can easily remove a gadget:

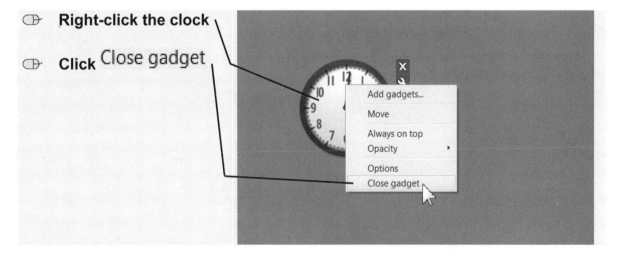

☞ **Right-click the clock**

☞ **Click** Close gadget

In this chapter you have learned how to adapt your work environment to suit your own needs and wishes. In the next exercise you are going to repeat all the operations.

1.14 Exercises

Have you forgotten how to carry out a certain task? You can use the number next to the footsteps to look up this task in *Appendix B How Do I Do That Again?*

Exercise: Shortcuts

This exercise is for practicing creating shortcuts and organizing icons on the desktop.

☞ In the program list, in the *Accessories* folder, find the *Paint* program.

☞ Create a shortcut to the *Paint* program on your desktop. $\mathscr{GG}^1$

☞ Disable the *Auto arrange icons* option. $\mathscr{GG}^2$

☞ Drag the *Paint* icon to the centre of the desktop.

☞ Pin *Paint* to the taskbar. $\mathscr{GG}^3$

☞ Pin *Paint* to the Start menu. $\mathscr{GG}^4$

☞ Unpin *Paint* from the taskbar. $\mathscr{GG}^5$

☞ Remove *Paint* from the Start menu. $\mathscr{GG}^6$

☞ Enable *Auto arrange icons*. $\mathscr{GG}^2$

☞ Remove the *Paint* icon from the desktop. $\mathscr{GG}^7$

☞ Add the *Picture Puzzle* gadget to the desktop. $\mathscr{GG}^8$

☞ Close the gadgets window. $\mathscr{GG}^9$

☞ Drag the gadget to the centre of the desktop.

☞ Try to solve the puzzle by dragging the blocks to the correct position.

☞ Remove the gadget. $\mathscr{GG}^{10}$

1.15 Background Information

Dictionary	
Desktop	The desktop is the main screen area that you see after you turn on your computer and log on to *Windows*. Like the top of an actual desk, it serves as a surface for your work. When you open programs or folders, they appear on the desktop.
Gadget	These are mini-programs on your desktop that execute specific tasks. For instance, you can display a clock, a continuous picture slide show, or the weather forecast on your desktop.
Icon	Icons are small pictures that represent files, folders, programs, and other items.
Shortcut	A shortcut is a link to an item on your computer. For instance, a program, file, folder, hard disk partition, printer, or even another computer. You can place shortcuts in various locations. On the desktop, in the Start menu, on the taskbar, and in the system tray.
System tray	The area to the right-hand side of the *Windows 7* taskbar. This area contains shortcuts (in the form of icons) to specific programs and program information.
Taskbar	The long horizontal bar at the bottom of your screen. The taskbar contains buttons for the programs you have opened. The taskbar also contains shortcuts to the programs that have been pinned to the taskbar.
Taskbar button	Taskbar buttons are icons that are created on the taskbar whenever you have opened a program, a file, or a folder. By clicking one of the taskbar buttons you can quickly switch between windows.

Source: Windows Help and Support

1.16 Tips

 Tip

Examples of different windows

If you are using multiple programs or documents at the same time, you cannot always see all of these windows on your desktop.

For every opened program or document, a button is displayed on the taskbar. Gently slide the mouse pointer over any of these buttons and you will see a small preview window:

☞ **Slide the mouse pointer over a taskbar button** ———

You will see the preview window:

If you slide the mouse pointer over the small preview window, you will briefly see the corresponding window in actual size:

☞ **Slide the mouse pointer over the preview window** ———

You will see a larger rendering of the window:

By clicking the preview window, you will switch to the corresponding program.

You can close the program from within the preview window by clicking the ⊠ button:

Tip

Change the order of the buttons on the taskbar
You can arrange the order of the buttons on the taskbar according to you own preferences, by simply dragging the buttons. You can do this with the buttons for opened programs or files, as well as shortcut icons to other programs.

☞ **Drag** 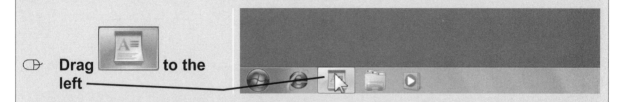 **to the left**

You can see that the *WordPad* taskbar button can be dragged to a position amidst the other shortcuts on the taskbar.

 Tip

Select a different desktop background
On the Tips and tricks page of the Visual Steps website you can find a PDF file called *Change Your Desktop Background*. In this file you can read how to select a different background for your desktop. You can download and view this PDF file for free. You can find the PDF file at **www.visualsteps.com/tips**, under the *Windows 7* topic.

Notes

You can use this space to take notes.

2. Setting Up Windows

In *Windows 7* you can modify many of the settings for your hardware and software programs. For the most part, you will use the tools in the *Control Panel* to modify these settings. You can change the settings for your mouse and keyboard, for example, or alter the way the time and date is displayed on your computer.

The *Ease of Access Center* provides you with quick access to a number of tools to help make your computer easier to use. For example, you can choose to use the computer with or without visual displays or sounds.

Another useful feature in *Windows 7* is the ease with which you can set up your default programs. These are the programs that will be used for specific file types. For example, you can associate all photo files with *Windows Photo Viewer*.

You can also associate a single file type with a specific program. You can assign the *WordPad* text editor to all your text documents, for example. *WordPad* then becomes the default program that is opened each time you click on a text file.

The last thing covered in this chapter is how to define the default settings for your multimedia files, such as choosing the auto play settings for CDs, DVDs and video files.

In this chapter you will learn how to:

- use the *Control Panel*;
- set the date and time on your computer;
- use the *Ease of Access Center*;
- set your default programs;
- associate file types to specific programs;
- select auto play settings for your CDs, DVDs, and other multimedia.

2.1 The Control Panel

Most of your computer's settings can be modified by using the *Control Panel*. This is how you open the *Control Panel* window:

👆 **Click**

👆 **Click** Control Panel

The *Control Panel* window appears:

The topics are grouped according to their main subject.

You can select a specific task by clicking one of the hyperlinks.

If the *Control Panel* of your computer looks very different from this screenshot, you will need to adjust the view.

👆 **Click** Large icons **or** Small icons

👆 **Click** Category

Now your *Control Panel* will look the same as in this book.

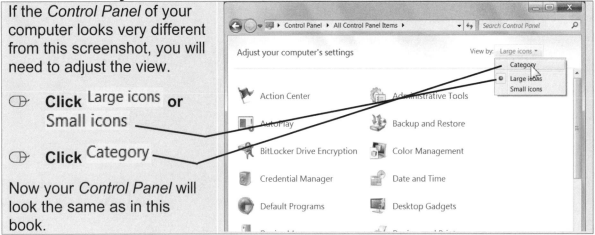

2.2 Setting the Date and Time

Sometimes, the clock on your computer runs too fast or too slow. Here is how to adjust the time on your computer:

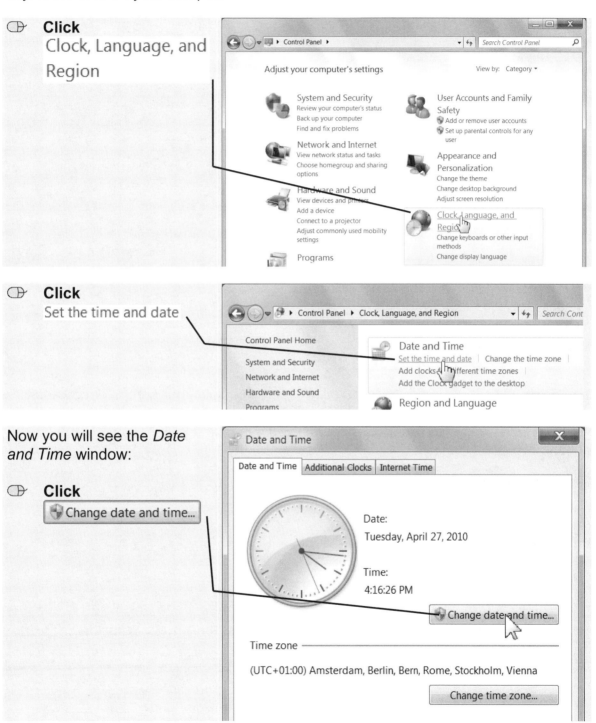

☞ **Click**
Clock, Language, and Region

☞ **Click**
Set the time and date

Now you will see the *Date and Time* window:

☞ **Click**
Change date and time...

You will see this window:

Here you can select the correct month, year, and weekday:

You can set the time by clicking this box:

After you have set the time and date:

☞ **Click** | OK |

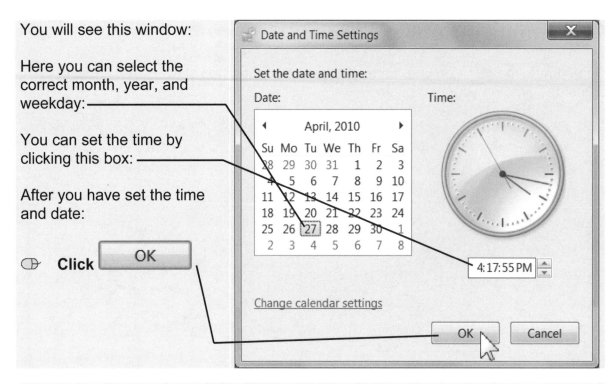

☞ **Close the *Date and Time* window** 🦶⁹

2.3 The Ease of Access Center

The *Ease of Access Center* contains all the tools to adjust your computer settings for vision, hearing, and mobility. You will also find recommendations on how to make your computer easier to use. In this section you can take a look at some of the options available:

In the *Control Panel*:

☞ **Click** ◀

☞ **Click** Ease of Access

☞ **Click** Let Windows suggest setting

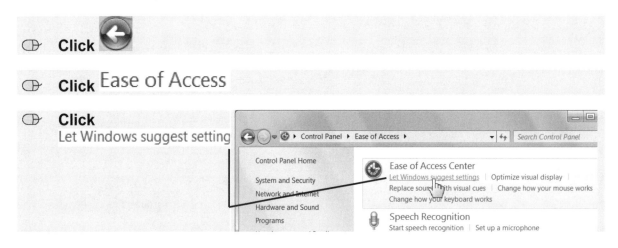

Now you will see a set of five windows. These windows contain a number of questions regarding physical problems, or specific problems you might encounter while using your computer.

☞ **Check the boxes** ☑
next to the statements
that apply to you ⎯⎯⎯

☞ **Click** [**Next**] ⎯⎯⎯

☞ **Repeat this action in**
the next four windows

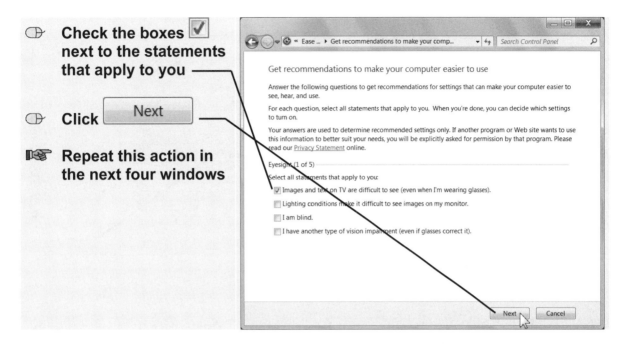

After you have filled in the boxes in the fifth window, *Windows 7* will give you a list of recommended settings which may make it easier for you to use your computer. You can then decide which settings you want to apply.

☞ **View the**
recommended
settings

☞ **Check the box** ☑ **or**
click the radio button
◉ **next to the settings**
you want to use ⎯⎯⎯

Please note: you will probably see a set of different recommended settings. The recommendations are based on the answers you have entered in the previous windows.

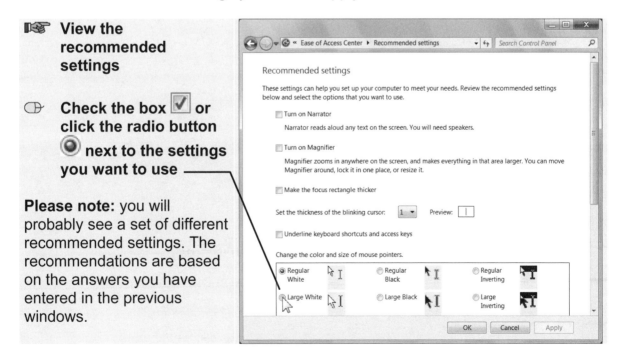

If you want to apply the
selected settings:

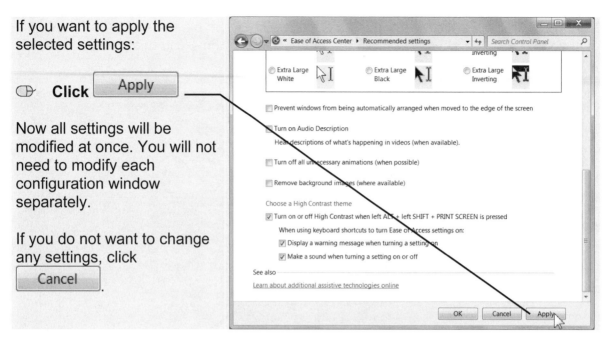

⊕ **Click** 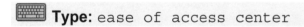 Apply

Now all settings will be
modified at once. You will not
need to modify each
configuration window
separately.

If you do not want to change
any settings, click
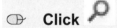 Cancel.

☞ **Close all windows** 👣9

If you experience specific problems with your vision or mobility, you may want to take
a look at some of the other *Windows* features. The *Windows Help and Support*
section offers a lot of information:

☞ **Open** *Windows Help and Support* 👣11

In the search box:

⌨ **Type:** ease of access center

⊕ **Click** 🔍

You will see a list of topics
available regarding this
subject:

☞ **Read the topics that
    interest you**

When you have finished:

☞ **Close the window** 👣9

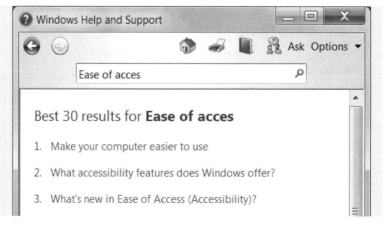

2.4 Setting Default Programs

A default program is the program that *Windows* uses to open certain specific file types, such as an image file or a web page. If you have more than one e-mail program for example installed on your computer, you can assign one of them as the default program.

This is how you set a default program:

Click

Click
Default Programs

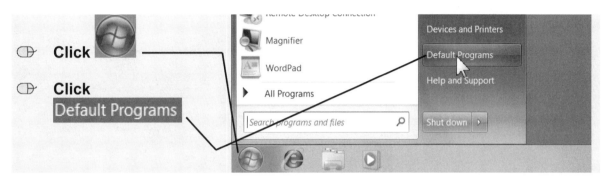

Now you will see the *Default Programs* window:

Click
Set your default programs

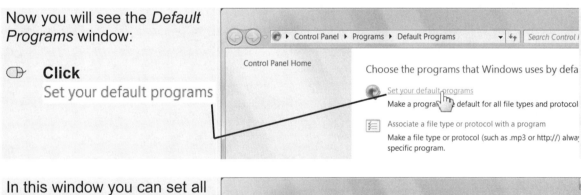

In this window you can set all your default programs:

Click
Windows Photo Viewer

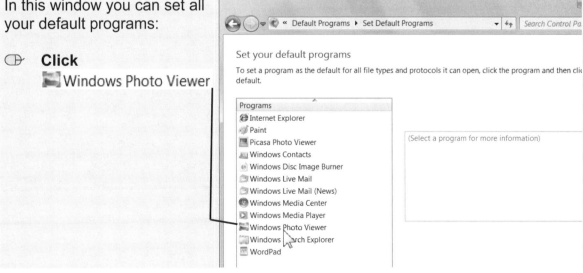

You will see a description of
the selected program:

You can set this program as a
default program.

⊕ **Click**

➔ Set this program as default
   Use the selected program to open all
   protocols it can open by default.

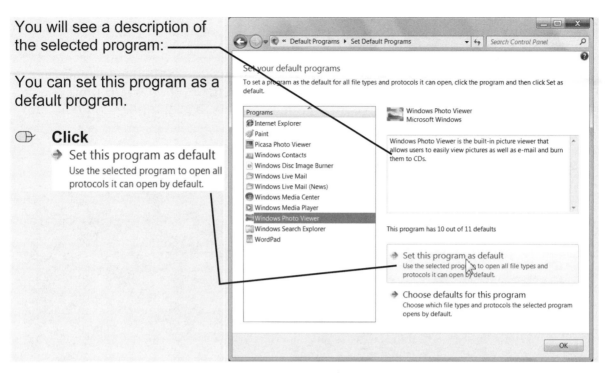

Now all the default settings
are attributed to *Windows
Photo Viewer*:

You can take a closer look at
these settings:

⊕ **Click**

➔ Choose defaults for this progra
   Choose which file types and protocols th
   opens by default.

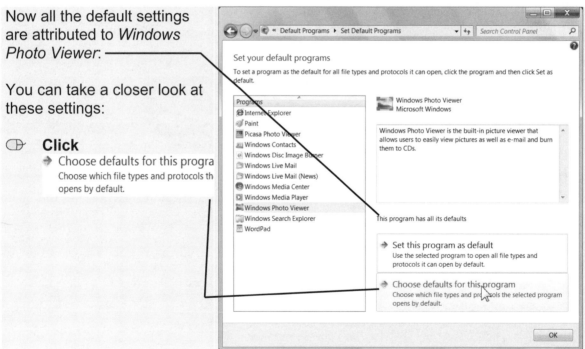

In this window you can see which file types will be opened with *Windows Photo Viewer*:

When you double-click a file with one of these file extensions, it will be opened in *Windows Photo Viewer*.

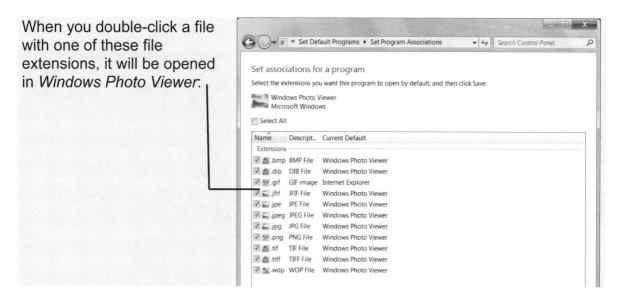

A file extension is the set of characters at the end of the file name preceded by a period. The file extension indicates the file type. For example, the file extension of a file called *photo.jpg* is 'jpg'.

You can go back to the previous window:

⊕ **Click**

Now you will see the *Set Default Programs* window once again:

⊕ **Click**

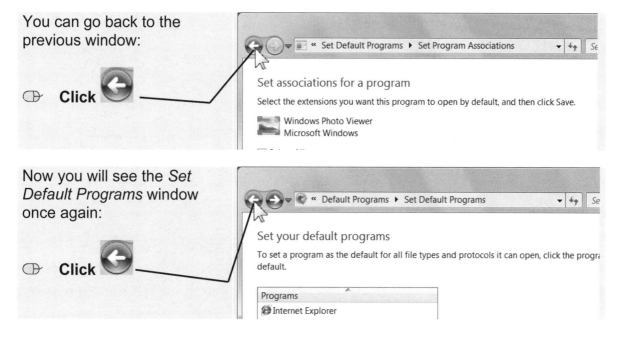

In this section you have selected a default program for all image file types. But you can also do the opposite. You can select one or more file types and link them to a specific program.
In the next section you will learn how to do this.

2.5 Associating a File Type With a Program

You can associate a certain file type with a specific program. This can be very useful, for instance if you always want to open certain image file types with your photo editing program. You can select these settings in the *Default Programs* window:

Here you see the *Default Programs* window:

⊕ **Click**
Associate a file type or protocol wi

Now you will see the *Set Associations* window:

This long list shows all the file types and their default programs:

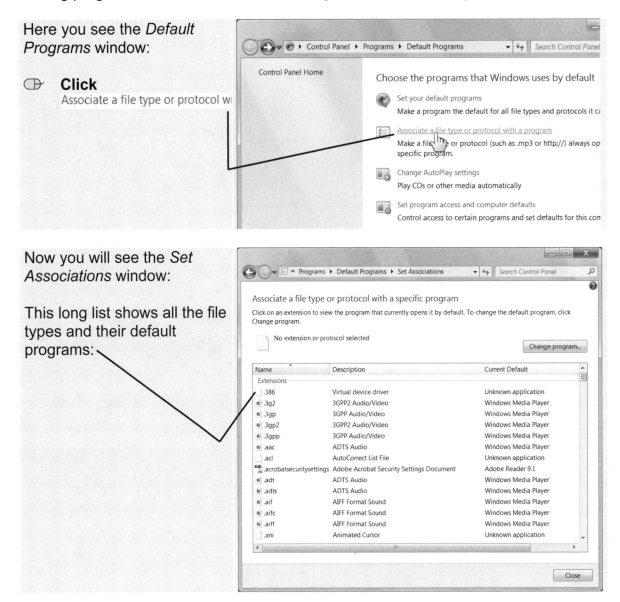

☞ **Drag the scroll bar downwards until you see the** BMP File **file type**

☞ **Click** BMP File

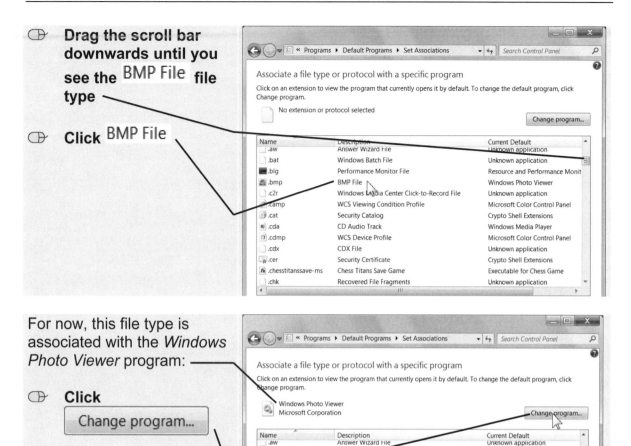

For now, this file type is associated with the *Windows Photo Viewer* program: ——

☞ **Click**

> Change program...

Now you can select a different program and associate the .bmp file type with that program:

Usually *Windows* will display a few programs for you to select right away:——

You can also search your computer for alternative programs:

☞ **Click** Browse...

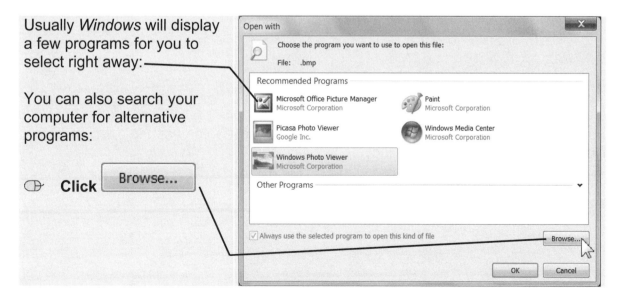

Here you can select the program you want to use, for example your favorite photo editing program.

However, in this exercise that will not be necessary:

☞ **Click** Cancel

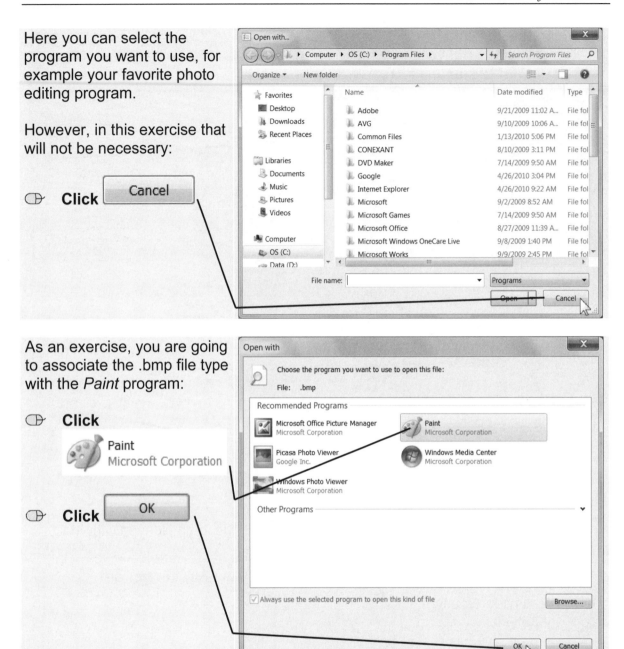

As an exercise, you are going to associate the .bmp file type with the *Paint* program:

☞ **Click**

Paint
Microsoft Corporation

☞ **Click** OK

Paint is a simple graphics painting program which can also be used to open image files. *Paint* is a default program included in *Windows 7*.

The BMP file type is now associated with the *Paint* program:

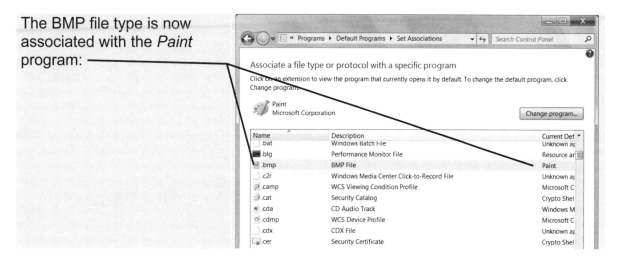

In the *Set Associations* window:

⊕ **Click**

From now on when you double-click a BMP file in a folder window (a file with the .bmp extension), it will be opened in the *Paint* program.

2.6 Setting the AutoPlay Options for CDs, DVDs and Other Multimedia

By default, when you insert a CD or DVD into the CD/DVD drive of your computer, or insert a USB stick into the USB port, a small window opens showing a list of programs available to open the files. In *Windows 7*, you can determine which programs to be used as default whenever a CD, DVD, or other devices are connected to your computer:

Here you see the *Default Programs* window:

⊕ **Click**
    Change AutoPlay settings

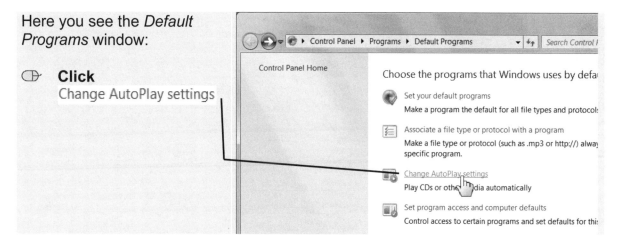

Now you will see the *AutoPlay* window:

By default, the *Use AutoPlay for all media and devices* option has been enabled:

In this example the other settings have not yet been selected:

Your computer may display different settings.

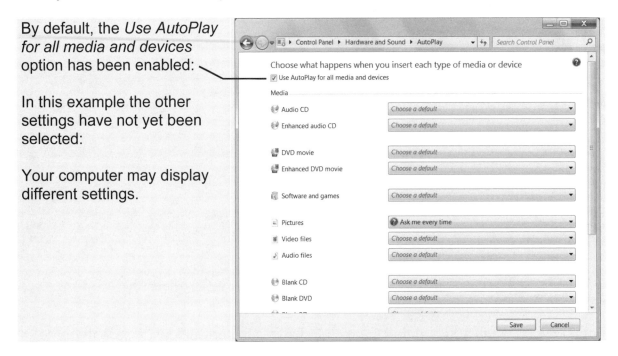

When the *Use AutoPlay for all media and devices* option has been enabled, *Windows 7* will automatically execute the selected operation, as soon as a CD, DVD, or USB stick is inserted. You can select separate settings for many different media types:

By Audio-cd :

☞ **Click** ▼

Now you will see different types of operations for an audio CD:
The options you see depend on the programs that are installed on your computer.

If you like to play your music with *Windows Media Player,* you can select that option:

☞ **Click**
      ▶ Play audio CD using W

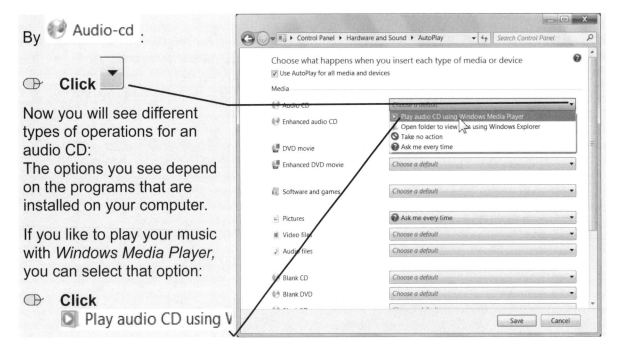

In the same way you can select the default settings for your other media:

☞ Choose the default settings for other media

Use the scroll bar to display the media at the bottom of the window.

💡 **Tip**

Choose action when inserting media
If you want to select the action yourself, each time a specific media type is inserted, select
❓ Ask me every time.

After you have selected all the desired settings, you will need to confirm these settings:

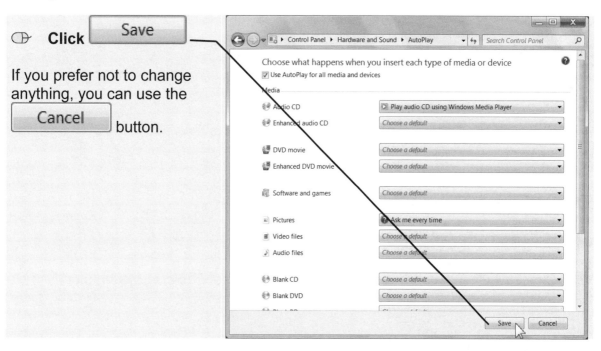

⊕ **Click** ⟨ Save ⟩

If you prefer not to change anything, you can use the ⟨ Cancel ⟩ button.

☞ Close the *Default Programs* window 🐾⁹

In this chapter you have learned how to associate programs with certain file types, and vice versa, how to associate a file type with a program. You have also read about setting the desired actions for different types of media, such as CDs, DVDs, or USB sticks. This way you can have *Windows* to do exactly what you want.
In the next exercise you can practice all these actions.

2.7 Exercises

Have you forgotten how to do something? Then you can use the number next to the footsteps to look up the description in *Appendix B How Do I Do That Again?*

Exercise: Associate a File Type With a Program

This exercise will let you practice associating a file type with a program.

☞ Open the *Default Programs* window. $\mathcal{QO}$[12]

☞ Open the *Set Associations* window. $\mathcal{QO}$[13]

☞ Associate the BMP file type with the *Windows Photo Viewer* program. $\mathcal{QO}$[14]

☞ Close the window. $\mathcal{QO}$[9]

Exercise: Set Default Program

Use this exercise to practice setting default programs.

☞ Open the *Default Programs* window. $\mathcal{QO}$[12]

☞ Set *Internet Explorer* program as a default program. $\mathcal{QO}$[15]

☞ Check which file extensions are opened by *Internet Explorer* by default. $\mathcal{QO}$[16]

☞ Close the window. $\mathcal{QO}$[9]

2.8 Background Information

Dictionary	
Computer clock	A chip in your computer, powered by a battery, that keeps track of the correct time and date.
Control panel	The window you can use to change the settings for *Windows*, and change your software, hardware or security settings.
Default program	The program normally used to open all file types of a specific kind. All photo files are opened by *Windows Photo Viewer*, for example.
Ease of Access Center	The *Ease of Access Center* is a central location that you can use to set up the accessibility settings and programs available in *Windows*. This feature will make it easier to use your computer, to enhance the visibility of your screen, and to find alternatives for using sounds.
File extension, file name extension	A set of characters at the end of a file name, used to tell *Windows* what kind of information is in the file. For instance, 'txt' is the extension of the *letter.txt* file name.
File type, file format	The format of a file. The file type indicates which program has been used to create the file, and which program should be used to open the file.
Protocol	A standard set of formats and procedures which computers use to exchange information.

Source: Windows Help and Support

Computer clock
Each computer has a built-in memory chip that keeps track of the current time and date.

This tiny memory is powered by a battery. If the clock keeps running behind, you may need to replace the battery. Contact your computer supplier for assistance.

2.9 Tips

 Tip

Revert to default auto play settings

Some programs will automatically be set as default programs during installation, such as programs for playing certain types of CDs or DVDs. Any disc containing a similar file type will from then on be opened by this new program. But you do not always want that to happen, especially when you use these programs only once in a while, or if you want to open these file types with a different program.

If you want to revert to the default settings, here is how you do that:

☞ **Open the *Default Programs* window** 𝒪𝒪12

☞ **Click** Change AutoPlay settings

☞ **Drag the scroll bar all the way down**

☞ **Click** Reset all defaults

☞ **Click** Save

☞ **Close all windows** 𝒪𝒪9

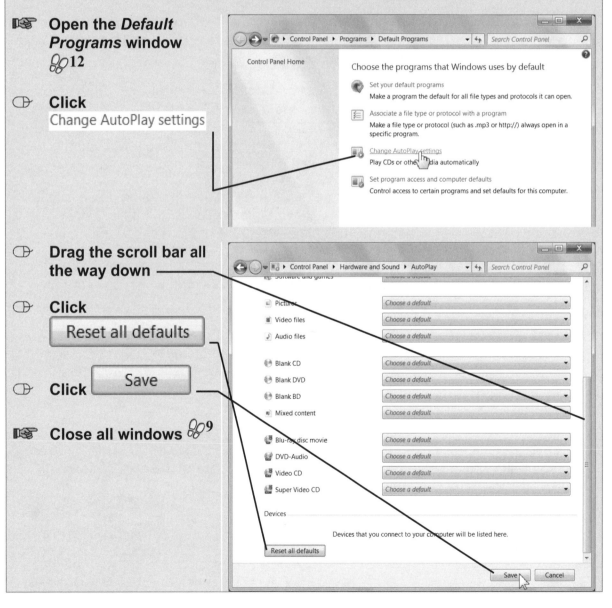

3. User Accounts

If you regularly share your computer with other users, it is recommended that a separate user account is created for each user. A user account contains a user's personal settings and preferences. For instance, the appearance of the desktop and screensaver, as well as the way in which the folders are displayed. Furthermore, each user can have his or her own list of favorite websites and browsing history in *Internet Explorer*. Also, each user can define his or her own settings for e-mail programs, such as *Windows Live Mail.* Finally, each user will have a separate *Personal Folder*.

It is very easy to work with user accounts. The user just needs to click his or her own user name in the *Windows 7* opening screen. Subsequently all the personal settings will be retrieved and applied. Any changes in these settings will not affect the settings of the other users. In *Windows 7* you can quickly switch to the account of another user. You will not need to close your own account first, and you can return to your own account just as quickly.

To prevent others from modifying your settings, you can protect your account with a password. With *User Accounts Control* you can secure your computer even further. This feature will prevent other users from accessing programs and settings on your computer for which they are not authorized.
Another useful feature in *Windows 7* is the *Parental Controls* function. This option lets you determine how and when your (grand)children are allowed to use the computer.

In this chapter you will learn how to:

- change the name and picture of a user account;
- create a new user account and delete an existing account;
- protect a user account with a password;
- change and remove a password;
- create and use a password reset disk;
- use the guest account;
- quickly switch between users;
- use *User Account Control*;
- set up *Parental Controls*.

 Please note!

The exercises in this chapter require the use of a USB stick. If you do not have such a stick, you can just read through the relevant sections.

3.1 Types of User Accounts

The use of user accounts allows you to share your computer with other people, while letting you keep your own files and settings. All users can use their own user name (and a password, if that is enabled) to access their own user account.

A user account is a collection of data that is used by *Windows 7* to determine which files and folders are accessible to the user, which changes are allowed to be made on the computer and what the settings for personal preferences look like, such as the desktop background theme and color scheme.

There are three types of user accounts:

- **Standard account:** useful for everyday computing. If you want to modify settings which will influence the accounts of other users or the security settings, you will need the administrator's permission. For example, you will not be able to install software and hardware, or delete files that are crucial to the operation of the computer.

- **Administrator account:** this account provides the most control over the computer. With the administrator account you can change settings which will influence the accounts of all other users. Administrators can modify security settings, install programs and hardware, and open all files on the computer. Also, administrators can modify the other user accounts.

- **Guest account:** this is a temporary account for users who do not have permanent access to your computer. A guest account enables people to use your computer without giving them access to personal files. Guest account users cannot install any programs or hardware, nor can they modify settings or create a password.

3.2 Change Your Name

When you start up *Windows 7* for the very first time, for instance on a new computer, the wizard asks you to enter the data for your user account. A wizard is an auxiliary program that assists you with specific operations.
For each user account, the user name will be displayed. In the *User Accounts* window you can easily change this name. You can open this window by going to the *Control Panel*:

☞ **Open the *Control Panel*** 🦯¹⁷

Click Add or remove user accc

Your screen may now turn dark and you will see the *User Accounts Control* window. This will depend on the settings of your computer. In this window you will need to give permission to continue.

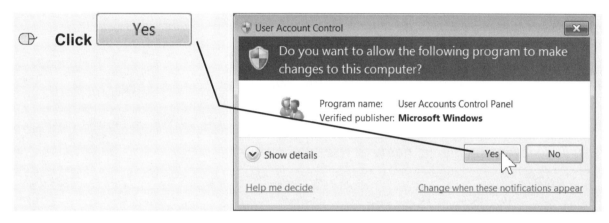

Click Yes

 HELP! I see a different window

If you see this window, you are using a standard account. A standard user account will not allow you to open the *User Accounts Control* window. In order to proceed, a standard user will first need to enter the administrator's password that goes with the administrator's account:

☞ **Ask the computer's administrator for help in changing your account, and for assistance with the other operations in this chapter**

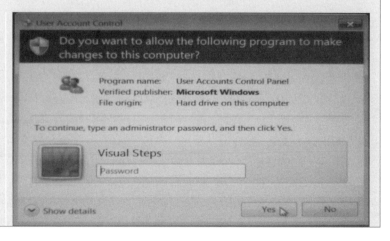

In the *Manage Accounts* window you will see all the current user accounts. If you have not yet added other user accounts, the only active account will be your own account, or the default *User* account. This *User* account has been created during the *Windows 7* installation procedure.

Click your user account

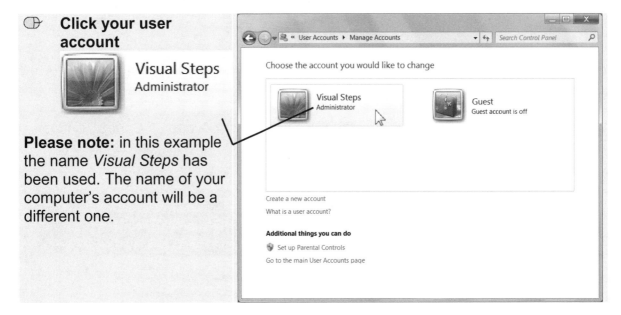

Please note: in this example the name *Visual Steps* has been used. The name of your computer's account will be a different one.

This is how you change the name of your user account:

Click
Change the account name

Now you can enter the new account name:

In the box:

⌨ **Type a name**

☞ **Click** Change Name

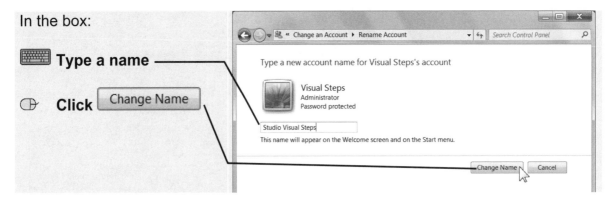

Your user account's name
has been changed:

3.3 Select a Different Picture

In *Windows 7*, each user account is accompanied by a small picture. If you would like to change this picture:

Click
Change the picture

In this window you will see the pictures you can select for your *Windows 7* user accounts. Here you can practice replacing the current picture by the picture of a fish:

Click

Click Change Picture

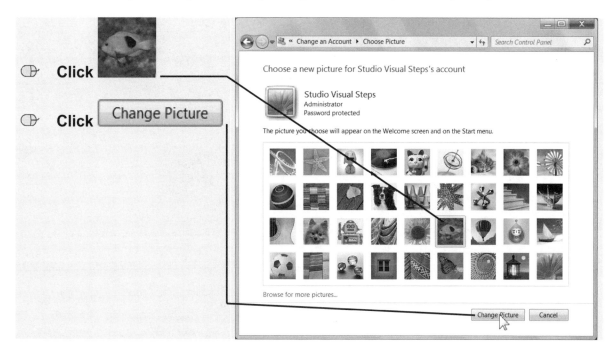

You see that the picture of
your user account has been
replaced:

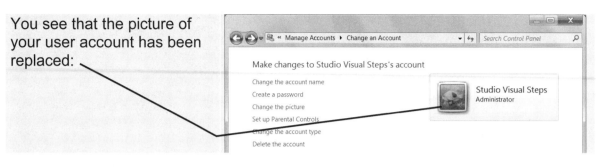

☞ **Close the window** 𝒶𝒶⁹

💡 **Tip**

Use your own picture
Instead of using one of the default *Windows 7* pictures, you can also use one of your
own pictures or photos for your user account. This is how you do that:

⊕ **Click**
   Browse for more pictures...

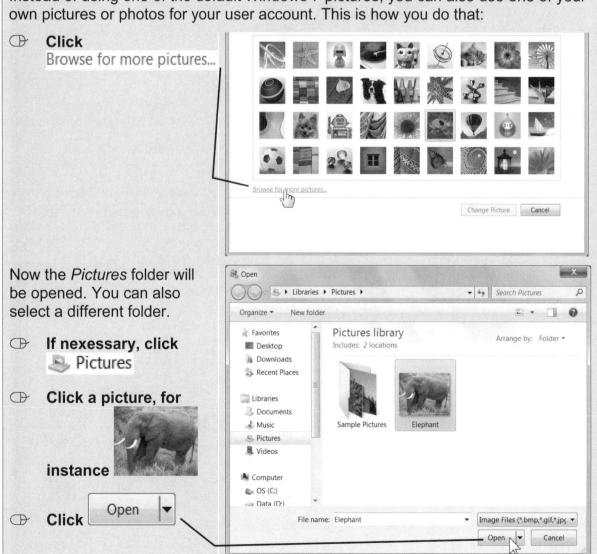

Now the *Pictures* folder will
be opened. You can also
select a different folder.

⊕ **If nexessary, click**
   🖳 Pictures

⊕ **Click a picture, for**

   instance

⊕ **Click** [Open ▼]

3.4 Creating a New User Account

In the *Manage Accounts* window you can create a new user account in just a few steps.

☞ **Open the *Manage Accounts* window** ✂18

⊕ **Click**
Create a new account

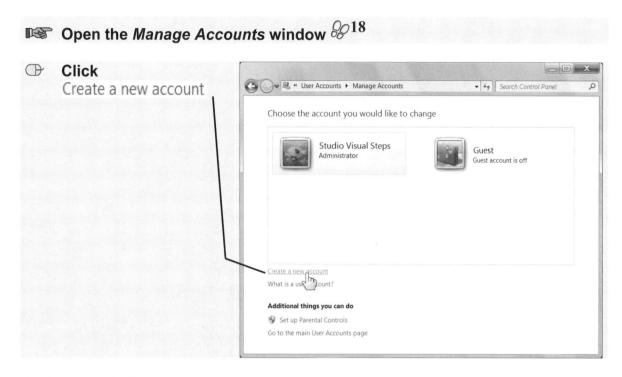

In the next window you can enter a user name and select the account type for the new account. For this exercise, select the standard user account type:

⌨ **Type a name, for example:** Nick

⊕ **Click the radio button**
⊙ **next to**
Standard user

⊕ **Click** Create Account

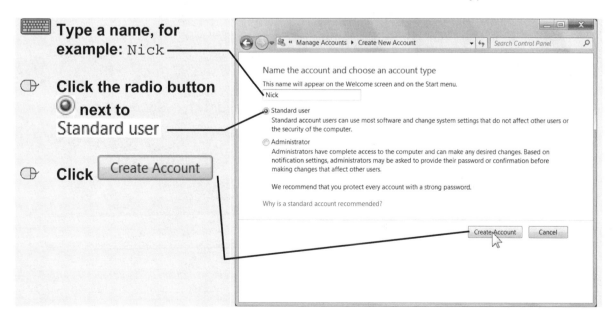

Now you will see that a new account has been added:

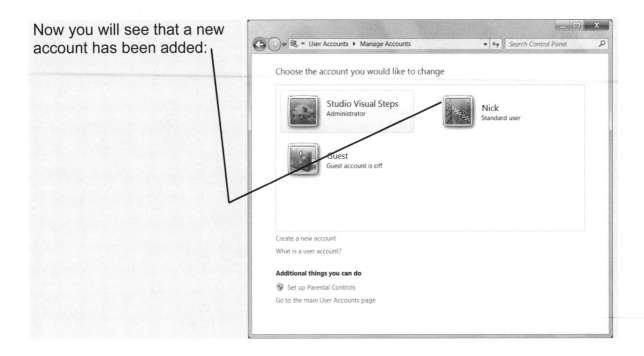

3.5 Deleting a User Account

If one of the users will not be using the computer any longer, you can delete his or her account. You need to be an administrator to delete an account, or have access to the administrator's password.

 Please note!

When a user account is deleted, the corresponding settings for *Windows Live Mail*, the stored e-mails, and various other settings will be deleted as well. But you can choose to save the files in the *Documents*, *Favorites*, *Music*, *Pictures*, and *Videos* folders to your desktop. *Windows 7* will ask you if you want to do this.

This is how you delete the new user account you have just created:

Now you will see a window with several options for this account.

Click
Delete the account

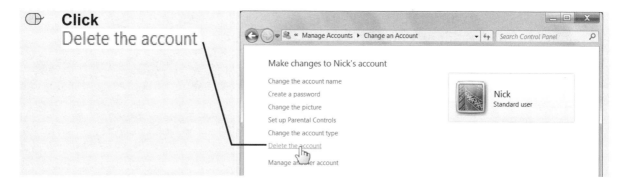

Windows 7 will ask you what to do with the files that belong to this user. You can choose to save the files in the *Documents*, *Favorites*, *Music*, *Pictures*, and *Videos* folders to your desktop or delete them. If you want to save these files, they will be added to your desktop. You will find the files in a folder which is named for the user you have just deleted.

In this example you are going to delete the files:

Click Delete Files

Finally, you will be asked if you are sure you want to delete this account:

Click
Delete Account

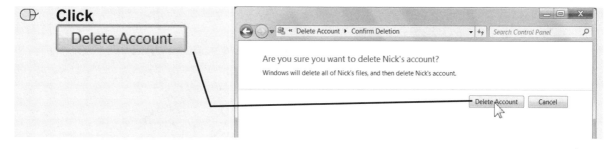

The user account has been deleted.

HELP! I see a different window

Windows 7 will warn you that there is a risk of losing data when you delete an account while the user of that account is still logged on.

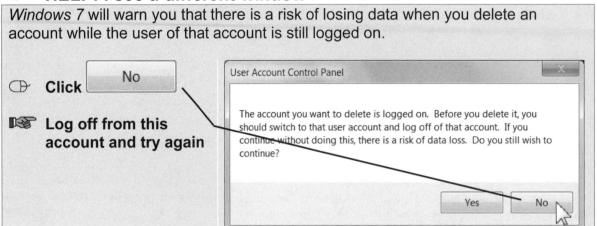

☞ **Click** No

☞ **Log off from this account and try again**

User Account Control Panel ✕

The account you want to delete is logged on. Before you delete it, you should switch to that user account and log off of that account. If you continue without doing this, there is a risk of data loss. Do you still wish to continue?

Yes No

3.6 Setting a Password For a User Account

You can secure each user account by entering a password for that account. If you want to make sure that nobody can change your settings, you will need to enter a password for your user account. Here is how to do that:

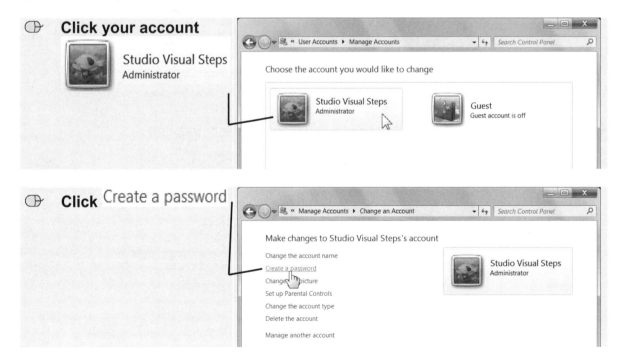

☞ **Click your account**

Studio Visual Steps
Administrator

☞ **Click** Create a password

In the next window you can enter a password, and a password hint. This password hint will help you remember your password, in case you have forgotten it. Keep in mind that passwords are case sensitive. If you use capital letters in your password, you will need to type the password in exactly the same way, every time you enter it.

 Please note!

Using a password will only make sense if it is difficult for others to find or guess the password. That is why you need to use at least seven characters, and a combination of numbers and letters.

 Type your password

Retype your password

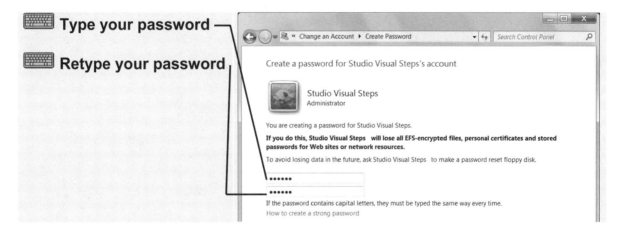

Now you can enter the password hint.

Please note!

Keep in mind that everybody who uses your computer can view your password hint on the opening screen. Try to think of a somewhat vague hint that is difficult to guess, like the name of your first pet, or your mother's maiden name.

Type a password hint

☞ **Write down your password on paper for safekeeping**

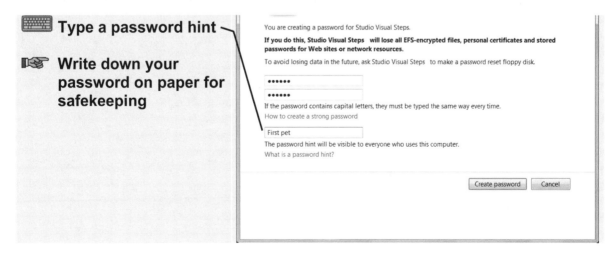

After you have entered your password and the password hint and have written down the password on a piece of paper, you can activate the password:

Click Create password

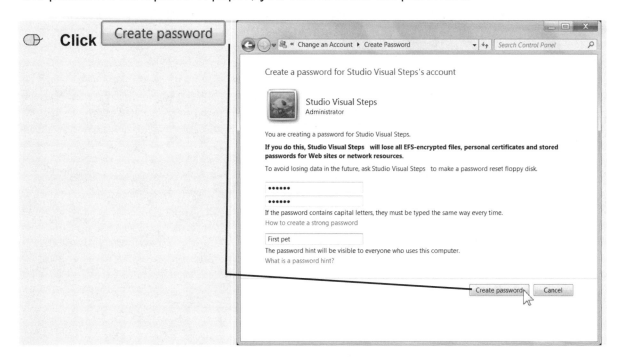

HELP! I see a different window

Do you see the following window? Then you have entered two different passwords.

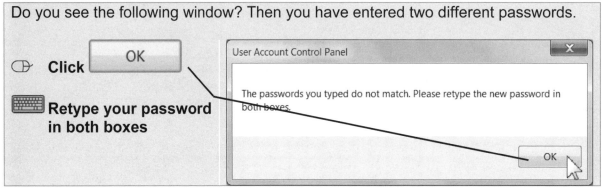

Please note!

Your password will only protect your own user account. It will prevent other users from logging on to the computer with your account.

When another user tries to open your *Personal Folder*, he or she will see this window:

A user with a standard user account will need to enter the administrator's password, after clicking Continue.

However, an administrator will be able to directly access other users' *Personal Folders*, after clicking Continue. Therefore, it is wiser to create standard user accounts for all other people who use your computer, instead of administrator accounts.

Please note: new folders that you have created on your computer's hard disk, can be viewed by other users. In the *Computer* or *Windows Explorer* windows they can view the computer's content and open folders. That is why you should always store your personal folders and files in the *Personal* folder (or in a subdirectory of that folder).

Tip

Share documents

Even if all users have a standard, password protected user account, they will still be able to share documents. For this you can use the *Public Documents* folder. All users will be able to open this folder. This is how you use the *Save as* window to save a document to the *Public Documents* folder:

Click ▷ 🖫 OS (C:) (you might see a different name on your computer, for example: 🖫 Local Disk (C:))

Double-click Users

Double-click Public

Double-click Public Documents

Click Save

3.7 Changing a Password

If you are using a password to protect your user account, it is recommended to change this password on a regular basis. Here is how to do that:

⊕ **Click**
   Change the password

In the next window you will be asked to enter your current password first. This is used to verify if you are the actual user who is authorized to change the password. Afterwards you can enter the new password and the new password hint:

⌨ **Type your current password**

⌨ **Type your new password**

⌨ **Retype your new password**

⌨ **Type a password hint**

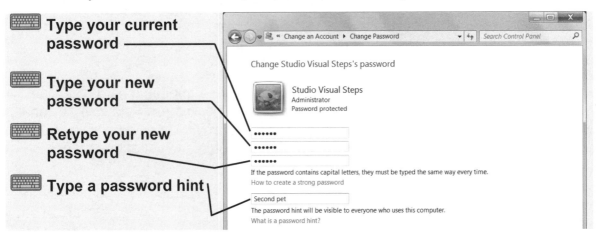

☞ **Write down your password on paper for safekeeping**

Now you can change the password:

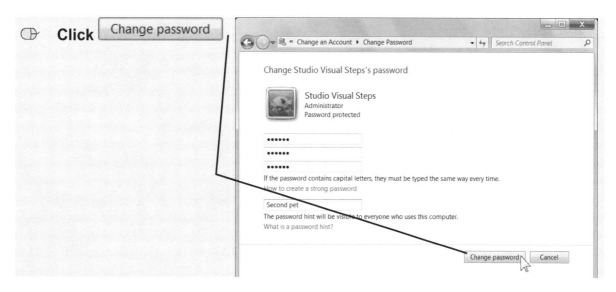

Now the password has been changed. You will need to use the new password, next time you want to log on.

 Close the *Change an account* window $\mathcal{U}\mathcal{P}^9$

3.8 Create a Password Reset Disk

There is always the chance that one day you will no longer remember what your password is. If even the password hint does not help you, it will be a relief to you that you are prepared for such an event. Namely, by creating a *password reset disk* with which you can log on to *Windows 7*. Afterwards you can enter a new password. You will only need to create a password reset disk once, no matter how often you change your password after creating this disk.

➡ Please note!

In order to create a password reset disk you will need to have a USB stick. A USB stick is also called a USB memory stick or a USB flash drive. If you do not have a USB stick, just read through this section.

In the *Control Panel* you will find the option for creating a password reset disk:

 Open the *Control Panel* $\mathcal{U}\mathcal{P}^{17}$

Click
User Accounts and Family Safety

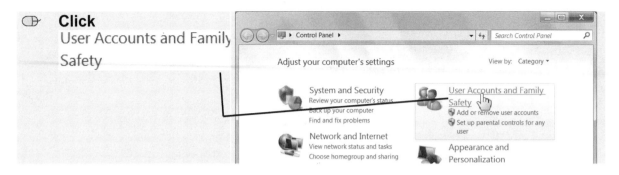

Open the *User Accounts* window:

Click User Accounts

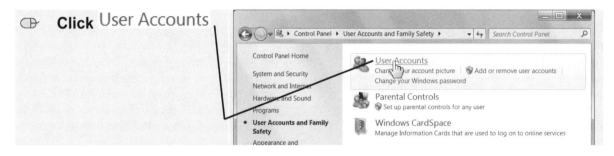

☞ **Insert a USB stick into the computer's USB port**

Wait a moment for *Windows 7* to identify your USB stick.

In the lower right corner of your screen you will see a message:

☞ **If necessary, close the *Auto play* window** 👣⁹

Click
Create a password reset disk

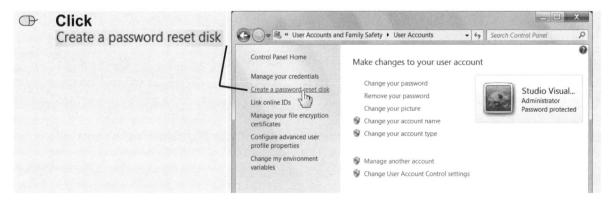

Now the *Forgotten Password Wizard* will be opened.

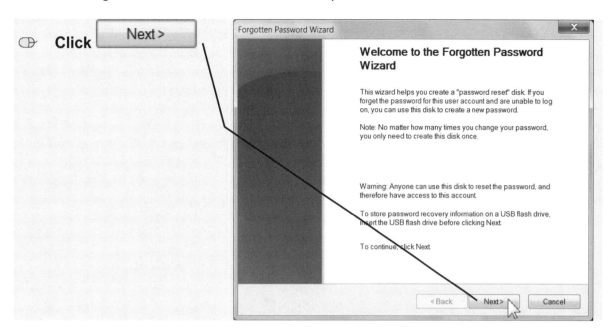

You can select the disk drive for the password key disk.

In this example we are using a USB stick that is inserted into the computer's G: port.

☞ **Click** ▼

☞ **Click the drive you want to use, for instance**
   REMOVABLE D (G:)

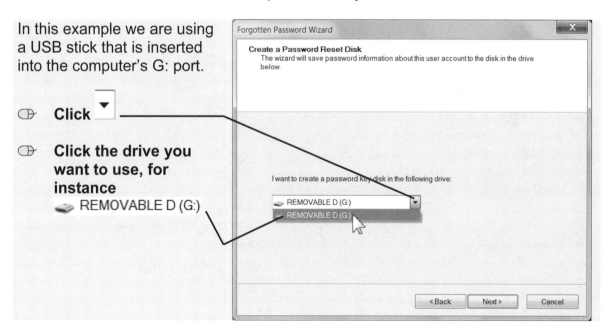

Click Next >

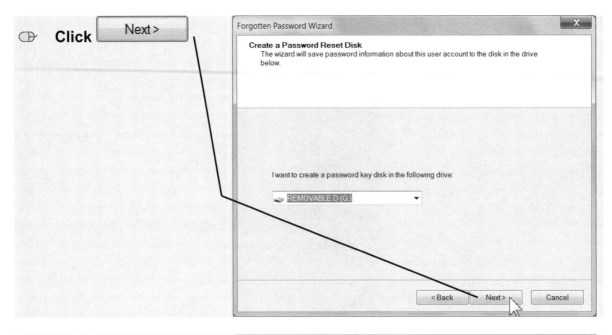

Type your current password

Click Next >

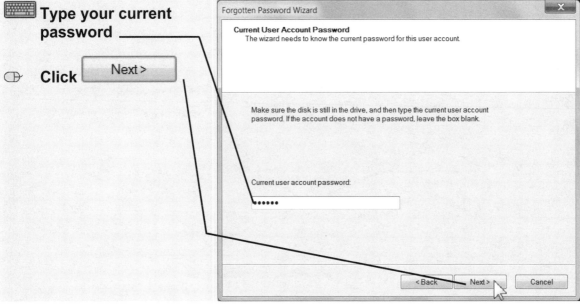

Now the *Forgotten Password Wizard* will write the password data to the USB stick:

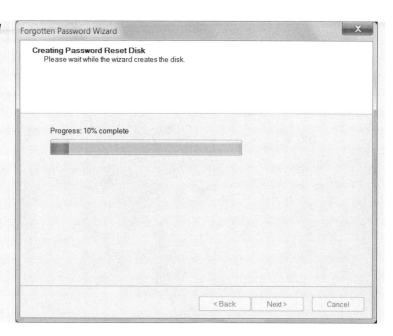

Click Next >

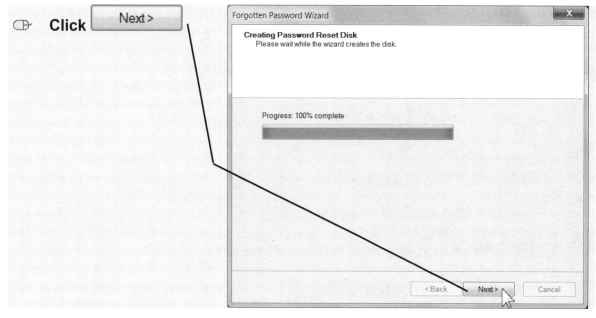

Click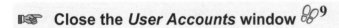

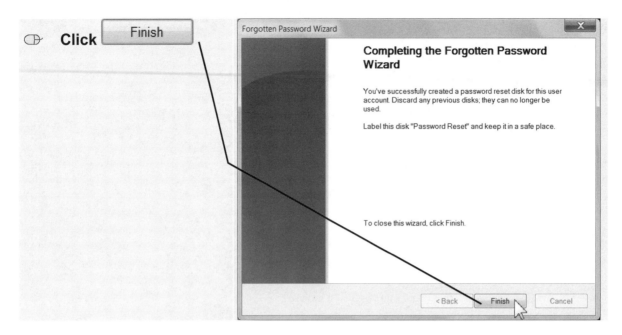

The password reset disk has been created and is ready to use. Store the USB stick in a safe location.

☞ **Safely remove the USB stick from your computer**

☞ **Close the *User Accounts* window** ᵍ⁹

➥**Please note!**

Make sure that other users cannot use your password reset disk. Anybody who gets hold of this USB stick will be able to log on with your account information.

HELP! I have not created a password reset disk

If you forget your password and you have not created a password reset disk, you will not be able to log on to the computer. If there is another administrator, a new password can be created for you. But you will still lose part of your settings. Your personal certificates and stored website passwords will be deleted.

Are you the only administrator for your computer? Then you will need to install *Windows 7* all over again.

Tip

Using the password reset disk
If you have forgotten your password, you will not be able to log on in the opening screen. The password reset disk will allow you to enter a new password without being logged on to your account. Then you can use this password to log on. This is how you do that:

☞ **Click your account**

Normally, you would have entered your password at this point, but you are not going to do so now.

☞ **Click** 🔄

You will see a message saying that your user name or your password is invalid.

☞ **Click** OK **to quit this window**

☞ **Click** Reset password...

Now you will see the first window of the *Password Reset Wizard*.

☞ **Insert the password reset disk (the USB stick) and click** Next >

You will see a window where you can select the drive to which USB stick is connected:

☞ **Click** ▼

☞ **Click the drive you want to use, for example** 💾 REMOVABLE D (G:)

☞ **Click** Next >

You can enter your new password and a new password hint:

⌨ **Type a new password**

⌨ **Retype your new password**

⌨ **Enter a password hint**

☞ **Click** Next >

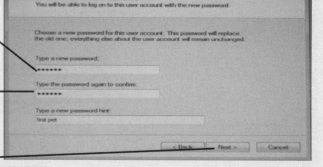

☞ **In the next window, click** Finish

Now you can log on with your new password.

3.9 Using the Guest Account

It is not necessary to create a separate user account for each user that uses your computer just once in a while. If your computer is used by persons who just need to check their e-mail once in a while, or who occasionally want to surf the Internet, it is better to let these persons use the *Guest Account*. If you activate the *Guest Account*, people who do not have their own user account will be able to log on to the computer as well. The *Guest Account* is an account with limited user rights.

➥ Please note!

You can only activate the *Guest Account* if you are a user with administrative rights, that is, you need to be an *Administrator*.

This is how you activate the *Guest Account*:

☞ **Open the *Manage Accounts* window** ᡃᡃ18

⊕ **Click**

Guest
Guest account is off

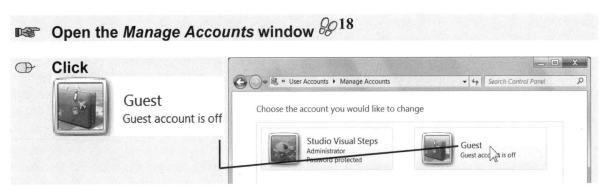

In this window you can turn on the *Guest Account*:

⊕ **Click** [Turn On]

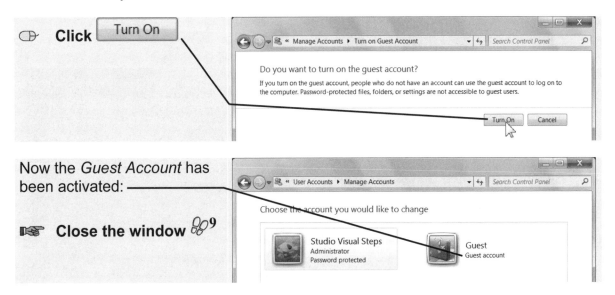

Now the *Guest Account* has been activated: ─────

☞ **Close the window** ᡃᡃ9

In the *Windows 7* opening screen you will now see a new user called *Guest*.

3.10 Quickly Switch Between Users

Windows 7 lets you switch between users in a quick and easy way. This is very useful when you are using the computer yourself, and one of the other users wants to briefly check his or her e-mail. This way, you will not need to close all your programs and log off. In *Windows 7* you can switch to somebody else's user account, and then switch right back again to your own account.

This is how you switch to the *Guest* account:

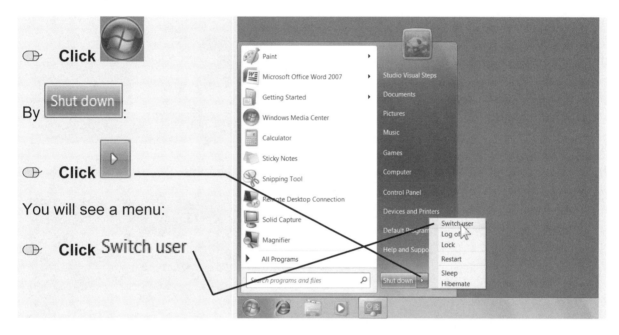

Now you will see the *Windows 7* opening screen. Here you can select the user account you want to open:

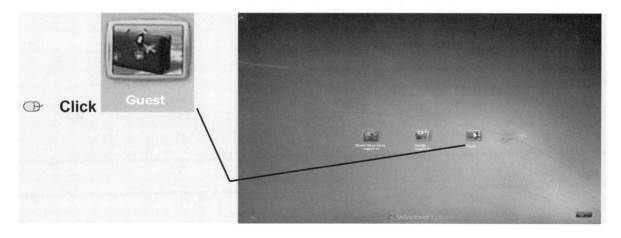

The *Guest Account* will be opened.

From the *Guest Account* you can return to your own account again. First, you need to log off from the *Guest Account*:

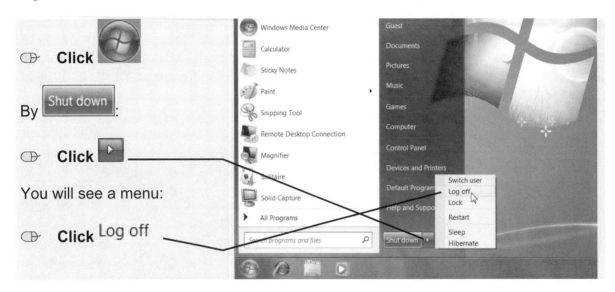

Click ⊕

By **Shut down** :

Click ⊕ ▶

You will see a menu:

Click ⊕ Log off

In the opening screen you can select your own account again:

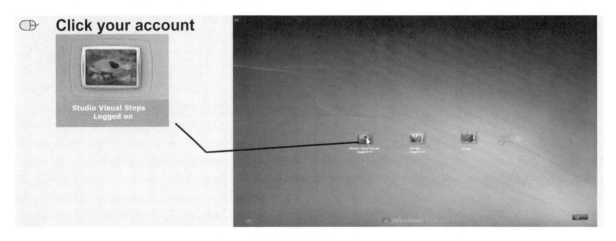

Click your account ⊕

After you have entered your password, your user account will be opened again. All programs that you had opened will still be active.

Up to now you have learned how to set up and use user accounts, with and without entering a password. In the next section you will learn how to employ additional security measures when you manage your user accounts.

Tip

No need to enter your password over and over again

If you do not use the computer for more than ten minutes your computer screen will go dark by default. If the computer is idle for more than thirty minutes, the computer will revert to the sleep state. There is no default screen saver but you can set up one for yourself.

The default settings:

- You are not required to retype your password when you interrupt the screen saver (by moving the mouse or pressing a random key on the keyboard).
- You are required to retype your password when you wake your computer from the sleep state. Depending on the type of computer you use, you do this by pressing the On/Off switch on the computer, by moving the mouse, or by pressing a random key.

You can modify these settings according to your own preferences. Here is how to do that:

☞ **Right-click the desktop**

☞ **Click** Personalize

☞ **Click** Screen Saver

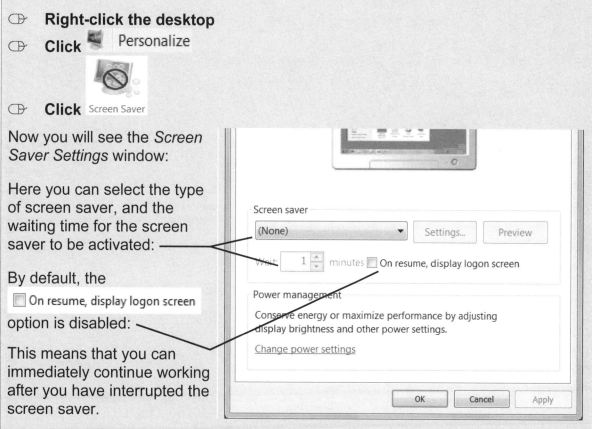

Now you will see the *Screen Saver Settings* window:

Here you can select the type of screen saver, and the waiting time for the screen saver to be activated:

By default, the

☐ On resume, display logon screen

option is disabled:

This means that you can immediately continue working after you have interrupted the screen saver.

If you enable this option, the screen saver window will switch to the opening screen. There you will need to retype your password in order to log on again.

- Continue reading on the next page –

You will find the sleep state settings in a different window:

☞ **Click** Change power settings

In the *Power Options* window:

☞ **Click**
Require a password on wakeu

In this window there are a few disabled options:

☞ **Click**
🛡 Change settings that a

Your screen may turn dark and you will need to give permission to continue.

☞ **Click** Yes

If you do not want to enter your password any longer, after waking up the computer:

☞ **Click the radio button**
🔘 **next to**
Don't require a password

☞ **Click** Save changes

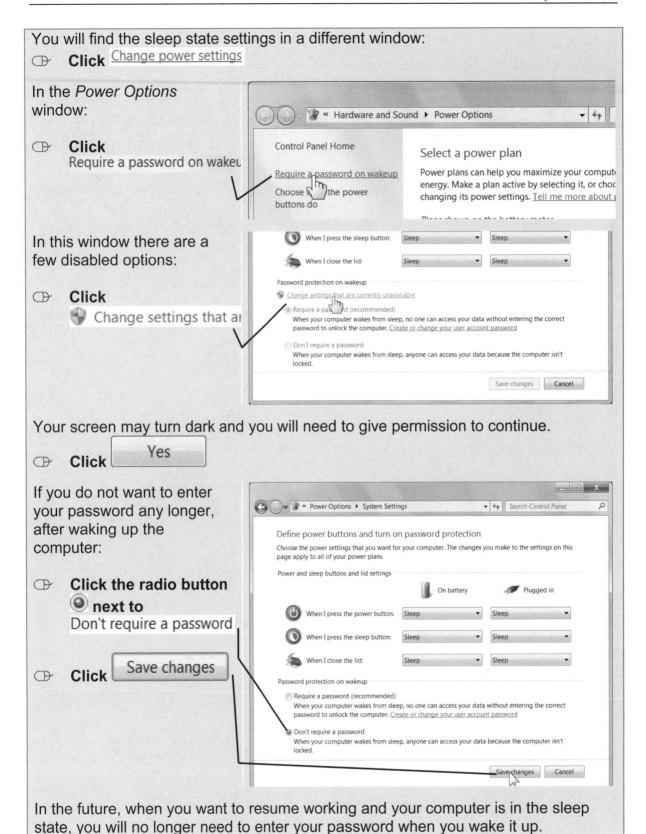

In the future, when you want to resume working and your computer is in the sleep state, you will no longer need to enter your password when you wake it up.

3.11 User Account Control

You may already be familiar with the *Windows 7 User Account Control*. This feature is responsible for opening a new window and asking for permission before continuing any action in a certain program. The computer screen will turn dark. This feature prevents unauthorized users from making changes to your computer. Every time you see a *User Account Control* message, you need to read it carefully and make sure that the name that is stated for the operation corresponds with the action or program you want to execute.

You may see different *User Account Control* messages, each with their own icon:

A setting or feature that is part of *Windows* needs your permission to start.
This item has a valid digital signature that verifies that Microsoft is the publisher of this item. If you get this type of dialog box, it's usually safe to continue. If you are unsure, check the name of the program or function to decide if it's something you want to run.

A program that is not part of Windows needs your permission to start.
This message will be displayed when you start a program that is not part of *Windows*, but does have a valid digital signature. Make sure the program is the one that you want to run and that you trust the publisher.

A program with an unknown publisher needs your permission to start.
This message will be displayed when you start an unknown program that does not have a valid digital signature from its publisher. That is why you cannot be sure that it is a legitimate program. This doesn't necessarily indicate danger, as many older, legitimate programs lack signatures. However, you should use extra caution and only allow a program to run if you obtained it from a trusted source, such as the original CD or a publisher's website.

You have been blocked by your system administrator from running this program.
If your computer is connected to a network, the system administrator can block a program, to prevent it running on your computer. You can ask your administrator to unblock the program.

Tip

User Account Control Settings
By default, the *User Account Control* settings in *Windows 7* are set to a low level. This means that you will only see warning messages if the operations are really important. If you have previous experience with *Windows Vista*, you surely have noticed that the *User Account Control* messages were displayed much more often than in *Windows 7*. You can modify the *User Account Control* settings yourself:

☞ **Open the *User Accounts* window** ⬚⬚^{19}

👆 **Click**
   🛡 Change User Account Control

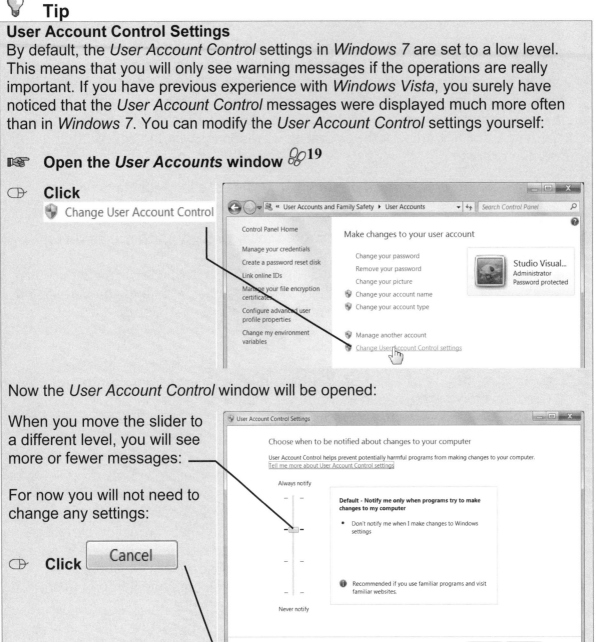

Now the *User Account Control* window will be opened:

When you move the slider to a different level, you will see more or fewer messages:

For now you will not need to change any settings:

👆 **Click** Cancel

If you want to fully use all the features of *User Account Control*, you will need to create *standard user accounts* for all users of your computer, including yourself. This account will give you sufficient rights for sending e-mails, editing photos, or surfing the Internet.

Apart from that, you will need one *administrator account* that is password protected. It is recommended to protect also the standard accounts with passwords.

For example, when a standard user tries to install a software program, the screen will turn dark and the user will be asked to enter the administrator's password. This way, no software can be installed without the administrator's permission.

In this window the standard user will need to enter the administrator's password in order to continue the operation:

If you do not see a box in which you can enter your password (like in this example), then click

 Show details .

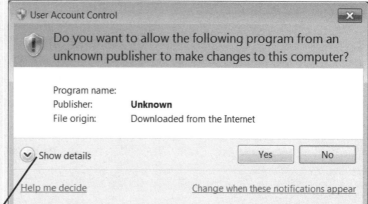

You will always need to enter the administrator's password to execute tasks that:
- may affect the operation of the computer, or
- may affect other users' settings.

The same thing is true for the *Parental Controls* settings. In the next section you can learn more about *Parental Controls*.

3.12 Parental Controls

The *Parental Controls* feature gives you control over the way in which other users, for instance your (grand) children, can use the computer. In this way you can set limits on the hours that children can use the computer, or the types of games they can play, or the programs they can run.

➥ Please note!

Before you can set the *Parental Controls*, you need to make sure that your (grand) children have a standard user account. This account needs to be protected by a password, just as all other user accounts. If any of the other accounts are not password protected, the children can use these other accounts to bypass the *Parental Controls*.
In *section 3.4 Creating a New User Account* and *section 3.6 Setting a Password For a User Account*, you can read how to create a user account and protect it with a password.

You can use the *Control Panel* to set the *Parental Controls*:

☞ **Open the *Control Panel*** 🦶¹⁷

⊕ **Click**

   🛡 Set up parental controls for
      user

Depending on your computer's settings, your screen may now turn dark. If you are logged on as a standard user yourself, you will now need to enter the administrator's password.

⊕ **Click** ┃ Yes ┃

Now you will see all the user accounts on your computer.

⊕ **Click the account for which you want to set up *Parental Controls***

First you need to switch on the *Parental Controls*:

⊕ **Click the radio button**
   ◉ **next to**
   On, enforce current settings

As soon as you have activated the *Parental Controls*, the rest if this window will become active.

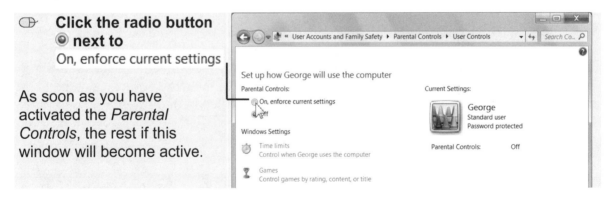

There are three separate settings you can modify in *Parental Controls*:

- ⏱ Time limits
  : use this setting to set limits on the hours the user of this account can use the computer;
- 🏆 Games
  : use this setting to determine the types of games this account's user can play;
- 🗔 Allow and block specific programs
  : here you can determine which programs the user can open, so you can prevent the user from running specific programs.

For example, you are going to change the Time limits settings:

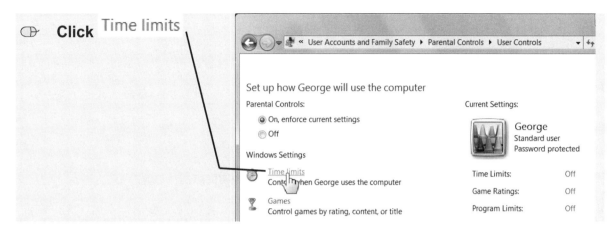

Click Time limits

In this window you can set the hours in which this user is allowed to use the computer. Outside this time limit, this user will not be able to log on.

By default all hours are ☐ Allowed. By clicking or dragging the blocks, you can change this status in ▨ Blocked.

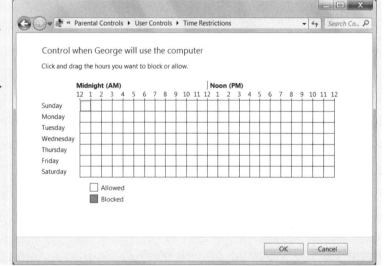

Click the hours you want to block

In this example all hours between 8 p.m. and 8 a.m. are blocked. Of course you can choose the time limits yourself. When you have finished:

Click [OK]

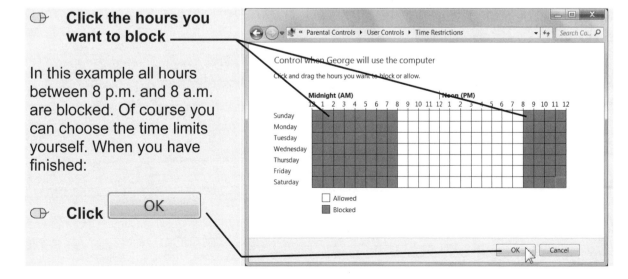

☞ **If necessary, modify the settings for** 🏆 Games **and**
🔳 Allow and block specific programs **as well**

After you have modified all the settings, the main *Parental Controls* window will display a summary of these settings. Here is an example:	Time Limits: On
	Game Ratings: Up to EVERYONE 10+
	Program Limits: Off

If you are satisfied with these settings, you can confirm them.

At the bottom of the window:

👉 **Click** ▭ OK ▭

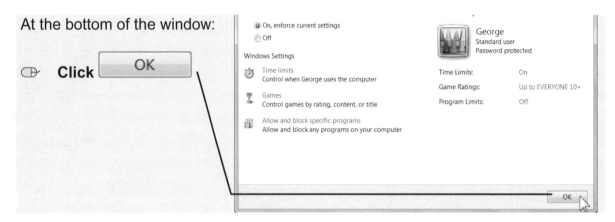

3.13 Deleting a Password

If, on second thoughts, you do not find it necessary to protect your account by a password, you can delete this password.

 Please note!

> If you have set up *Parental Controls*, it is better not to remove your password. That is because *Parental Controls* can be bypassed if the computer contains accounts which are not password protected.

This is how you remove your password:

☞ **Open the *User Accounts* window** 🔗**19**

⊕ **Click**
Remove your password

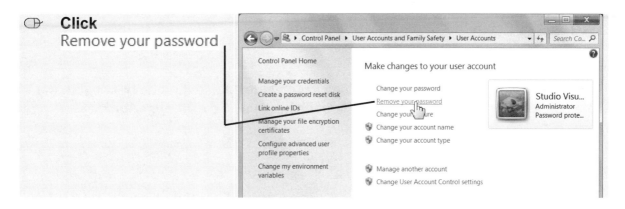

In order to delete your password, *Windows 7* has to check if you are actually the authorized user. That is why you need to enter your password first:

⌨ **Type your password**

⊕ **Click**
Remove Password

Now your password has been removed.

☞ **Close all windows** ⁹

➥ **Please note!**

If you decide to create a new password for your account later on, you will need to create a new password reset disk as well.

In this chapter you have learned how to work with user accounts. In the following exercises you can practice the operations you have learned.

3.14 Exercises

Have you forgotten how to do something? Then you can use the number next to the footsteps to look up the description in *Appendix B How Do I Do That Again?*

Exercise: A New User Account

In this exercise you are going to create a new user account. In order to do this, you must be logged on as an administrator.

☞ Open the *Manage Accounts* window. $\ell\ell$ [18]

☞ Create a new standard user account by the name of *Exercise*. $\ell\ell$[20]

Exercise: Modify the User Account

In this exercise you are going to modify the new user account.

☞ Change the picture for this user account and select the picture. $\ell\ell$[21]

☞ Change the account name and call this account *Trial*. $\ell\ell$[22]

☞ Close all open windows. $\ell\ell$[9]

Exercise: Delete an Account

In this exercise you are going to delete the new user account. In order to do this you will need to be logged on as an administrator once again.

☞ Open the *Manage Accounts* window. $\ell\ell$[18]

☞ Click the account called *Trial*.

☞ Delete this user account, do not save the files that go with this account. $\ell\ell$[23]

☞ Close all windows. $\ell\ell$[9]

3.15 Background Information

Dictionary	
Administrator account	This user account lets you influence all other user accounts. Administrators can modify security settings, install hardware and software, and open all the files on the computer. Administrators can also modify the accounts of other users.
Guest account	An account for users who do not have permanent access to your computer. A guest account lets people use your computer, but they do not have access to personal files. People using the guest account cannot install software or hardware, change settings, or create a password.
Hint	Hint that helps you remember your password, which will be displayed when you type an incorrect password.
Parental Controls	You can use this feature to determine how others use your computer, for instance, your (grand) children. For example, by setting limits on the hours they are allowed to use the computer, or the types of games they can play, or the programs they can run.
Password	A password is a string of characters that people can use to log on to a computer and access files, programs, and other resources. Passwords help ensure that people do not access the computer unless they have been authorized to do so.
Password reset disk	This device lets you create a new password, in case you have forgotten the current one. You can create a password reset disk on a USB stick.
Screen saver	A screen saver is a moving picture or pattern that appears on your computer screen when you have not used the mouse or keyboard for a specified period of time.
Sleep state	Sleep is a power-saving state that allows a computer to quickly resume full-power operation (typically within several seconds) when you want to start working again. Before the sleep state is activated, all open documents and programs will be saved, so the computer is ready to start again when you want to resume working.
- Continue reading on the next page -	

Standard user account	This account lets you use most of the capabilities of the computer, but you will need the administrator's permission to change settings that will affect the accounts of other users, or the security of the computer.
Time limits	Feature of *Parental Controls* to control the hours in which your (grand) children are allowed to use your computer. Time limits prevent children from logging on during the specified hours. If they are logged on when their allotted time ends, they will be automatically logged off.
USB port	A narrow, rectangular connection point on a computer where you can connect a USB (Universal Serial Bus) device.
USB stick / USB memory stick	A small device you can use to store data. A USB stick is connected to the USB port of your computer. *Windows 7* will display a USB stick as a removable device drive.
User account	A user account is a collection of information that tells Windows which files and folders you can access, what changes you can make to the computer, and your personal preferences, such as your desktop background or screen saver. User accounts let you share a computer with several people, while having your own files and settings.
User account control	This feature prevents users from executing unauthorized operations on your computer. Before any changes can be made that will affect the operation of the computer, or will affect other users' settings, the screen will turn dark. Next, you will be asked to give permission to continue (if you are logged on as an administrator) or you will be asked to enter the administrator's password (if you are logged on as a standard user).

Source: Windows Help and Support

4. Your Computer

In this chapter you will take a look at the various components of your computer, such as your computer's hard drive and the removable storage devices.

You will learn more about the different types of files that are stored on your hard drive. A file can consist of all sorts of things. It might be a part of a software program, or a data file. Your own work, saved as a text document or a photo, is also called a file.

There are many different kinds of file types, each with their own file format. It is very useful to learn about the various file types and the programs you can use to open them.

In this chapter you will learn how to:

- detect the hard disk drives on your computer;
- view disk properties;
- view your DVD and removable drives;
- take a look at the components and performance of your computer;
- display information about your computer;
- discern the various file types;
- view file properties;
- open a file.

 Please note!

In order to work through this chapter, you will need to download the folder with practice files from the website that accompanies this book. In *Appendix A Download Practice Files* at the back of this book, you can read how to do this.

4.1 What Is Inside Your Computer?

There is a special button in *Windows* that will take you to the screen where you can view all of your computer's components:

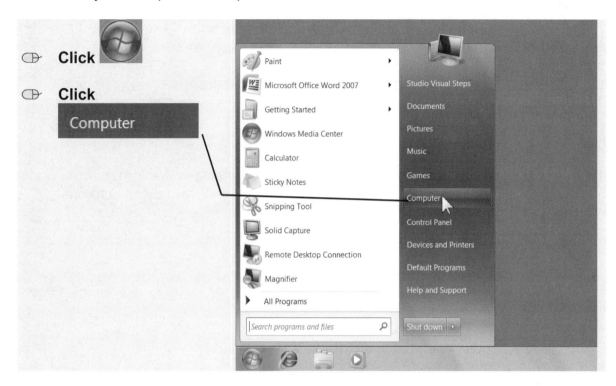

The *Computer* window is now open. If you want to see the exact same window as in this book, you will need to take the following steps:

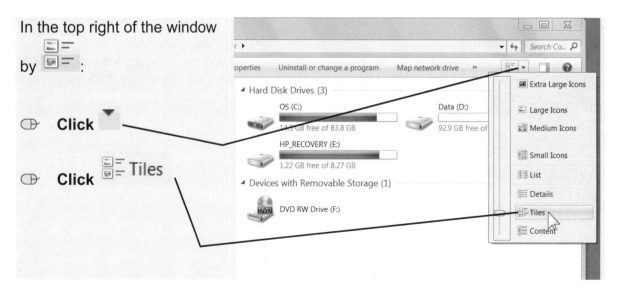

You will see this window, which contains the following elements, from top to bottom:

The hard disk drive/disks:

The removable storage devices: CD/DVD drives and removable hard disks:

USB sticks and external hard disks are examples of removable media.

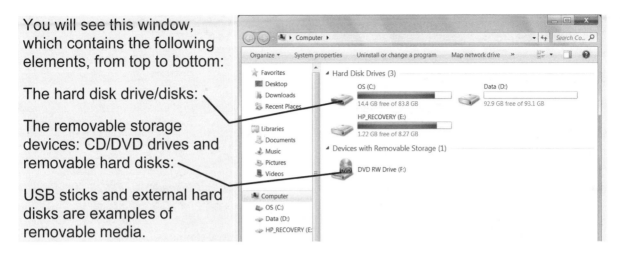

On your own computer you will see different components. That is because your computer will not be exactly the same as the computer that was used for writing this book. Your computer may have other components and other drive names.

You will see that all components are indicated by a letter. The hard disk drive is always assigned the letter C. If your computer contains more than one hard disk drive, the next drive will be assigned the letter D. CD or DVD drives will then get the following letters (in this example the letter E), and removable media will be assigned all the subsequent letters (in this example it is the F). Each computer will have a different amount of letters, depending on the devices that are connected to the computer.

4.2 The Hard Disk Properties

In the *Computer* window you can view the properties of the various components. This is how you do that:

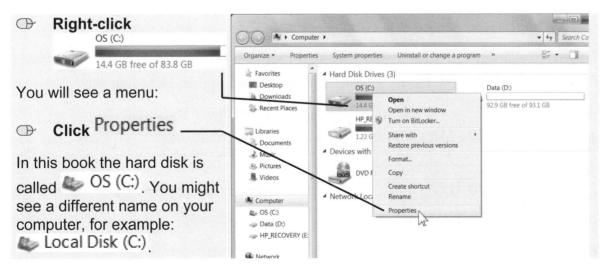

☞ **Right-click**
OS (C:)

14.4 GB free of 83.8 GB

You will see a menu:

☞ **Click** Properties

In this book the hard disk is called OS (C:). You might see a different name on your computer, for example:
Local Disk (C:).

Now you will see this hard disk properties window:

The full capacity of the disk is expressed in GB:

Below that, you see a pie chart which shows you the distribution of used and free disk space:

The capacity and the pie chart will look different on your own computer.

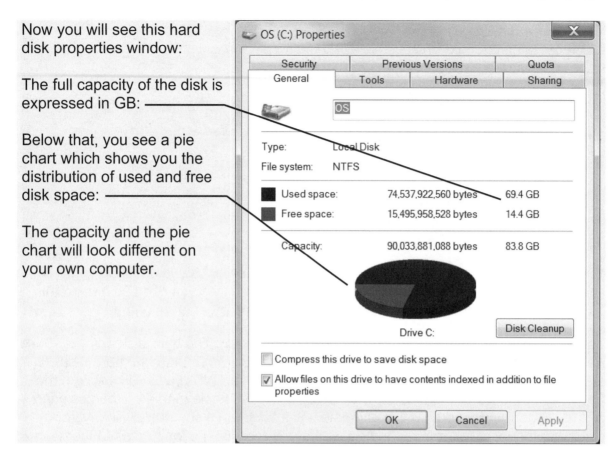

The GB abbreviation stands for Gigabyte, a measurement of the storage capacity. In the next section you will learn more about this subject.

4.3 Gigabyte, Megabyte, Kilobyte

The smallest unit used to store data on a computer is the *bit*. A group of 8 bits is called a *byte*. Try to picture it this way: each digit, letter, or photo pixel will take up one or more bytes.

This is a very small unit. Large quantities of bytes are expressed as follows: *Kilobyte*, *Megabyte* and *Gigabyte*.
The size of these units increases in multiples of a thousand. To make it easier, just assume that the size of each next unit is multiplied by thousand:

- 1 Byte is 8 bits
- 1 Kilobyte (kB) is 1000 bytes
- 1 Megabyte (MB) is 1000 Kilobyte
- 1 Gigabyte (GB) is 1000 Megabyte
- 1 Terabyte (TB) is 1000 Gigabyte

You can use various types of media to store and save data: USB sticks, memory cards, CDs, DVDs, and hard disks. Much older computers may still use floppy disks.

The storage capacity of these media is expressed in Megabytes or Gigabytes. For example:

- floppy disk: 1.4 MB
- CD disc: 650 MB
- DVD disc: 4.7 GB (or twice that amount, depending on the type of disc)
- Blu-ray disc: 25 GB (or twice that amount, depending on the type of disc)
- USB stick: 16 MB up to 8 GB (or even more)
- memory card: 256 MB up to 8 GB (or even more)
- small computer hard disk: 30 up to 80 GB
- large computer hard disk: 100 up to 400 GB (or more)

In the properties window you can see the size of your computer's hard disk, in other words, the *storage capacity* of your hard disk.

In this example you can see that 69.4 GB has been used, and that there is still 14.4 GB of free space available:

The total capacity of this hard disk is 83.8 GB:

You can close this window:

⊕ **Click** ❌

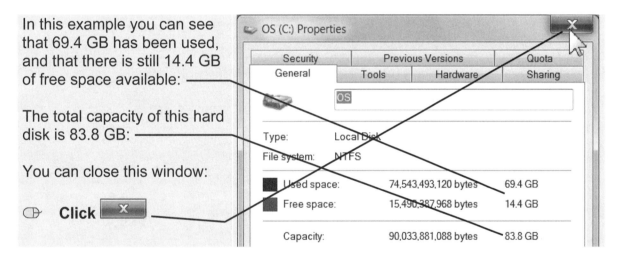

4.4 Your DVD drive

You can also view the properties of your DVD drive. These devices come in various versions:

- DVD player: can read and play CD ROMs and DVD ROMs;
- DVD writer: can read and play CD ROMs and DVD ROMs and write to CD recordables (cd-r) and DVD recordables (dvd-r);
- DVD rewriter: can read and play CD ROMs and DVD ROMs and write to CD recordables (cd-r), DVD recordables (dvd-r), CD rewritables (cd-rw) or DVD rewritables (dvd-rw).

A DVD writer or DVD rewriter is also called a DVD burner.

Types of CD discs
- A CD ROM disc can only be read or played. These are the CDs that are used to distribute software programs, for example. The 'ROM' extension stands for *Read Only Memory*.
- A CD recordable is a CD disc to which data can be written only once.
On the package of these CDs you will see the term: cd-r.
- A CD rewritable is a CD disc that can be re-written several times.
On the package of these CDs you will see the term: cd-rw.

Types of DVD discs
- A DVD ROM disc can only be read or played.
- A DVD recordable is a DVD disc to which data can be written only once.
On the package of these DVDs you will see the term: dvd-r or dvd+r.
- A DVD rewritable is a DVD disc that can be re-written several times.
On the package of these DVDs you will see the term: dvd-rw or dvd+rw.

The most recent development is the invention of the Blu-ray disc. A blu-ray drive is usually able to read DVDs and CDs as well.

If you have a blu-ray drive, you can perform the operations below for this drive.

In the *Computer* window you can see which kind of DVD drives are installed in your computer:

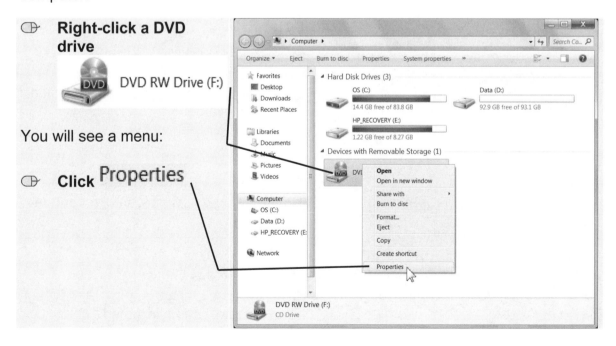

☞ **Right-click a DVD drive**

DVD RW Drive (F:)

You will see a menu:

☞ **Click** Properties

If you have a DVD burner, you will see the following window:

If the drive does not contain a CD or DVD disk, the capacity will be 0 bytes: ───

 Click OK

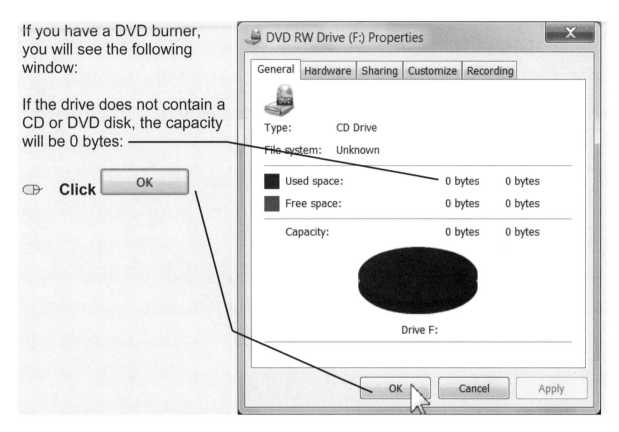

If you insert a CD ROM or DVD ROM into the DVD drive, this window will display the used space on the disc. If you insert a recordable CD or DVD into a DVD drive, the storage capacity will be displayed.

 Tip

Which DVD drive?
Are you uncertain about the type of DVD drive in your computer? Then take a look at the *Computer* window and see what *Windows* has to say about it:

On the left side you see a DVD burner. To the right is a DVD player. If the *Computer* window does not indicate the type of drive, read the manual that came with your computer. The manual will contain information on all the computer's components, including the type of DVD drive.

 Tip

Burn CDs or DVDs yourself
Does your computer have a DVD burner? Then you can use *Windows 7* to write data to CD or DVD recordables. This is also called burning a CD or a DVD. In *Chapter 6 Burning files to a CD, DVD or Blu-ray Disc* you will learn how to do this.

4.5 Removable Media

Recordable CDs and DVDs are also examples of removable media. Removable media is used for storing data and is easily connected to your computer.
Other examples of removable media are: memory cards, USB sticks or flash drives and external hard disks.

Memory cards come in different types and sizes. These cards are used for data storage. They are connected to your computer with a special card reader.

A memory card and a card reader:

You can insert a USB stick into one of your computer's USB ports. You can read more about using USB sticks in the Visual Steps book
Windows 7 for Seniors (ISBN 978 90 5905 126 3).

You can connect a USB stick directly to the computer's USB port:

Memory cards and USB sticks are intended for temporary storage of data and files. That is why it is better to use an external hard disk for creating backups of your important files. You can connect such an external hard disk to your computer's USB port by cable.

You connect an external hard disk to the computer's USB port:

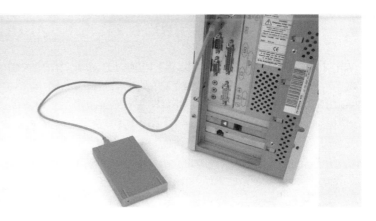

In the *Computer* window you will see all of the removable media that are connected to your computer:

DVD drive: ———————

Memory card readers, USB sticks and external hard disks:

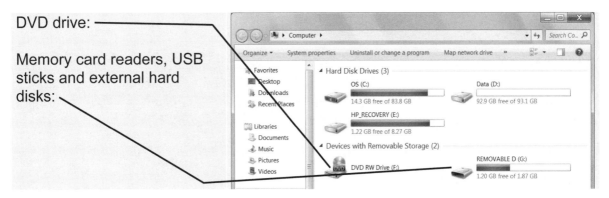

If you have connected a memory card, a USB stick, or an external hard disk to your computer, you can double-click this device in the *Computer* window. You will see its contents, and the folder window will display the files that are stored on the device.

For example, here you see the contents of a USB stick:

In the address bar you can see which removable disk has been opened. In this example it is REMOVABLE D (G:):

In the file list you will see the folders on the USB stick:

The USB stick may also contain a number of single files.

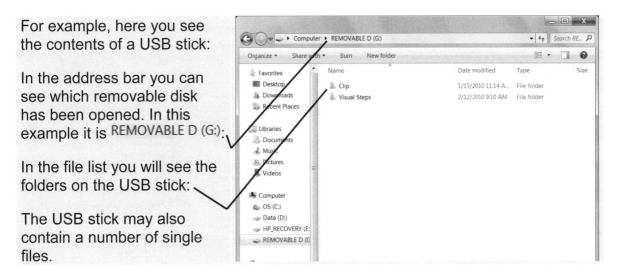

☞ **Close the window** 🦶🦶**9**

4.6 View Your Computer's Components

With the *Control Panel* you can view the components in your computer, and learn more about the type of computer you own. Many computer components are built into your computer, but some hardware components are connected to your computer by cable. You can take a look at them now:

☞ **Open the *Control Panel*** 🐾¹⁷

Now you will see the *Control Panel* window:

⊕ **Click**
    System and Security

You will see this window:

⊕ **Click** System

In this window you can see which *Windows* edition you are using:

You can also see the type of processor and how much *RAM* memory you have on your computer:

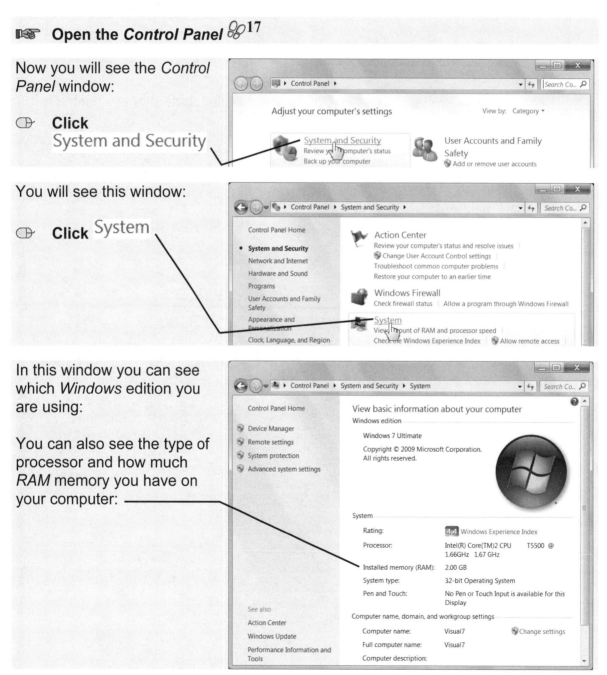

The RAM memory is also called the working memory.

4.7 View Your Computer's Performance

Windows 7 can also give you information on your computer's performance. This mainly concerns the speed of the various components of your computer. A computer that performs well will also enhance the performance of your software.

Click
Performance Information
Tools

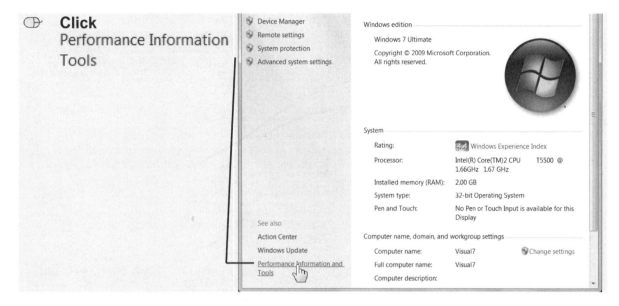

Performance rate: ─────

Information on the significance of the performance rate: ─────

Tips for improving your computer's performance: ─────

Please note: your computer's performance information will be different from the data in this example.

Click X

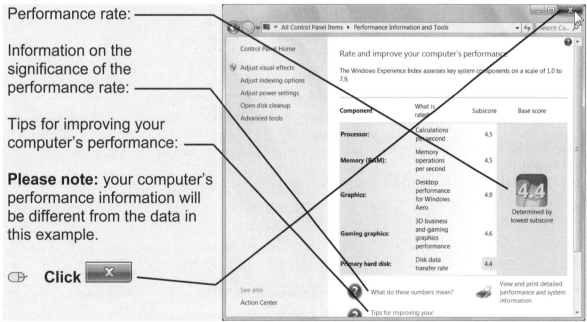

You can enhance your computer's performance by *upgrading* your hardware. That is, by installing extra internal memory, or a better graphics card, for example.

4.8 Practice Files

In the *Examples* subfolder of the *Practice-files-MoreWindows7* folder you will find various types of files. You will have stored this folder in your *My Documents* folder:

 HELP! I have not stored the practice files

It is always possible to download the practice files to your computer later on. In *Appendix A Download Practice Files* at the back of this book, you can read how to do this step-by-step.

☞ **Open the *My Documents* folder** 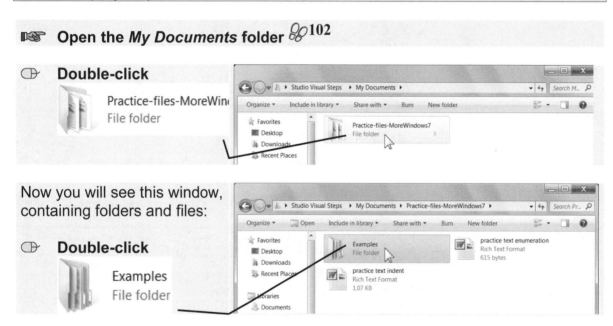102

⊕ **Double-click**

    Practice-files-MoreWind(
    File folder

Now you will see this window, containing folders and files:

⊕ **Double-click**

    Examples
    File folder

In this window you will see a number of folders:

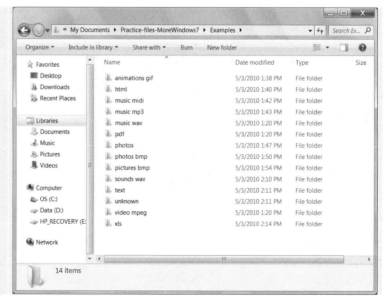

These folders contain many files of different types. Just open one of the folders:

 Double-click
 photos bmp

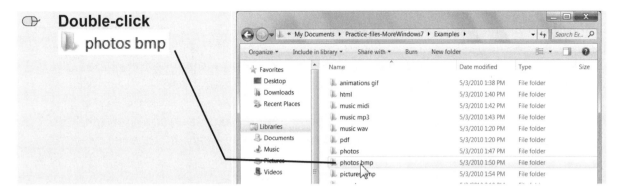

Now you will see this window, containing a list of photo files. The photos will be displayed as thumbnails (small pictures):

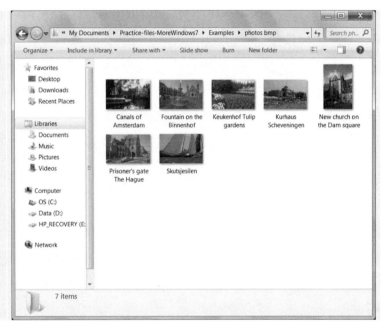

 Tip

Change the view
Do the files on your computer look different from the files in this *Computer* window?

By :

 Click

 Click Large Icons

4.9 Various File Types

In the *Examples* folder you have copied to your computer, you will see many different file types. Files always have a suffix (*extension*) added to the filename, which tells you what type of file it is. Below you will see a list of frequently used file types along with the programs you can use to open these files (in parentheses):

BMP   Graphics file used for drawings and pictures. Abbreviation of the word *bitmap* (*Paint, Windows Photo Viewer*, photo editing programs).

GIF   Graphics file used for drawings (*Paint, Windows Photo Viewer*, photo editing programs).

JPG of JPEG   Graphics file used for pictures, often used on the Internet (*Paint, Windows Photo Viewer*, photo editing programs).

TIF, TIFF   Graphics file used for pictures (*Paint,* photo editing programs).

DOC   Text file (*WordPad, Microsoft Word*).

DOCX   Text file – special file format (*Microsoft Word 2007* – older editions of *Word* require a specific 'viewer').

TXT   Text file with no formal layout (*Notepad, WordPad, Microsoft Word*).

HTM of HTML   Web page (*Internet Explorer*).

PDF   Text file converted to a special file format, may include pictures (*Adobe Reader, Acrobat Reader*).

XLS   Spreadsheet (*Microsoft Excel*).

XLSX   Spreadsheet (*Microsoft Excel 2007*).

PPS, PPT   Slide show (*PowerPoint* or *PowerPoint Viewer*).

WAV   Sound file (*Windows Media Player*).

MID of MIDI   Sound file (*Windows Media Player*).

MP3   Sound file (*Windows Media Player*).

WMA   Sound file (*Windows Media Player*).

AVI   Video file (*Windows Media Player*).

WMV   Video file (*Windows Media Player*).

MPG of MPEG   Video file (*Windows Media Player*).

Some file types can be used by a variety of graphics or photo editing programs, such as BMP and JPG files. Other file types are linked to a specific program, like *Microsoft PowerPoint* or *Microsoft Excel*. These programs use their own file format. However, the programs listed above are not the only programs you can use. If you want to play music files (audio files), for example, there are many additional programs to choose from.

4.10 File Properties

Each file has certain technical attributes, among which are the *properties*. For instance, a file can have the *hidden* or the *read-only* attribute.

A file may have the *read-only* property in order to protect it from illicit changes. All files on a CD ROM or DVD ROM are *read-only* files. You will be able to read such files, but you cannot save them to the same CD or DVD disc. After all, a ROM disc is not writable. That is why each file on a CD ROM or DVD ROM has the *read-only* property.

In the folder with the sample photos you can also find a *read-only* file:

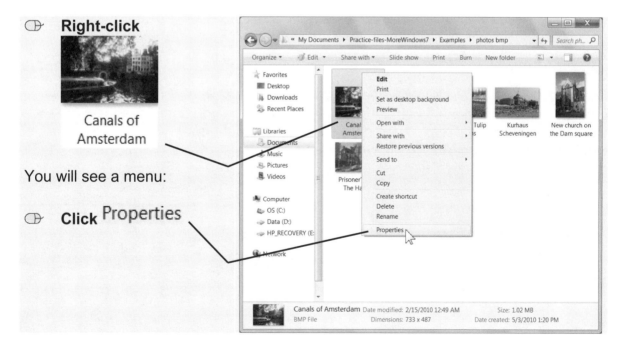

Right-click

Canals of Amsterdam

You will see a menu:

Click Properties

You will see this window:

At the bottom you will see that the Read-only box is checked ✓:

Click OK

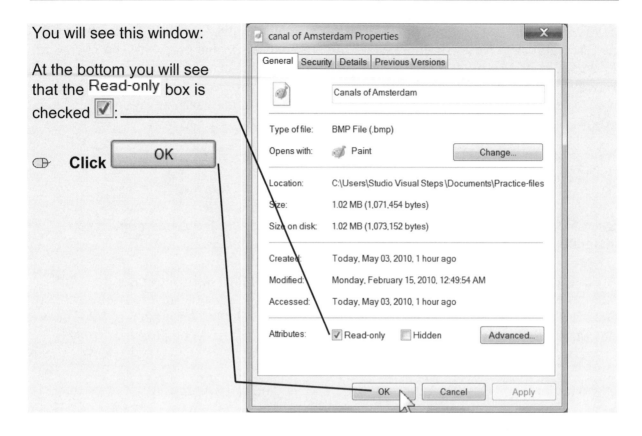

4.11 How To Open a File

In *Chapter 2 Setting Up Windows* you have learned that *Windows* keeps track of all programs that are linked to certain file types. That is why you can always use the *Computer* window to directly open a file. You will see right away which program is associated with that particular file type.

Right-click

Canals of Amsterdam

Click Open with

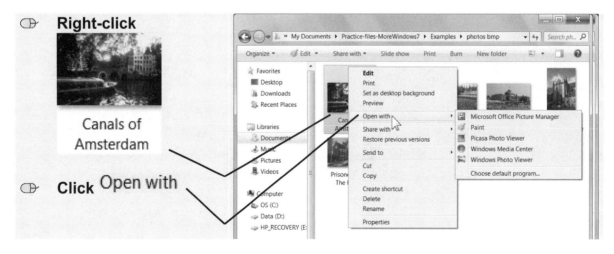

In the menu you will see that your computer contains five different programs that can read photo files. You can select the program you want to use to open the photo file. Your computer may contain additional programs to view photos, for instance, a photo editing program you have installed yourself.

To close the menu:

☞ **Click an empty spot somewhere in the window**

The exercises in the back of this chapter will give you more practice in how to use various programs to open the different file types in the folder. You will automatically notice if your computer does not (yet) recognize a certain file type. For now try to open the following file:

First open the *Examples* folder once again. Here is how to do that:

☞ **Click**

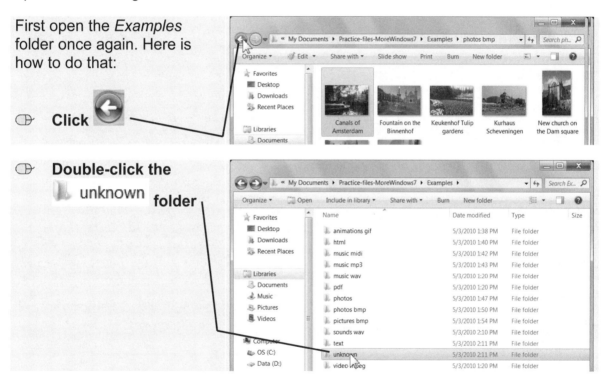

☞ **Double-click the**

unknown folder

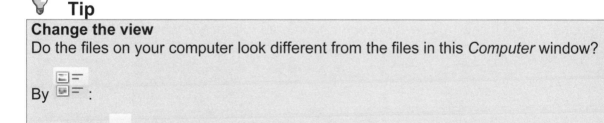

💡 Tip

Change the view
Do the files on your computer look different from the files in this *Computer* window?

By 🔲 :

☞ **Click** ▾

☞ **Click** 🔳 Large Icons

You can try to open this file:

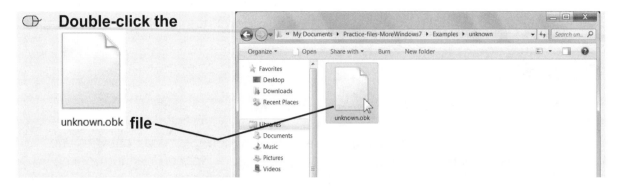

This file type has not yet been linked to a program:

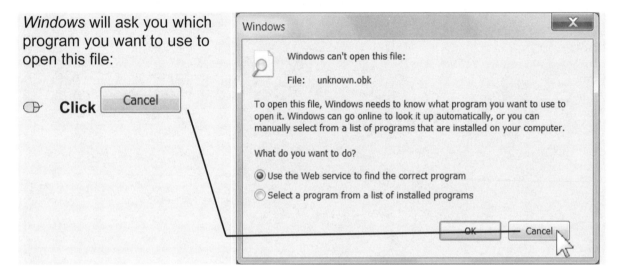

The obk extension does not exist. This file was created intentionally to demonstrate what happens when *Windows* does not recognize a certain file type.

☞ **Close the *Computer* window** 𝒷𝒷⁹

In this chapter you have learned how to view the various components of your computer. In the following exercises you will be able to practice what you have learned.

4.12 Exercises

Have you forgotten how to do something? Then you can use the number next to the footsteps to look up the description in *Appendix B How Do I Do That Again?*

Exercise: Opening Files

In this exercise you will practice how to find out which programs to use for opening the files on your computer.

 Please note!

Some of the file types on your computer may be opened by a different program than the ones that are shown here. This depends on the specific software that is installed on your computer.

☞ Open the *My Documents* folder. $\wp$102

☞ Open the *Examples* folder. $\wp$103

☞ Open the *photos JPG* folder. $\wp$104

☞ Open the JPG file named *duck*. $\wp$104

☞ Take a look at the program that is used to open this photo file, for example, *Windows Photo Viewer*.

☞ Close the program window. $\wp$9

☞ Return to the *Examples* folder.

The next file type is a music file.

☞ Open the *music wav* folder. $\wp$104

☞ Open the music file named *fanf01*. $\wp$104

☞ Take a look at the program that is used to open this music file, for example, *Windows Media Player*.

☞ Close the program window. ✌⁹

☞ Return to the *Examples* folder.

You can also try to open a video file.

☞ Open the *video mpeg* folder. ✌¹⁰⁴

☞ Open the video file named *horse*. ✌¹⁰⁴

☞ Take a look at the program that is used to open this video file, for example, *Windows Media Player*.

☞ Close the program window. ✌⁹

☞ Return to the *Examples* folder.

You can also try to open a PDF document:

☞ Open the *pdf* folder. ✌¹⁰⁴

☞ Open the PDF file named *Change the size of the mouse pointer* ✌¹⁰⁴

☞ See if this file will be opened with *Adobe Reader*.

☞ Close all windows. ✌⁹

 Tip

Were you unable to open the PDF file?
Then *Adobe Reader* has not yet been installed on your computer. *Adobe Reader* is a free software program you can use to read and print PDF documents. PDF files are digital documents. They are used on many websites. You can download the program from the Adobe website. In *Chapter 9 System Management and Computer Maintenance* you will learn how to install this program.

 Tip

Try for yourself
The *Examples* folder contains several other different file types. Try to open them and see what happens.

4.13 Background Information

Dictionary	
Blu-ray	Blu-ray is seen as the successor of the DVD disc. The big difference between DVD and blu-ray is the storage capacity: a blu-ray disc has five or ten times as much capacity as a DVD. Blu-ray discs can only be played by blu-ray burners, blu-ray players, or the *Sony PS3*.
Computer	The *Windows* feature that lets you view the content of drives and disks.
Extension	An extension is a set of characters preceded by a period after the name of a file, identifying the file type.
External hard disk	Portable hard disk drive that is easy to connect (and disconnect) to your computer.
Gigabyte, Megabyte, Kilobyte	Units used for measuring data storage capacity.
Read-only	File property which indicates that the file can only be read.
Removable media	Any medium that is used for data storage and is designed to be easily inserted or connected (in)to your computer. Examples of popular removable media are CD and DVD discs, USB sticks and removable memory cards.
Upgrade	Enhance the computer by adding more or better hardware.
USB stick, USB memory stick	Type of memory that is connected to a computer's USB port. It can be used to read or write data. Also called a *memory stick*.

Source: Windows Help and Support

4.14 Tips

 Tip

Basic view: speed up your computer
The default *Windows 7* settings for viewing windows, menus, and other components, requires extra computer capacity. If your computer operates very slowly, you could decide to select a less complicated theme:

☞ **Right-click the desktop**

☞ **Click** Personalize

☞ **Click** Window Color

Make sure that the box ☑ next to Enable transparency is not checked:
This option in particular uses a larger amount of processor capacity.

If you have changed anything:

☞ **Click** Save changes

If you have not changed anything:

☞ **Click** Cancel

You can also select a more basic theme:

☞ **Drag the scroll bar downwards**

☞ **Click a different theme, for instance *Windows 7 Basic***

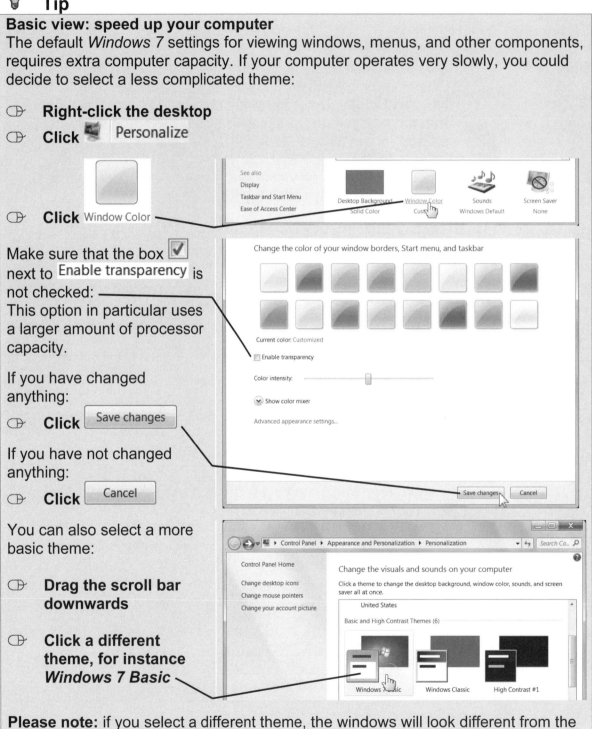

Please note: if you select a different theme, the windows will look different from the windows in this book.

5. Photos, Music and Videos

In this chapter you will take a closer look at some of the handy built-in features that *Windows 7* provides for working with photos, music, and videos.

Are you like so many others with an enormous amount of digital photos stored on your computer's hard drive? *Windows 7* will help you organize this collection. You can learn how to add tags and ratings to your photos to make it easier to find them later on. You can turn on the preview pane to give you more detailed information about your photos. You will see how quick and easy it is to view the photos in a selected folder as a slide show.

Windows 7 provides various options for sharing your photos with other people. You can print your photos, or send them by e-mail, and if you use the *public folder* you can share them with other users on your computer.

This chapter will also introduce you to the versatile *Windows Media Player* program. This program can do more than just play your music CDs. You can also use it to play video files and DVD movies.

In this chapter you will learn how to:

- work with the *Pictures* folder;
- view photos in the preview pane;
- use *Windows Photo Viewer*;
- play a slide show;
- use tags and ratings;
- print photos and send them by e-mail;
- share photos with the other users on your computer;
- connect your digital camera to the computer;
- import photos from your digital camera;
- play a CD in *Windows Media Player*;
- play a video file;
- play a DVD.

 Please note!

In order to watch all the examples in this chapter, you will need to have a music CD, and a DVD movie or an episode from a TV series.

5.1 The Pictures Library

Windows 7 offers various options for working with pictures. You can take a look at some of these options in the *Pictures* library:

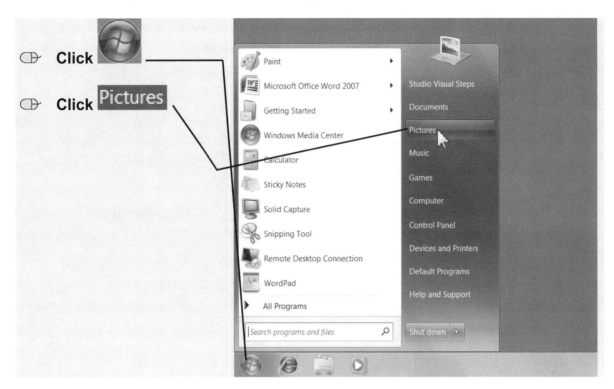

Click

Click Pictures

Now the *Pictures* library will be opened:

In this example the *Pictures* library contains two subfolders.

The *Sample Pictures* folder contains all the *Windows 7* sample photos:

You may see additional folders on your own computer.

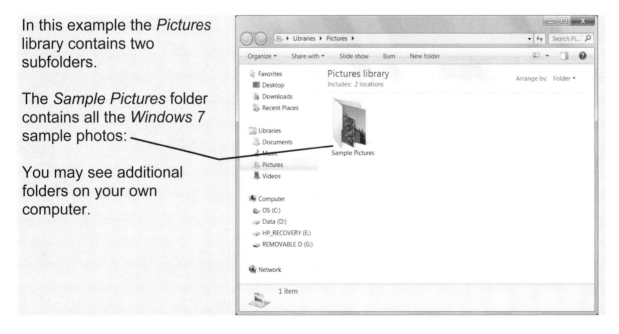

Tip

Working with libraries
A library is a virtual display of files that are scattered all over your computer; the actual files may be stored in different folders. In this way the computer can easily retrieve files of the same type from the same location.

In *Chapter 8 Windows Explorer, Libraries and Folder Windows* you can read more about working with libraries.

Take a look at the *Sample Pictures* folder:

Double-click

Sample Pictures

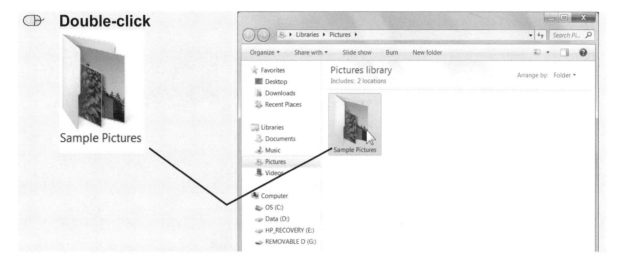

Now you will see the thumbnails of all the pictures that are stored in this folder:

5.2 Viewing a Photo In the Preview Pane

The *Windows 7* folder window has an extra feature that allows you to preview your photos before opening them. It is called the *preview pane*. Here is how to view it:

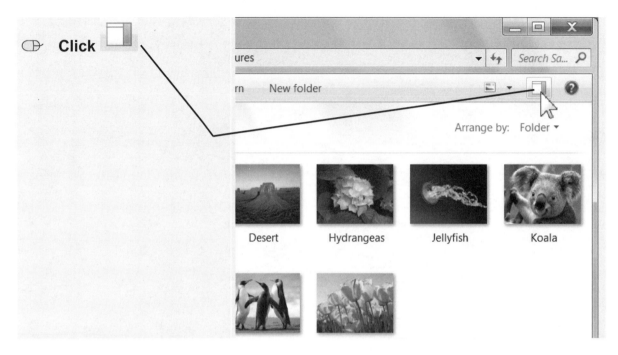

Now the preview pane is enabled. Take a look at the Koala sample picture:

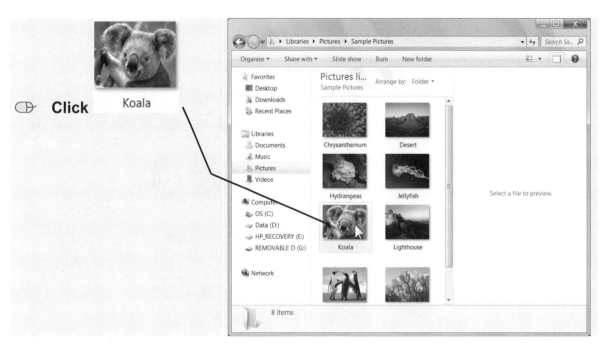

You will see the Koala photo appear in the preview pane:

In the *Properties Bar* below the photo you will see extra information about this photo:

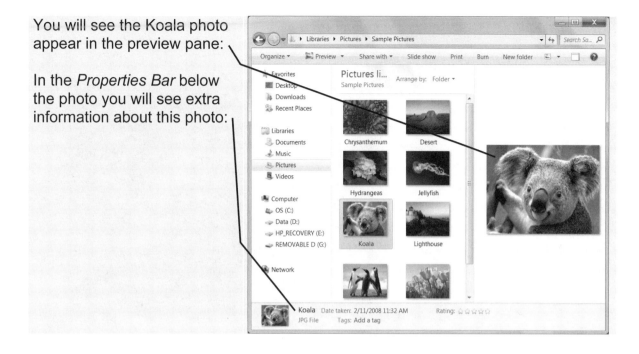

5.3 Windows Photo Viewer

You can also view a larger rendering of a photo. *Windows 7* contains a very useful program for this purpose, called *Windows Photo Viewer*.

Click ▦ Preview ▾

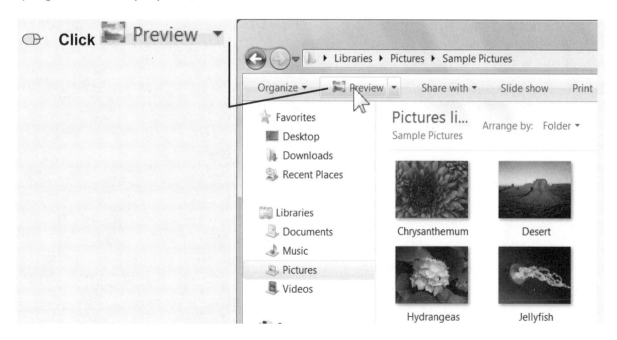

Now the *Windows Photo Viewer* will be opened:

You will see a larger picture:

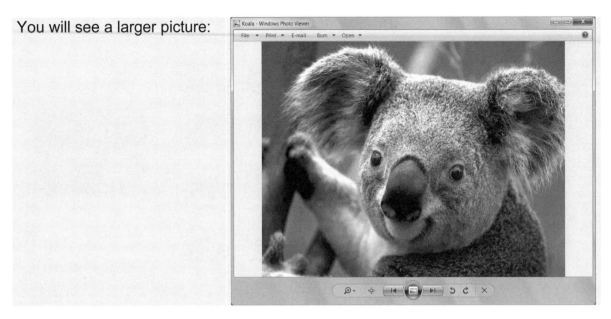

 HELP! I see a completely different window

This could mean that *Windows Photo Viewer* is not set as the default program for viewing photo files. In *Chapter 2 Setting Up Windows* you can read how to set up default programs.

If you do not wish to set *Windows Photo Viewer* as your default photo program, you can also open the file in the following way:

By 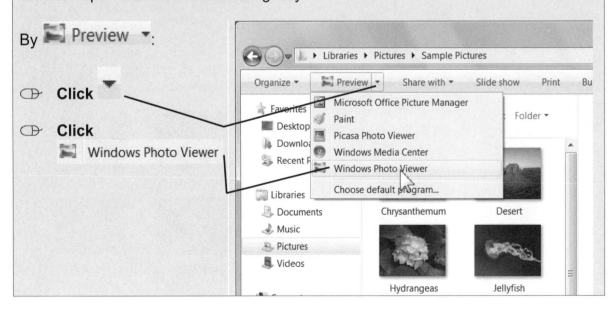 Preview ▼:

☞ **Click** ▼

☞ **Click**

   🖼 Windows Photo Viewer

5.4 Zooming In and Zooming Out

In *Windows Photo Viewer* you can easily zoom in and out on a photo. To do this, you can use the magnifying glass on the toolbar below the photo.

☞ **Click**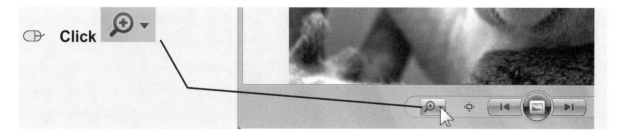

Now you will see a slider, which you can use to adjust the display size.

☞ **Drag the slider up, until it's about halfway to the top of the bar**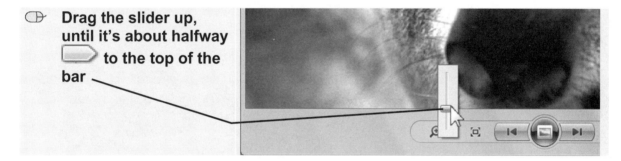

Now you can take a closer look at the photo. If you want to examine a specific detail, you can move the photo. For example, this is how to take a closer look at the nose:

☞ **Place the mouse pointer on the nose**

The mouse pointer will turn into a 🖑:

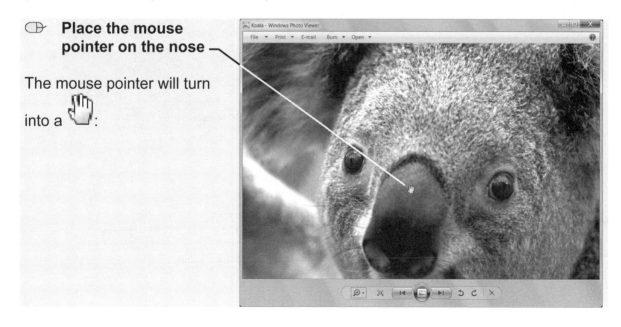

☞ **Drag the photo upwards** ——

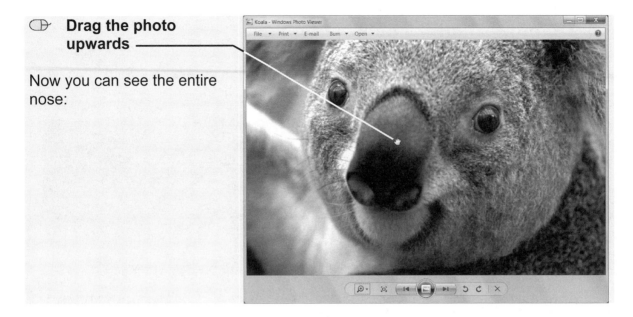

Now you can see the entire nose:

You can zoom out again:

☞ **Click** ▼ ——

☞ **Drag the slider** ▭ **all the way down** ——

You will see the entire photo once again:

Now you can close the *Windows Photo Viewer* window.

☞ **Close the *Windows Photo Viewer* window** ℘⁹

Tip

Windows Photo Viewer
In the *Windows Photo Viewer* window you will see even more buttons.

This is how you use these buttons:

 zoom in and zoom out.

 render the photo in its actual size.

 skip to the previous photo.

 view the photos in a selected folder as a slide show.

 skip to the next photo.

 rotate the photo counterclockwise.

 rotate the photo clockwise.

 delete the photo.

5.5 Viewing a Slide Show

A slide show is a great way of viewing a series of photos, one after the other. Your photos will be displayed full screen. This is how you open a slide show:

Click Slide show

The screen will turn dark for a second and then the slide show will start:

In the context menu you can change several slide show settings:

👉 **Right-click a photo**

Now you will see a menu:

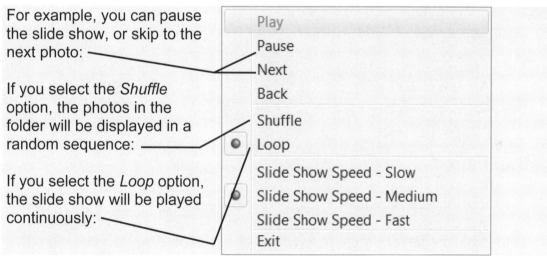

For example, you can pause the slide show, or skip to the next photo: ——

If you select the *Shuffle* option, the photos in the folder will be displayed in a random sequence: ——

If you select the *Loop* option, the slide show will be played continuously: ——

Play
Pause
Next
Back
Shuffle
Loop
Slide Show Speed - Slow
Slide Show Speed - Medium
Slide Show Speed - Fast
Exit

 Tip

Quickly jump to the next photo
If you click the photo while the slide show is playing, the next photo will be displayed immediately.

 Tip

Open a slide show in Windows Photo Viewer

You can use the ⬜ button to open a slide show in the *Windows Photo Viewer* program.

This is how you close a slide show:

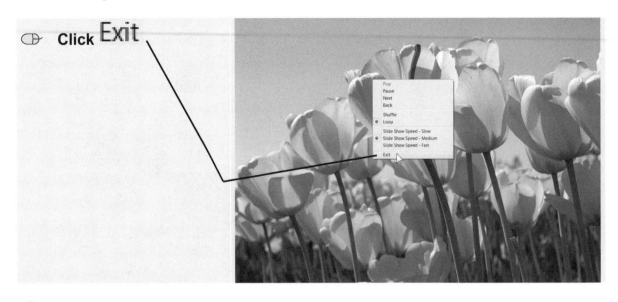

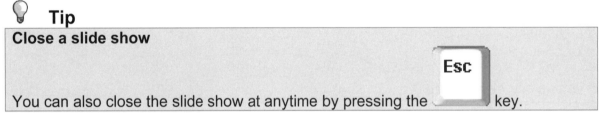

Tip

Close a slide show

You can also close the slide show at anytime by pressing the [Esc] key.

5.6 Using Tags

If you have a large number of photos, trying to find a specific one is not always easy. You searching will improve if you add *tags* to your photos. Tags are little pieces of information that you create yourself and attach to your photos. They will help you find and organize your photos more easily. This is how you add a tag to a photo:

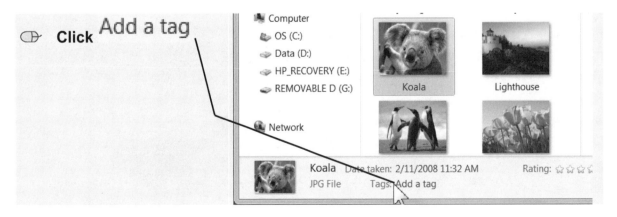

Now you can enter a tag for this photo:

Type: Animals

Click Save

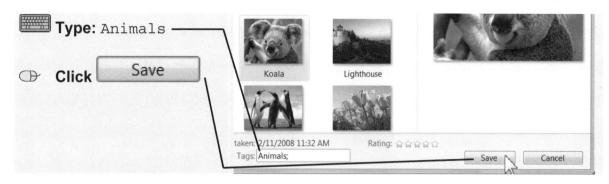

You can do the same thing with the penguins' photo:

Click Penguins

Click Add a tag

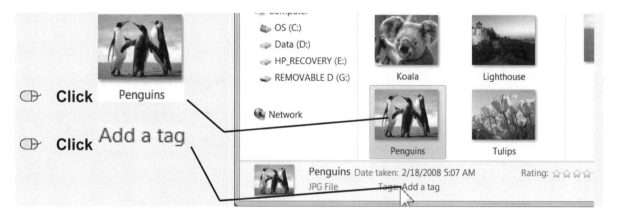

You will not need to type the entire tag:

Type: A

Windows 7 will immediately display all the existing tags that start with an 'a':

Check the box ☑ **next to** Animals

Click Save

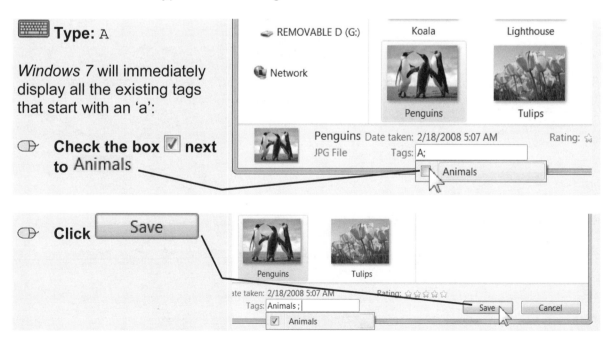

Practice this some more by adding tags to two more photos:

☞ **Add the *flowers* tag to the *Chrysanthemum* and *Tulip* photos** ✂24

Now it will be very easy to find all the photos with a specific tag. You do that like this:

⊕ **Click the search box**

Now you will see a search window below the search box. You can use this to add a *search filter*:

⊕ **Click** tags:

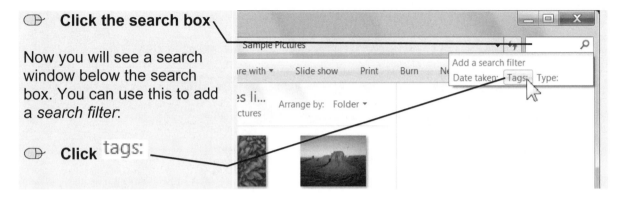

Here you can select the tag you want to use for filtering the photos in the folder:

⊕ **Click** Animals

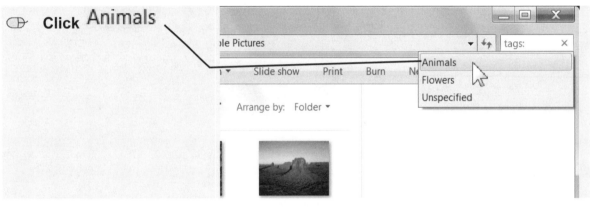

You will see that the search produces the two photos with the *animals* tag:

This is how you remove the search filter:

In the search box:

⊕ **Click** ✕

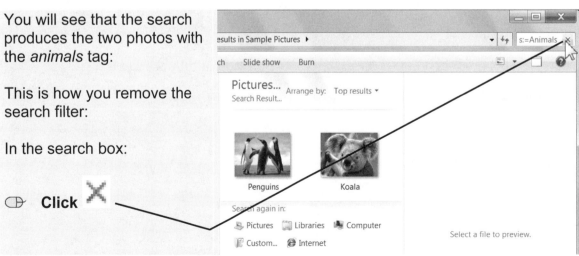

5.7 Rating Photos

You can also distinguish your photos by rating each photo with a number of stars. For example, you can add two stars to the tulips photo:

☞ **If necessary, click**

Tulips

☞ **Click the second star**

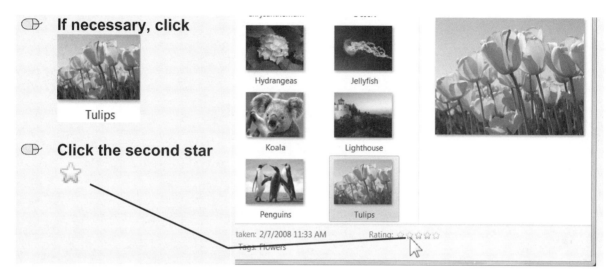

You will need to save this new rating:

☞ **Click** Save

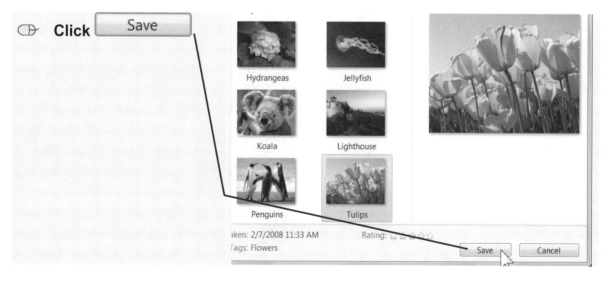

You can rate each picture with one to five stars. The five star rating should be reserved for your favorite photos. In the next section you can read how to organize your photos in different ways, including the use of star ratings.

5.8 Arranging Photos

In the *Pictures* folder window you can arrange your photos in various ways. For example, you can sort them by their rating:

☞ **Click** Folder ▼

☞ **Click** Rating

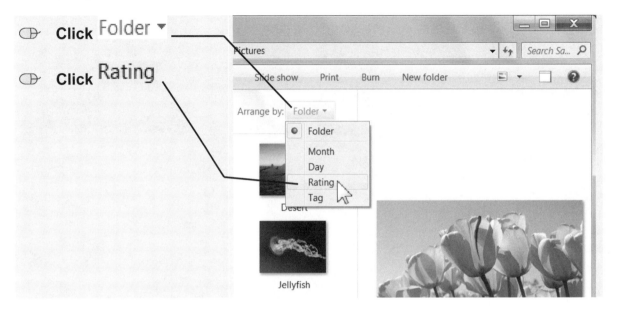

Now the photos will be listed according to their rating (number of stars). If you want to view all the rated groups, you will need to close the preview window:

☞ **Click** ⬜

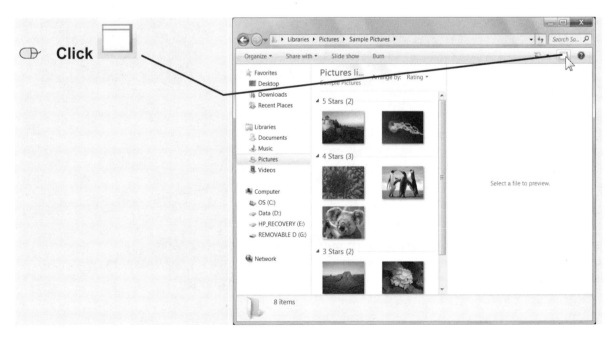

Now you will see all the groups:

The tulips photo has a two-star rating. Therefore you see it at the bottom of the list:

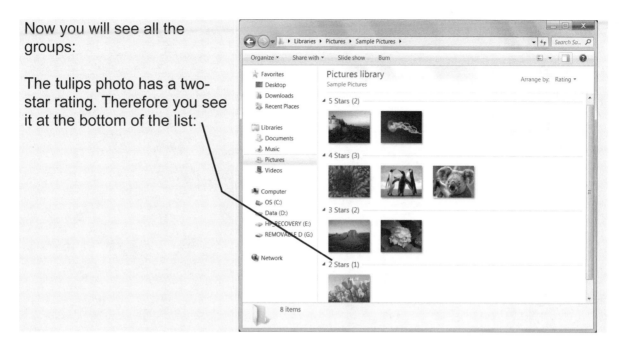

You can also sort the photos by their tags:

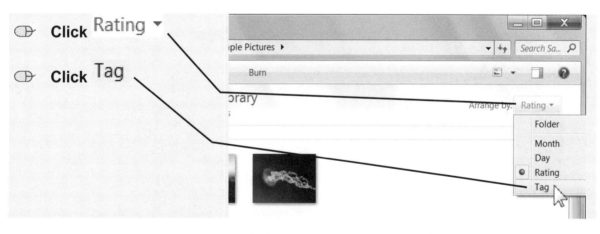

☞ **Click** Rating ▾

☞ **Click** Tag

You will see two groups of pictures, each with their own tag:

The last group does not have a tag:

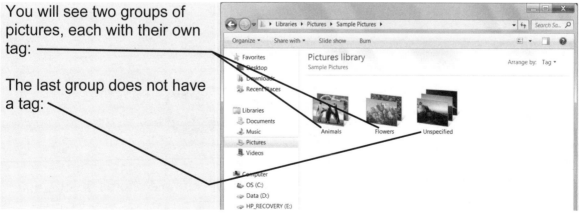

Open the last group of photos:

👆 **Double-click**

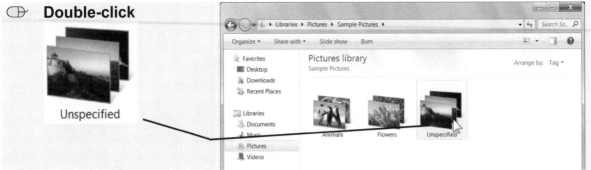

Unspecified

You will see that these photos are not tagged. They are sorted by Day ▼, i.e. the day the picture is taken:

Some photos may only display the month and the year.

👆 **Click** ⬅

You can now return to the familiar view of the *Pictures* folder window:

👆 **Click** Tag ▼

👆 **Click** Folder

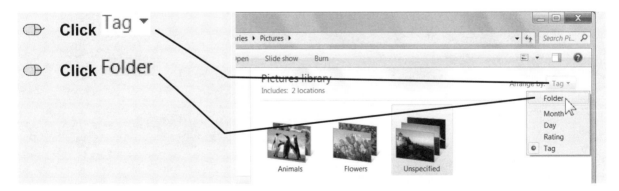

Here you will see once again the folder containing all the sample photos. In the next section you will learn how to print photos.

Tip

Learn more about editing your digital photos
Unfortunately, *Windows 7* does not offer additional features for working with digital photos, such as editing. Luckily you can find lots of other programs that will help you edit and organize your photos. *Visual Steps* has published several books on the subject of digital photo editing.

Picasa for Seniors
Picasa is a popular, free program for editing and managing digital photos. With this program you can crop a photo, remove red eyes, enhance the colors of your photo, and much more. You can also print your photos and create slide shows. And if you want to safely store your collection of photos, *Picasa* will let you burn a backup disk on a CD or a DVD. In this useful book you can also read how to create an Internet web album.

www.visualsteps.com/picasa

Digital Photo Editing for Seniors
This book is specifically written for seniors who want to learn more about digital photo editing. You will learn how to retouch and enhance your digital photos, for example by adjusting the definition, the contrast, or the exposure. Other topics include creating a photo collage, and working with layers. On the CD supplied with this book, you will find the complete version of the user-friendly software, ArcSoft PhotoStudio.

www.visualsteps.com/digital

5.9 Printing Photos

Windows 7 has a useful print wizard to help you print your photos more easily. You can also choose from a number of different print sizes. The first step is to select two photos:

Click the *Desert* photo

Press **Ctrl**

Click the *Lighthouse* photo

Release the **Ctrl** key

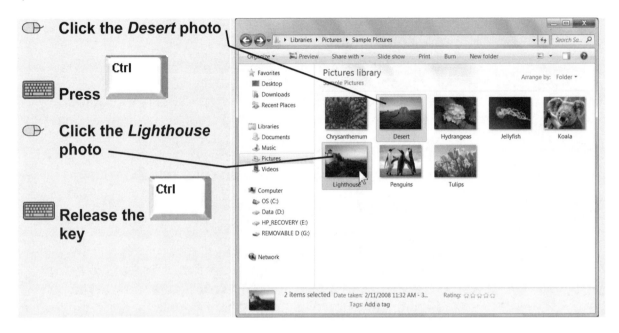

Now you can open the *Print* window:

Click **Print**

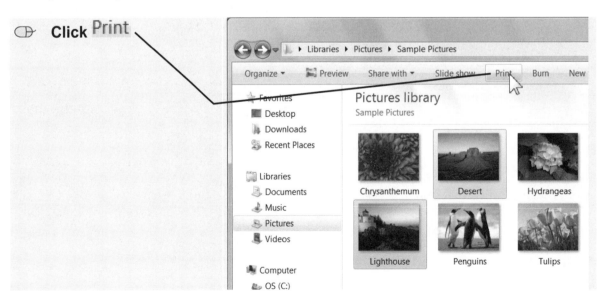

Now the *Print Pictures window* will be opened. In this window you can select various print settings. Depending on the type of printer you use, some of the options may be different than the ones shown in the example below:

Here you will see the settings for your default printer:

If you want to use special paper for printing photos, here is where you select the paper size and type:

Here you can select the number of copies you want to print:

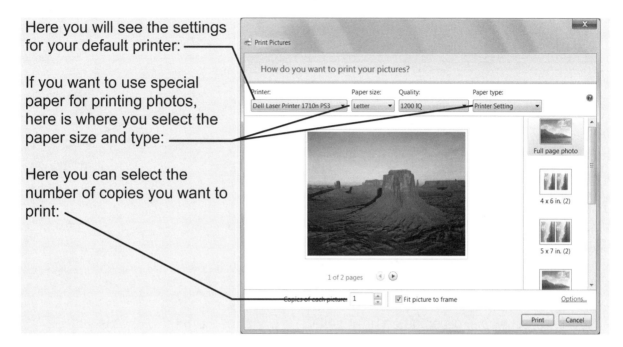

  Tip

Fit picture to frame
Frequently, the size of a digital photo does not match the standard print sizes. That is why you will often see a white border around the photos you want to put in standard photo frames.

If you want to print a photo according to an exact frame size (for example, a 3.5" x 5" print), you can select the Fit picture to frame option. *Windows 7* will enlarge the picture and print the photo in the size you have selected.

Please note: because the photo will be 'blown up', part of the photo will be outside the printable area. This means that the borders of the photo will not be printed.

Just try to print both photos in the 3.5" x 5" format:

☞ **Drag the scroll bar downwards**

☞ **Click** 3.5 x 5 in. (4)

In this example you can see that the page has enough space for two more photos:

This is how to print two copies of the picture:
By Copies of each picture: :

☞ **Click** ▲

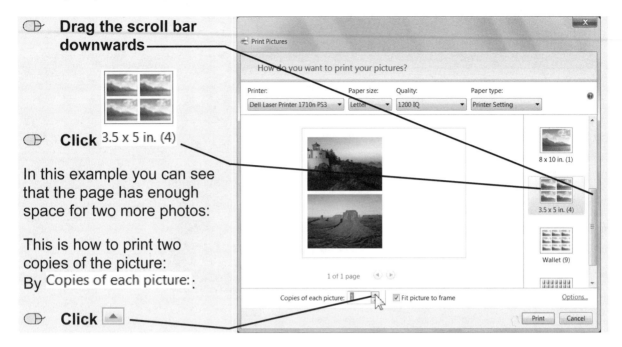

The print preview will be adjusted right away. Now you can print the photos.

☞ **Check if your printer is switched on**

☞ **Click** Print

Now the photos will be printed.

Please note!

The quality of your prints depends on a number of elements. The most important is the quality and depth of the photo itself. The depth is defined by the number of pixels of which the photo consists. If you want to print a low resolution photo in a too large size, the print will look grainy. This is not caused by the type of paper or the printer's toner cartridge, but by the low number of pixels.

In such a case, you will need to select a smaller print size for the photo. You will then notice that the photo already looks much better. The photo's resolution is a fixed value; you cannot change this.

5.10 Sending Photos by E-mail

You can quickly share your photos by sending them by e-mail. You can do this directly from the *Pictures* window. Just try sending the two photos you have just printed:

The photo selection is still active:

☞ **Click** E-mail

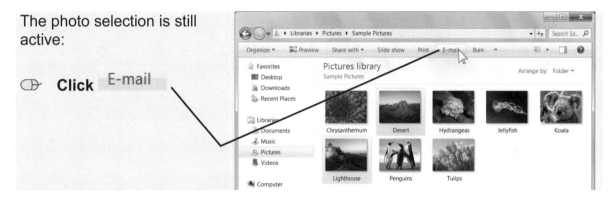

You will see the *Attach Files* window:

In this window you can see how big the e-mail attachment will be:

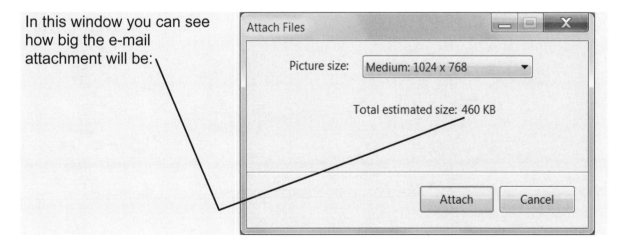

If the attached file is too big, you can change the size of the attached photo files.

 Please note!

Many e-mail servers have set limits regarding the size of individual e-mail messages, usually 1 or 2 megabytes (MB) per message. Large files will be blocked by a number of e-mail systems. It is recommended to optimize large photos for e-mail programs by minimizing them, before you send them. Minimizing photos before sending them by e-mail will not affect the size or quality of the original photos on your computer. The only thing that will be modified is the size of the photos attached to the e-mail message.

☞ **Click**
Medium: 1024 x 768

You can select a smaller size, but you can also send the photos in their original size:

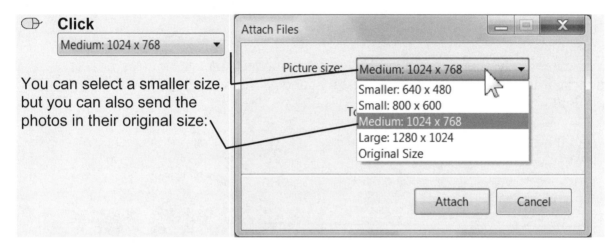

Now you can add the photo files to your e-mail message:

☞ **Click** Attach

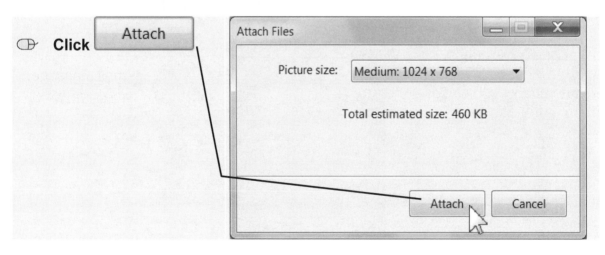

Your e-mail program will automatically start. If *Windows Live Mail* is your default e-mail program, you will first see the *Photo E-mail* window:

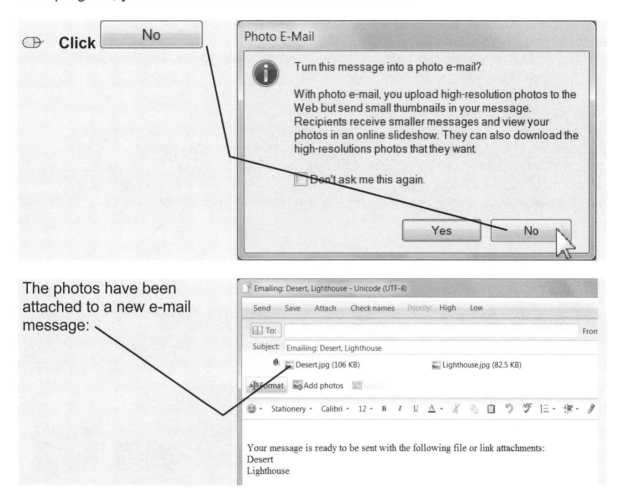

☞ **Click** No

The photos have been attached to a new e-mail message:

Now you can select a recipient, type a message and then send the e-mail message. If you do not wish to do this:

☞ **Close the message and do not save the changes** 25

💡 **Tip**

Burn photos to CD or DVD
You can also share your photos by burning them to a CD or a DVD.

In the *Picture* folder window, click the Burn button. The tray of your CD or DVD burner will open. Now you can insert a blank disc.
In *Chapter 6 Burning Files To a CD, DVD or Blu-ray Disc*, you can read more about burning CDs or DVDs.

5.11 Sharing Photos With Other Users

If you share your computer with other users, it will be very easy to share your photos as well. You can achieve this by moving or copying the photos you want to share to the *Public Pictures* folder. A public folder can be accessed from all of the user accounts configured on your computer.

 Please note!

If you want to use a public folder to share your photos, do not use the Share with ▼ button in the *Pictures* window. This button is intended for using the advanced network settings with which you can exchange files from the computers in your (home) network with other computers. For the moment you will not need to use this feature.

You can copy the photos selected in section *5.10 Sending Photos by E-mail* to the public folder:

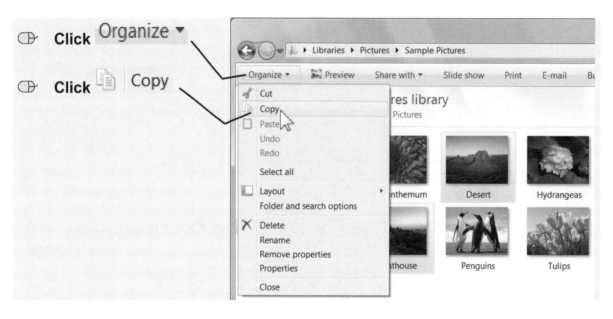

⊕ **Click** Organize ▼

⊕ **Click** 📄 Copy

Now the photos have been copied to the *Clipboard* and you can paste them into a different location.

 Please note!

In this book the hard disk is called 💾 OS (C:). You might see a different name on your computer, for example: 💾 Local Disk (C:)

Use the *Navigation pane* to open the public folder:

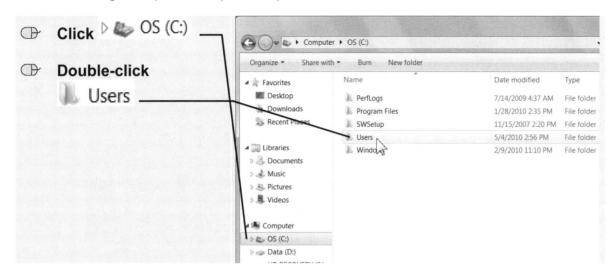

Click ▷ 🖥 OS (C:)

Double-click
📁 Users

In the *Users* folder you will see the personal folders belonging to the other user accounts on this computer:

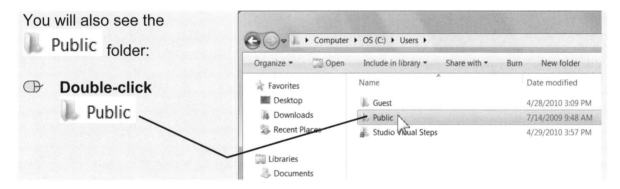

You will also see the
📁 Public folder:

Double-click
📁 Public

You can see that the names of the various folders inside the *Public* folder are preceded by the word *Public*. You can neatly organize all the files you want to share in these folders. In this exercise you will use the *Public Pictures* folder:

Double-click
📁 Public Pictures

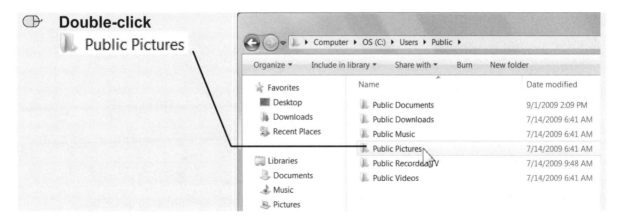

You will see the contents of the *Public Pictures* folder:

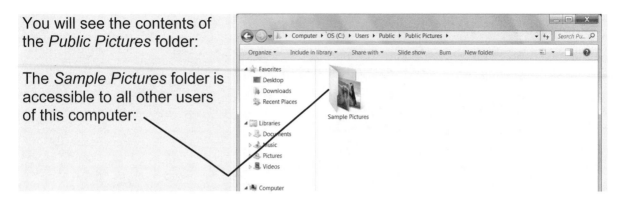

The *Sample Pictures* folder is accessible to all other users of this computer:

Now you are going to paste the copied photos into the *Public Pictures* folder:

⊘ **Click** Organize ▾

⊘ **Click** 🗋 Paste

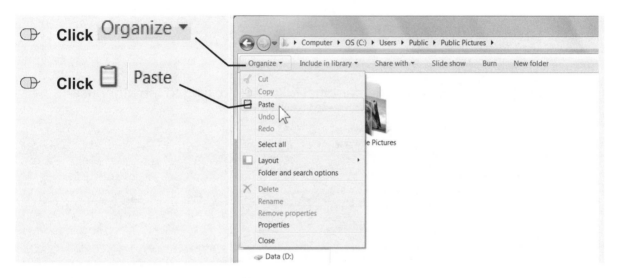

The copied photos now appear in the *Public Pictures* folder:

Other users of this computer will now be able to open and view these photos.

Please note!

All users of this computer will be able to open, modify, and delete the files in public folders. That is why it is recommended to save the original photos in your personal *Pictures* folder. If you are using a password-protected administrator's account, the standard account users will not be able to access your files.

Read *Chapter 3 User Accounts* to read more about protecting your computer by using different user accounts.

 Close all open windows [9]

5.12 Connecting Your Digital Camera To the Computer

If you want to view the photos from your digital camera in *Windows 7*, you will need to *import* them first. Importing means transferring the photos from your camera to your computer. There are two different ways to do this. You can use a cable to connect the camera to the computer, or you can use the *memory card* to which the photos have been stored. The memory card is a small card that can be removed from the camera.

In this section, you will learn how to connect your camera directly to the computer by means of a cable.

To connect your camera correctly, you will need to follow a few steps.

 Make sure you have all the necessary materials at hand

The first thing you need is your digital camera containing the photos you want to copy. Next, you will need the right cable. The cable will have been supplied with the camera.

Most cameras, these days, have a USB cable that can be connected to one of the USB ports on your computer. Some digital cameras need to be connected to your computer's firewire port with a firewire cable. Older cameras may require a serial cable.
The other end of each of these cables consists of a plug which needs to be inserted into the camera. Refer to your camera's manual to find out where the insertion slot is located on your camera.

The most common cable connection for digital cameras is a USB cable:

Firewire is an alternative connection method for digital cameras and computers. Firewire uses a smaller plug:

Apart from the cable, it is a good idea to have the camera's manual at hand, and the CD or DVD containing the camera's software, if you have one.

☞ **Make sure the camera is ready to use**

If you want to transfer photos from the camera, the photos must be present in the camera. If you have more than one memory card, make sure the right one is inserted into the camera.

The camera will also need to have power. Make sure the camera's battery is fully charged.

☞ **Make sure that the camera is turned off**

☞ **Connect the camera to the computer**

Your computer must be turned on and your camera must be turned off. Now you can connect the USB, firewire, or other cable to the camera. For this you need to use the plug on the opposite end of the cable, not the part that goes into the USB or firewire port. Usually, the insertion slot for the cable (a small trapezoidal-shaped hole) is hidden behind a small rubber flap on the side of the camera. If you cannot find this slot, refer to your camera's manual.

Insert the correct end of the cable into the camera's slot:

The other end of the cable will be inserted into the USB or firewire port of your computer.

If you have a different cable, other than a USB or firewire cable, you will need to connect this cable to the correct computer port as well (read the camera's manual).

 Please note!

If your camera does not use a USB or firewire cable, you will need to install the camera software first, before switching on the camera.

 Turn your camera on

 Please note!

Some types of cameras require that you activate the connection mode, or play mode, first. In your camera's manual you will find the correct settings.

 If necessary, activate the correct connection or play mode on your camera

Windows will now try to connect to your camera.

 HELP! Windows does not recognize my camera

If *Windows* cannot connect to your camera, even after you have installed the correct driver software, this is what you can do to solve the problem:

1. Check the camera battery (it should be fully charged).

2. Check if the camera is really turned on, and if you need to activate a special connection mode (read the camera manual).

3. Turn off the camera and restart the computer. Afterwards, turn on the camera again.

4. Download and install the most recent software (*driver*) for your camera, from the manufacturer's website.

5. Check the cable. Try connecting the cable to a different port on your computer, or use a different cable.

6. Try connecting the camera to a different computer and see if the connection can be made. If this does not succeed, chances are that your camera is on the blink. Look up the manufacturer's website and contact the manufacturer's support service.

7. Try to transfer the photos to your computer by using the camera's memory card.

In the next section, you will learn how to transfer the photos from your camera to your computer.

5.13 Importing Photos From Your Digital Camera

As soon as *Windows 7* has recognized your camera, you will see the *AutoPlay* window:

Click

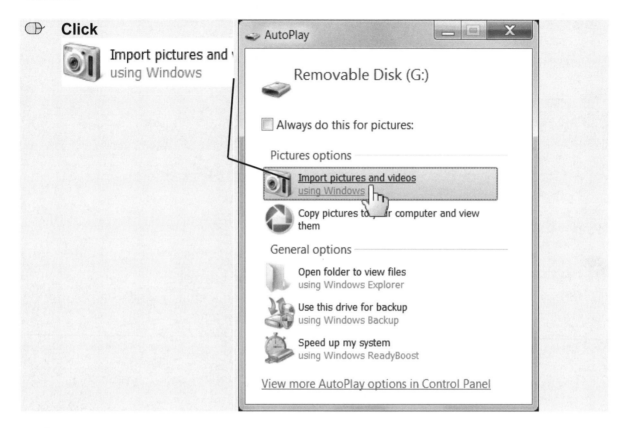

Import pictures and using Windows

 HELP! I do not see this window

If the *AutoPlay* window does not appear on your screen, you can open the folder in *Windows Explorer*:

Click 🪟 **Computer** ,

Right-click the name of your camera or the removable disk, such as

Removable Disk (G:)
1.70 GB free of 1.89 GB

Please note: your computer may use a different letter for your camera.

Click Open AutoPlay...

First, *Windows* will check the number of photos on your camera:

Next, you will be asked if you want to add one or more tags to the pictures while you import. This step is optional. In the example below more than one photo is imported:

Type a tag, for instance: My town

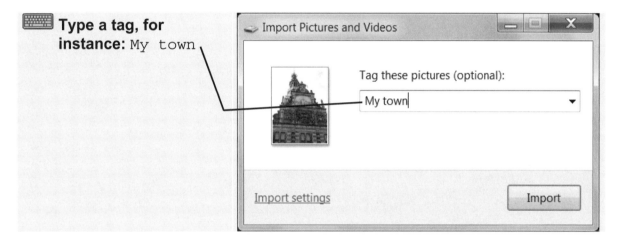

Now you can take a look at the import settings:

Click Import settings

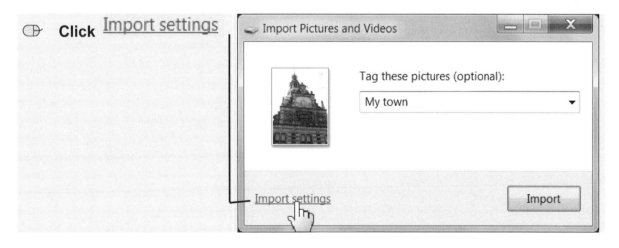

By Import images to: you can select the folder where you want to store the imported photos:

By Folder name: you can change the name of the folder where the photos will be stored:

By File name: you can enter a file name (tag) for the imported photos:

By Example: you will see an example of the folder name and file name that go with these settings:

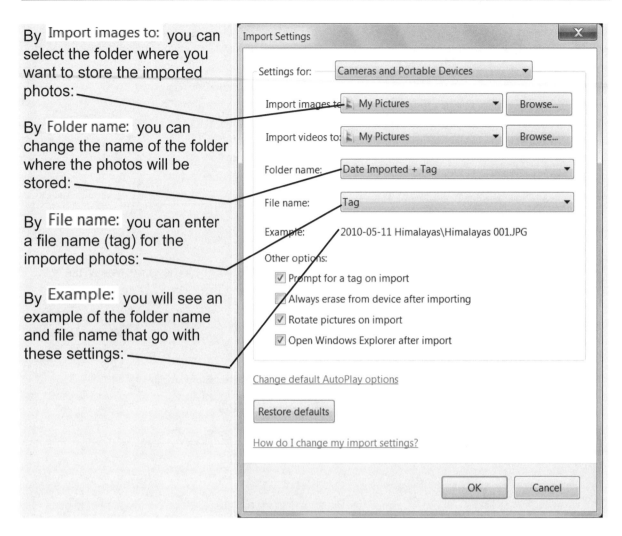

In this case you will not need to modify the settings:

Click Cancel

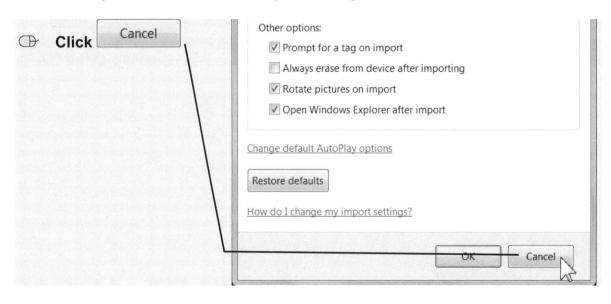

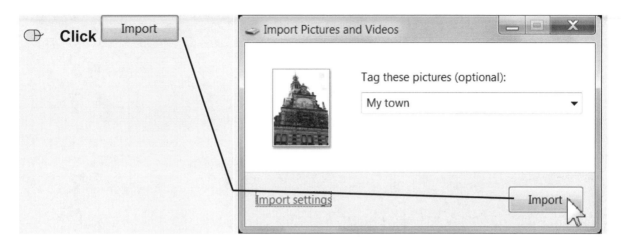

⟳ **Click** | Import |

Now the photos will be imported:

The green color in the progress bar increases as the items are being imported:

HELP! Why can't I select which photos I want to import?

This is because *Windows 7* checks which photos are the most recent ones. Older photos that have already been copied to your computer will not be copied again. This is why it is easy to copy your photos in a single step and store them in the *My Pictures* folder.

If you do want to import older photos, you will need to click [icon] Open folder to view files using Windows Explorer in the *AutoPlay* window. The contents of your digital camera will be displayed in *Windows Explorer*. Now you can select the desired photos in your camera's folders, and copy them to a folder on your computer. You can do this in the same way as you would copy files between two different folders on your computer.

The photos have now been stored in the *My Pictures* folder of your computer.

Windows will show you which pictures are imported:

You can check to see where the pictures have been stored:

⊕   **Click** Pictures

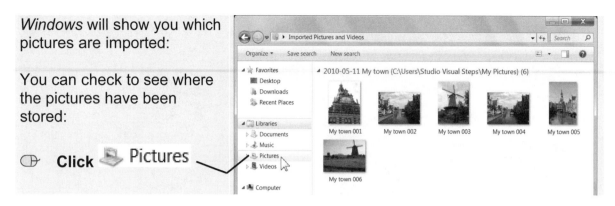

Now the *Pictures* library will be opened. A library does not contain the actual files, only the references to these files that are stored in different locations on the hard drive.

You will see the contents of the *Pictures* library:

Here you can see the folder with the photos you have just

imported   2010-05-11 My town   :

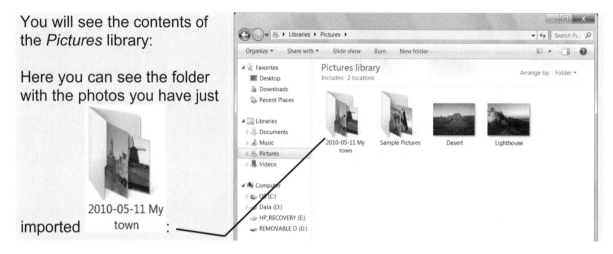

To find the actual location on your hard drive, where the folder with imported photos has been stored:

⊕   **Right-click the folder with imported photos**

⊕   **Click** Open folder location

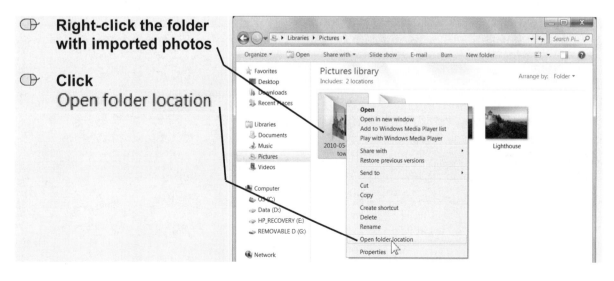

You will see that the folder has been stored in your *My Pictures* folder:

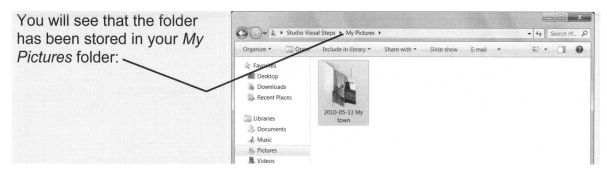

☞ **Close all windows** 9

☞ **Remove the camera from the computer**

5.14 Opening Windows Media Player

Windows Media Player is a *Windows 7* program that can play audio and video files. You can open *Windows Media Player* by clicking the shortcut on the taskbar:

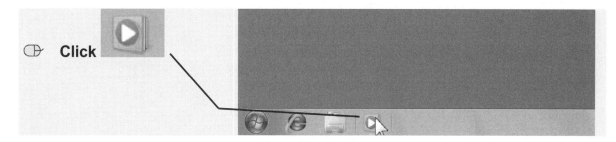

Click

When you start up *Windows Media Player* for the first time, you can select various settings for the way in which the program works. In this case you can use the default settings.

➥ Please note!

If you have already opened *Windows Media Player* before, you will not see the following window. You can continue on to the next step.

Click the radio button
 ◉ **next to**
 Recommended settings

 Click [Finish]

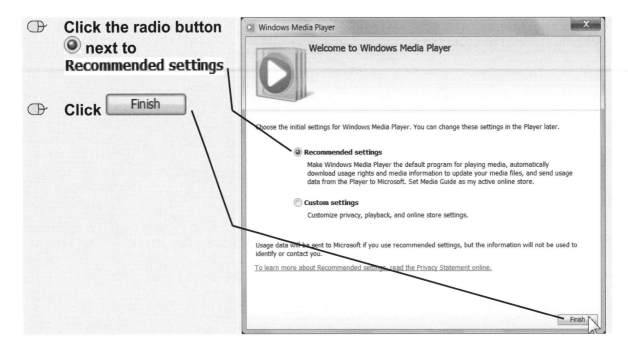

After the settings have been selected, *Windows Media Player* will start searching your computer for music files.

After a short while you will see the music files the program has found:

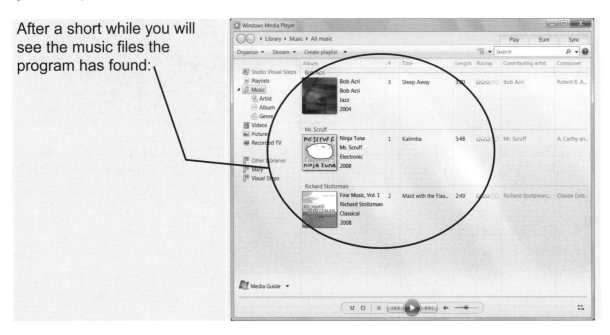

➡ **Please note!**

Your own *Windows Media Player* window will display different music files than the ones shown in this example.

Now you can close the *Windows Media Player* window:

 Click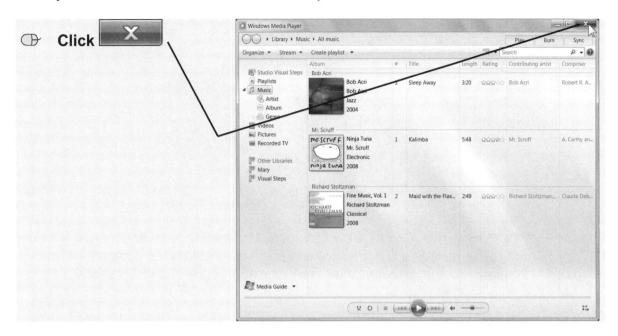

5.15 Playing a Music CD

Most computers have *Windows Media Player* set as the default music player for the most commonly used music files. If you insert a music CD into your CD or DVD player, *Windows* will immediately open the *Media Player* and play the CD.

Please note!

If you want to work through the operations in the next few sections, you will need to have a music CD. For instance:

See what happens when you insert a music CD into your computer:

☞ **Insert one of your own music CDs into your computer's CD or DVD drive**

☞ **Carefully close the tray**

Most likely you will see the window shown below. *Windows* recognizes the CD you have just inserted as an audio CD. First, you are going to select the option for playing all music CDs in *Media Player* when they are inserted into the CD or DVD drive:

⊕ **Check the box ☑ next to**

Always do this for audio CDs:

⊕ **Click**

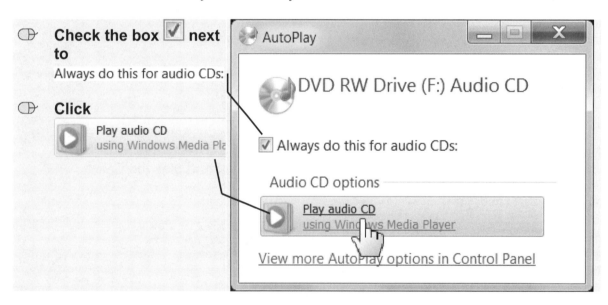

🖑 **Please note!**

Nowadays, many music CDs contain various extras, such as photos, ringtones, etc. In that case you will see an extra option in this window, such as

Run enhanced content, for example:

In this case:

⊕ **Click**

HELP! Nothing happens after I have inserted the CD

If you have inserted a retail music CD and it does not play, it may have copyright protection (to discourage copying and illegal distribution). Try a different music CD.

 ## HELP! I do not see the AutoPlay window

If you do not see the *AutoPlay* window, but you do see the *Windows Media Player* window, this means *Windows Media Player* has already been set as default music program.

 ## HELP! A different program is starting up

Does the CD start playing with a different program instead of *Windows Media Player*? Then your computer has been set to play music files and audio CDs with a different program. In *Chapter 2 Setting Up Windows* you can learn how to set default programs.

Now the *Windows Media Player* window will be opened and the CD will be played. The current *Windows Media Player* view is called the *Library*, or the *Media library*.

The various pieces of music on a CD are called *tracks*. We will continue to use this term in the next few sections of this book.

The first track is played:

If you have an Internet connection, by default, *Windows Media Player* will start looking for information on the CD. As soon as the CD has been found, the program will display the cover picture and the track titles:

In this example the CD has not been found on the Internet.

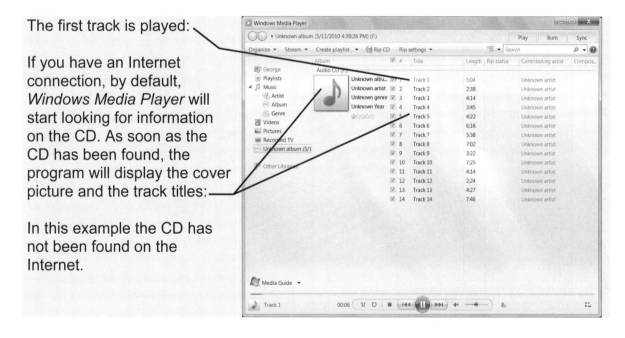

HELP! I see a much smaller window

That means *Windows Media Player* is displayed in the *Now Playing* view. This is how you can switch to the view with the larger window (the *Library*):

☞ **Click**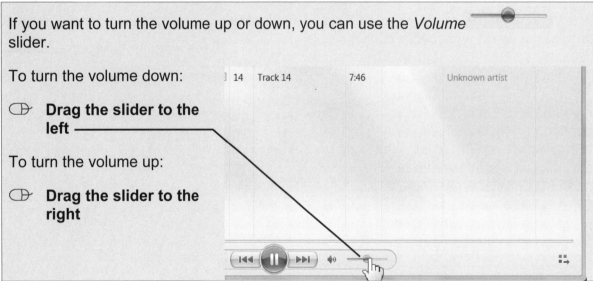

 HELP! The volume is too loud or too soft

If you want to turn the volume up or down, you can use the *Volume* slider.

To turn the volume down:

☞ **Drag the slider to the left**

To turn the volume up:

☞ **Drag the slider to the right**

 Tip

Quickly turn off the volume

If you want to mute the sound immediately, click 🔊 :

To restore the sound to its old level, click 🔇 .

Just like on a regular CD or DVD player, you can press a button to skip to the next track:

 Tip

Skip to your favorite song
If you know exactly which track you want to hear, you can play this track at once:

⊕ **Double-click the number or the title of the track, for example** Track 9

The song will be played right away.

This is how you skip to the previous track:

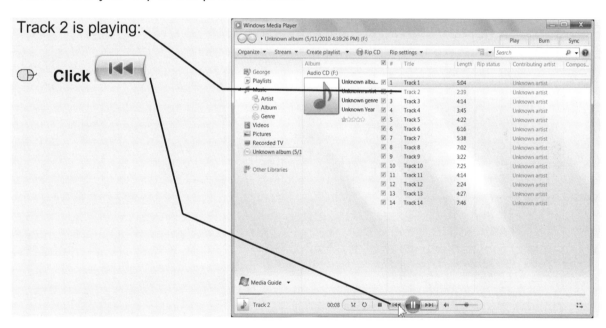

You can also pause the track from playing:

5.16 Playing Tracks In A Random Order

You may already recognize the random order feature in *Windows Media Player*, as it is quite similar to the option available on regular CD players. This feature is also called the *shuffle* option. This is how you select this option in *Windows Media Player*:

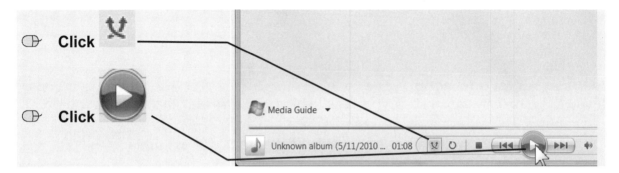

Now track 1 will be played. But when you continue with the next track, a new track will be selected at random. Try this option for yourself:

5.17 Repeat

You can also repeat playback of all tracks:

Now the tracks will be played in a random sequence. When the CD has finished playing, the CD will start playing all over again, in a continuous loop.

If you want to repeat playing the tracks in the regular order, you will need to disable the shuffle play option:

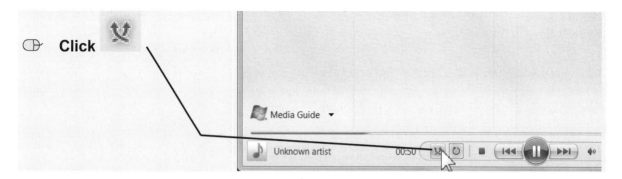

⊕ **Click**

You can also disable the repeat option:

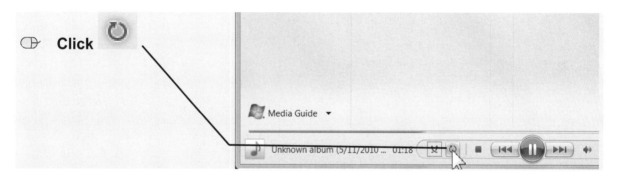

⊕ **Click**

Now the CD will be played in the correct sequence once again. After the last track has been played, *Windows Media Player* will stop playing the CD.

This is how you can stop playing the CD:

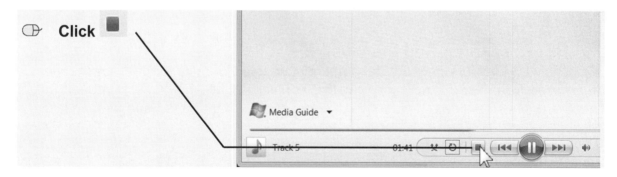

⊕ **Click**

Now you can close *Windows Media Player*.

☞ **Close *Windows Media Player*** ℰℰ⁹

☞ **Remove the CD from the CD or DVD player**

5.18 Playing a Video File

You can also use *Windows Media Player* to play video files from your computer's hard drive:

☞ **Open *Windows Media Player* ∂∂²⁶**

Take a look at the video files in the *Library*:

👆 **Click** 📽 Videos

In the *Library* you will find a single video file:

This is the sample video that comes with *Windows 7*.

Please note: you may see more than one video file on your computer.

🩹 HELP! I cannot find the video file

It is possible that your computer does not contain this video file, or perhaps you see other video files. This will not be a problem; you will still be able to work through this chapter. Just use a different video file, instead of the file that has been used in this book.

👆 **Double-click**

Now the short video movie will be played. *Windows Media Player* will automatically switch to the *Playing Now* mode:

You will see that the video is displayed full screen:

Also, the buttons have disappeared:

HELP! My video is displayed in a much smaller window

This is because the *Windows Media Player* window has been minimized. This is how you maximize the window:

Click [▢]

After the video has finished playing, you can choose to play the video once more, or you can return to the *Library*:

Click ↻ Play again

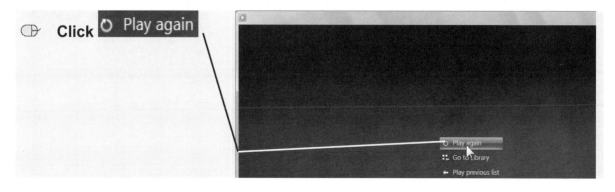

Here is how you display the *Windows Media Player* buttons again:

 Slide the mouse pointer down to the bottom of the window

The buttons will appear again:

HELP! The video keeps playing over and over again

That is because you have enabled the *Repeat* option. This is how you disable this option:

 Click ⟳

You can also play the video full screen. This is how you do that:

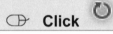 **Click** ⟳ Play again

 Right-click the video

 Click Full screen

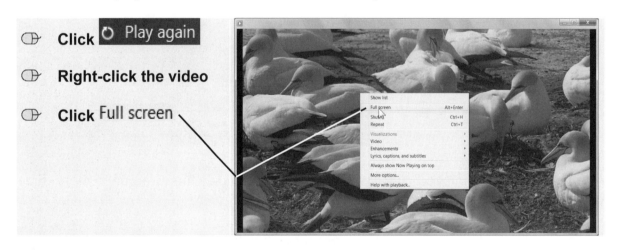

Now the video will be played on a full screen:

If the size of the video does not correspond with the size of your monitor, you will see a couple of black bars, just like this example:

Please note!

Whether the image will still be sharp when you enlarge it to maximum size depends on the quality of the video file.

Now you can exit the full screen mode:

☞ **Right-click the black part of the window**

☞ **Click** Exit full screen

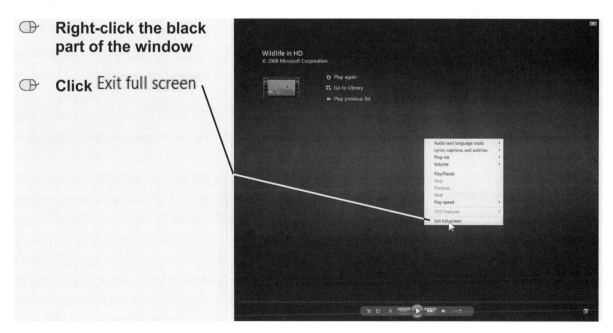

Now you are going to return to the regular *Windows Media Player* view:

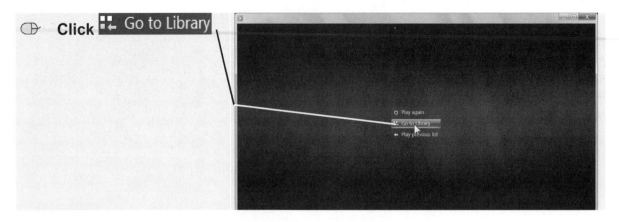

Click **Go to Library**

Here you will see the full *Windows Media Player* once again.

In this section you have experimented with the various options for playing video files. In the next section you will learn how to play a DVD in *Windows Media Player*.

☞ **Close** ***Windows Media Player*** ✋⁹

5.19 Playing a DVD

Besides playing video files from your computer's hard drive, *Windows Media Player* can play DVDs as well.

 Please note!

To work through this section, your computer will need to have a DVD drive.

You can recognize a DVD drive by this logo:

You will also need a movie DVD, or a TV series on DVD:

If you do not have a DVD, you can just read through the next section.

☞ **Insert a DVD into your computer's DVD drive**

Windows 7 will recognize this disc as a DVD disc. Now you are going to play this DVD in *Windows Media Player.*

Maybe you will see this window:

☞ **If necessary, uncheck the box ☑ next to** Always do this for DVD n

☞ **Click**

Play DVD movie using Windows Media Pl

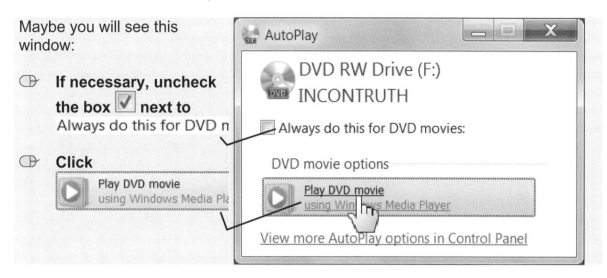

Windows Media Player will be opened and you will see the opening images of the DVD on your screen, in full screen mode.

If you want to view the movie in your own language, or read the subtitles (Captions) in your language you may need to adjust the language settings. Almost every DVD contains a menu, where you can select the subtitle language and various other options. You can also use the menu to skip to a specific part of the DVD that you want to watch. When the copyright warning message has finished, you will automatically be sent to the main menu. This DVD has the option of turning subtitles off or on right from the start:

☞ **Click SET UP**

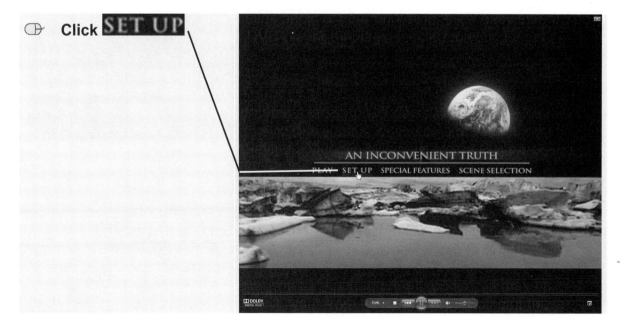

Click  (subtitles)

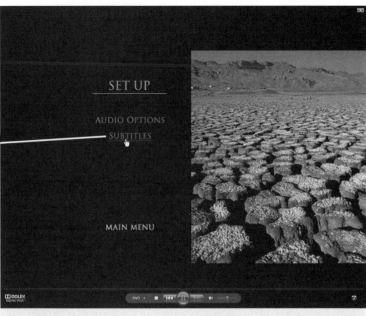

Click 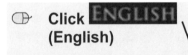 (English)

 Please note!

The structure of the main menu will be different for each DVD. Your DVD may require that you skip through other menu options, before you can select the language or the subtitles. It is also possible that your player has been set to automatically select the correct language. In that case, you will not need to select the language yourself.

HELP! I do not see the main menu

Did your DVD start playing right away, instead of displaying the main menu? This is how you can display the menu:

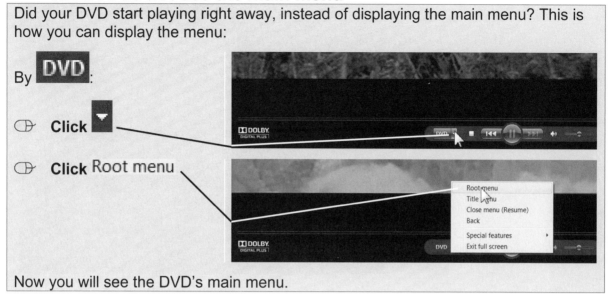

By **DVD**:

- ☞ **Click** ▼

- ☞ **Click** Root menu

Now you will see the DVD's main menu.

HELP! The DVD does not start playing

Does your DVD not start playing and do you see an error message with this text: 'Unable to play DVD video'? This probably means that there is no DVD decoder installed on your computer that is compatible with *Windows 7* and *Windows Media Player*. This decoder is required to play DVDs on your computer.
At the end of this chapter you will find a tip to help you install the decoder.

Now you can start playing your DVD:

- ☞ **Click** PLAY

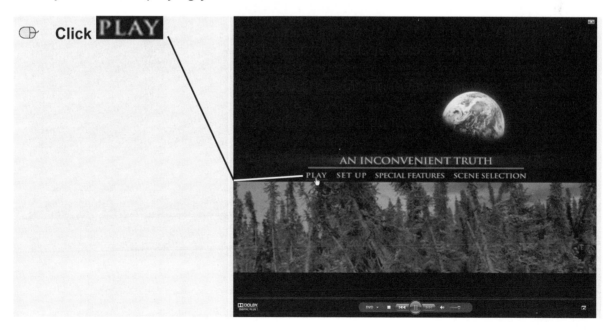

Now the DVD will be played, with English subtitles:

☞ **Close the full screen view** 🦶²⁷

The video screen will become smaller. You can also return to the *Library* view of the *Windows Media Player*:

Click

In the *Library* view, the movie is playing, but you don't see it. You can still hear the sound, however. You can easily switch back to the *Now Playing* view:

Use the ▪▪→ button in the bottom right corner to return to the *Playing Now* window and continue watching the movie: ―――――――

You can also stop the movie at any time:

🖝 **Click** ■

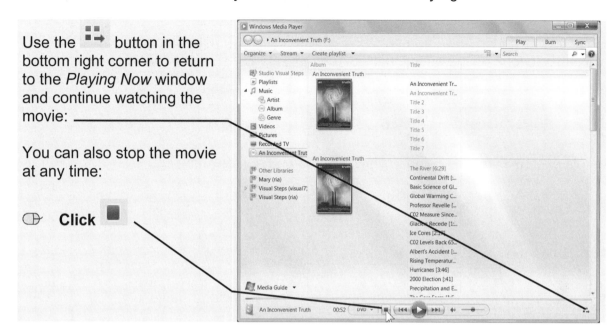

🖝 **Close *Windows Media Player*** ♐⁹

🖝 **Remove the DVD from the DVD drive**

In this chapter you have learned how to work with photos, music CDs, video files, and DVDs in *Windows 7*. You can work through the exercises in the next section and practice what you have learned.

5.20 Exercises

Have you forgotten how to do something? Then you can use the number next the footsteps to look up the description in *Appendix B How Do I Do That Again?*

Exercise: View a Photo and a Slide Show

In this exercise you are going to view a photo and a slide show.

☞ Open *Pictures* library. $\mathscr{QD}^{28}$

☞ Open the *Sample Pictures* folder. $\mathscr{QD}^{29}$

☞ Take a look at the *Lighthouse* photo in *Windows Photo Viewer*. $\mathscr{QD}^{30}$

☞ Zoom in to the lighthouse. $\mathscr{QD}^{31}$

☞ Zoom out, until you see the entire photo. $\mathscr{QD}^{32}$

☞ Close the *Windows Photo Viewer* window. $\mathscr{QD}^{9}$

☞ View a slide show of all the pictures in this folder. $\mathscr{QD}^{33}$

☞ Stop the slide show. $\mathscr{QD}^{34}$

Exercise: Tag and Organize Photos

In this exercise you are going to tag a photo and arrange the photos in the folder in various different ways.

☞ Add the *plants* tag to the *Hydrangeas* photo. $\mathscr{QD}^{24}$

☞ Sort the photos by their tags. $\mathscr{QD}^{35}$

☞ Sort the photos by date (month). ℘^{36}

☞ Return to the regular thumbnail view of the folder. ℘^{37}

Exercise: Share Photos

In this exercise you are going to share your photos by printing them, by sending them in an e-mail and by copying them to the *Public Pictures* folder.

☞ Add the *Koala* photo to an e-mail message, as an attachment. ℘^{38}

☞ Close the e-mail message, do not save the changes. ℘^{25}

☞ Copy the *Koala* photo to the *Clipboard*. ℘^{39}

☞ Open the *Public Pictures* folder. ℘^{40}

☞ Paste the *Koala* photo into the *Public Pictures* folder. ℘^{41}

☞ Print one copy of the *Koala* photo once, in a 3,5 x 5 inch size. ℘^{42}

☞ Close all windows. ℘^{9}

Exercise: Play a Video

In this exercise you will practice playing a video in *Windows Media Player*.

☞ Start *Windows Media Player*. ℘^{26}

☞ Display all the videos in the *Media Library*. ℘^{43}

☞ Play the *Wildlife in HD* video. ℘^{44}

☞ Enlarge the window to maximum size (full screen). ℘^{45}

☞ Reduce the window to its normal size. $\wp^{46}$

☞ Watch the rest of the video.

☞ Open the *Library*. $\wp^{47}$

☞ Close *Windows Media Player*. $\wp^{9}$

Exercise: Play a Music CD

In this exercise you will play a music CD in *Windows Media Player* once more.

☞ Insert a music CD into your CD or DVD player.

☞ Skip to the next track. $\wp^{48}$

☞ Pause playback. $\wp^{49}$

☞ Continue playing the CD. $\wp^{50}$

☞ Play the tracks in random order. $\wp^{51}$

☞ Skip to the next track. $\wp^{48}$

☞ Repeat play. $\wp^{52}$

☞ Disable the shuffle option. $\wp^{53}$

☞ Disable the repeat option. $\wp^{54}$

☞ Stop play. $\wp^{55}$

☞ Remove the music CD from your CD or DVD player.

☞ Close *Windows Media Player*. $\wp^{9}$

5.21 Background Information

Dictionary

Driver	A driver is software that allows a device (such as a digital camera, or a printer) to communicate with *Windows*. Every device needs a driver to work properly.
DVD decoder	A DVD decoder is also called an MPEG-2 decoder. The contents of DVD discs are encoded in the MPEG-2 file format. You will only be able to play DVDs in *Windows Media Player* if you have a compatible DVD decoder installed on your computer.
Firewire	A fast cable connection between the computer and external devices, such as photo cameras.
Image dot	The smallest element that makes up a digital image, also called pixel.
Import	Transferring digital photos from your digital camera to your computer's hard drive.
Media library	The *Windows Media Player* location where all music files, videos, and pictures on your computer are displayed. Also called library, but this library differs from the *Windows 7* libraries.
Memory card	A device in the shape of a card, used for permanent data storage. There are many different types of memory cards. Their capacity may vary from 128 MB up to 8GB or more.
Mute	(Temporarily) turn off the sound during playback.
Pixel	The smallest element that makes up a digital image, also called image dot.
Preview pane	Part of the *Pictures* folder window, where you can view the details of the photo you have selected.

- Continue reading on the next page -

Public folders	*Windows 7* folders, used to store the files which you want to share with the other users of your computer. The *Public* folder contains various subfolders, such as *Public Pictures*, and *Public Documents*.
Rating	You can use stars to rate a photo. The ratings range from zero to five stars.
Resolution	The clarity and definition of a photo, which is determined by the number of pixels of which the photo is composed.
Search filter	Feature to help search the contents of a folder; you can use a filter to search for files with a specific attribute, such as tags.
Shuffle	Play tracks in random order.
Slide show	Allows you to view your pictures automatically and in full screen.
Tag	A custom file property that you can create and add to your photos and videos, to help find and organize them.
Thumbnail	A tiny preview version of a picture.
Track	A song in a music file, or an individual audio section.
USB	Square communication port in the computer, used as a universal port for a lot of devices, such as photo cameras.
Windows Media Player	Program for playing and managing music files and videos in *Windows 7*.
Windows Photo Viewer	Program for viewing photos in *Windows 7*.
Zoom in	Enlarge the rendering of a photo.
Zoom out	Diminish the rendering of a photo.

Source: Windows Help and Support

5.22 Tips

 Tip

DVD decoder

Do you see an error message, saying that the DVD cannot be played because a compatible DVD decoder cannot be found? Most likely, a DVD decoder is not yet installed on your computer, or the one that is installed is not compatible with *Windows 7* and *Windows Media Player*. This decoder is required to play DVDs.

On the *Microsoft* websites you can find several codecs. A codec is a piece of software that is used to compress or decompress a media file, such as a music file or a video. A codec may consist of two elements: an encoder and a decoder. *Windows Media Player* and a many other programs use codecs to create and play media files.

For the most part, the codecs available on the *Microsoft* website are manufactured by other companies. On the following web page you will find links to the websites of various DVD decoder manufacturers:
www.microsoft.com/windows/windowsmedia/player/plugins.aspx#DVDDecoder.
Is this page unavailable? Then type 'DVD decoder' in the search box of the website. Now you will see a page with several links to other relevant web pages.

While we were producing this book, *Microsoft* had not yet presented any *Windows 7* codecs. That is why we are using a *Windows Vista* DVD decoder in the example below.

The roxio company offers an easy-to-use website, with clear procedures for ordering, paying, and downloading codec software:

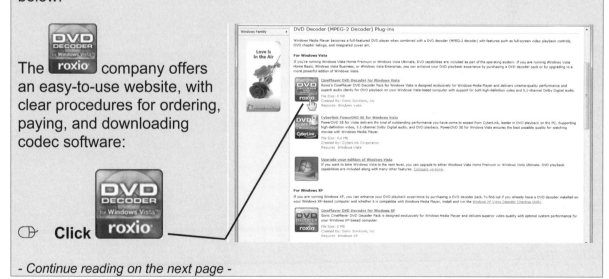

☞ **Click** roxio

- Continue reading on the next page -

Now you will see the Roxio website. On this page you can order the DVD decoder:

Please note: websites are updated on a daily basis; the pages in this example may differ from your own screen.

6. Burning Files to a CD, DVD or Blu-ray Disc

Windows 7 has a built-in burning capacity that will allow you to burn data to a CD, DVD or even a blu-ray disc. You can choose one of two different formats: *Live File System* and *Mastered*. In this chapter, we will show you how to use *Windows 7* to burn files from your computer to a CD or DVD, and which format to use. Burning a blu-ray disc is identical to burning a CD or a DVD.

With the burning capability, you can quickly create copies of important data, such as photo or text files, for safekeeping. You can also use your burned CD, DVD, or blu-ray disc to transfer files to another computer, or share them with others. When your computer's hard drive becomes too full, you can free up space by copying some of your larger files, such as video, to an external disc.

After you have burned such a disc to free up space, you will need to remove the original files from your computer. Files that are burned to a disc are copied, not moved, so they still remain in their original location on the computer.

In this chapter you will be working with the *Windows Burn* program. This program lets you create a video DVD or a slide show of your photos in a few easy steps. You can play the DVD in your regular DVD player that is connected to your TV set.

In this chapter you will learn how to:

- distinguish various formats for CDs, DVDs, and blu-ray discs;
- create a disc using the *Live File System*;
- burn data to a disc, and erase data;
- create a disc using the *Mastered* format;
- add data to a queue, or remove data from a queue;
- view the contents of a disc you have burned in *Windows Explorer*;
- burn a video DVD with *Windows Burn*.

 Please note!

In order to work through this chapter without encountering problems, it may be necessary to remove other burning software from your computer. Some of these programs will automatically take over the burning operations from the *Windows 7* burning program. First, try to work through this chapter. If the windows on your computer look completely different from the examples in this chapter, chances are that the *Windows 7* disc burning capability is superseded by another program.

- Continue reading on the next page -

Only remove the other burning software if you own the original software program on CD or DVD. Then you can re-install the program later on, if you wish, and use the more advanced burning options these programs usually offer.

6.1 What Will You Need?

With *Windows 7* you can burn CDs, DVDs, and blu-ray discs. But this requires a computer with a *burner*. Most new computers come with built-in burners. Modern burners are able to burn CDs as well as DVDs. Some of the newest burners can also burn blu-ray discs.

 Please note!

The process of transferring data to a CD or DVD disc is called *writing* a disc. Sometimes other terms are used to describe the same process: *burning* or *copying* data to a disc. The device you use for writing a disc is called a *writer* or *burner*.

 Please note!

Some computers are equipped with a CD/DVD player and a separate burner. Take good care to insert the disc in the correct drive. Often the burner is indicated by a *writer* or *RW* (read/write) logo.

 HELP! Do I own a CD/DVD burner?

Is it hard for you to find the burner in the *Computer* window?

Do you see   Cd-rom-station   or   DVD-station   ? Your computer may not have a CD/DVD burner, but only a CD ROM player, or a CD/DVD player.
But sometimes these icons also indicate a burner. Check your computer's manual to find out which type of CD/DVD drive your computer has and if it was installed properly. If necessary, refer to the manual to learn how to install the burner.

Apart from this, you will need at least one writable disc. Preferably, this disc is a rewritable disc, so you can use the same disc for all the exercises. The exercises in this chapter all use a DVD rewritable disc. A rewritable disc is a disc to which you can write files, erase files, and replace them. The disc package will have something like CD-rw, DVD-rw, DVD+rw, or BD-re written on it.

 Please note!

If you want to see the same windows as you see in this book, the rewritable CD or DVD needs to be new or unused. If you use a CD or DVD you have previously used, the windows on your computer may look different from the examples in this book.

Tip

Writing different types of CDs, DVDs, and blu-ray discs
There exist various types of (re)writable discs. If you are going to burn more discs later on, you can choose a different type from the type used in this chapter. At the end of this chapter you will find a summary of the different types of discs, in the *Background Information* section.

6.2 Choose Between Two Formats

Windows 7 can burn CDs, DVDs, or blu-ray discs. First, you will need to format the rewritable disc that you will use for the exercises. Formatting a disc means preparing the disc for use in *Windows 7*.
You can select one of two formatting options (file systems):

- *Live File System*
  This file system is only compatible with (or adapted to) *Windows 7*, *Windows Vista*, and *Windows XP*. The burning process for this system is also called copying files to CD, DVD, or blu-ray disc. You can add and delete files on a *Live File System* disc over and over again, just like you did on a floppy disc or a USB stick. The discs will only be rewritable if you use rewritable CDs, DVDs, or of blu-ray discs.
- *Mastered*
  This file system allows you to use the CDs or DVDs you have burned with older *Windows* editions, or in other CD or DVD players that can read digital music and video files. A disc which uses this file system has to be burned all at once. If you have previous experience with *Windows XP*, you will see that the *Mastered* file system works in the same way as in *Windows XP*. Blu-ray discs can only be played by specific blu-ray players. Check the player's manual to find out if you can use blu-ray discs.

By default, *Windows 7* will select the *Live File System*, but when the formatting process is about to start you will be able to choose a different file system.
If you choose to work with other types of discs later on, you will see that these discs also have to be formatted first. Recordable discs can only be formatted once. Rewritable discs can be formatted over and over again.

 Tip

Compare both file systems
At the end of this chapter, in the *Background Information* section, you will find a comprehensive overview of both these file systems. You will also find some tips as to which file systems you need to use for different purposes.

6.3 Formatting a Disc

When you insert a new, unformatted disc into the burner, first the disc will be formatted.

☞ **Insert a new, rewritable CD, DVD, or blu-ray disc into your burner**

In this example a rewritable DVD is used.

You will see the following window:

👆 **Click**

> Burn files to disc
> using Windows Explorer

Please note: maybe you will see different options in this window

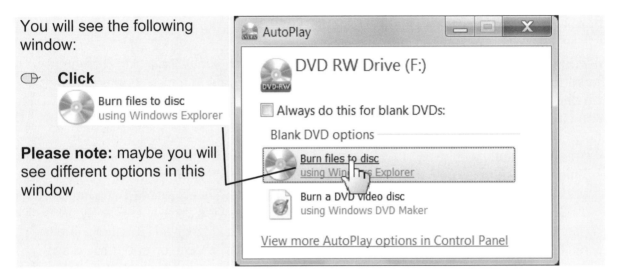

 HELP! I do not see this window

The settings on your computer may be different and the window shown above does not appear. You can continue further like this:

👆 **Click**

👆 **Click** Computer

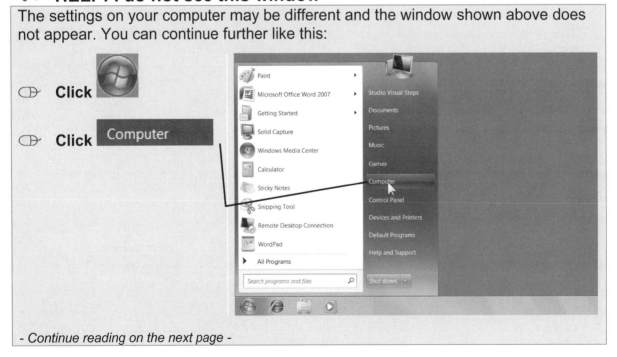

- Continue reading on the next page -

⊕ **Right-click your burner**

⊕ **Click** Open AutoPlay...

Now you can see the *AutoPlay* window.

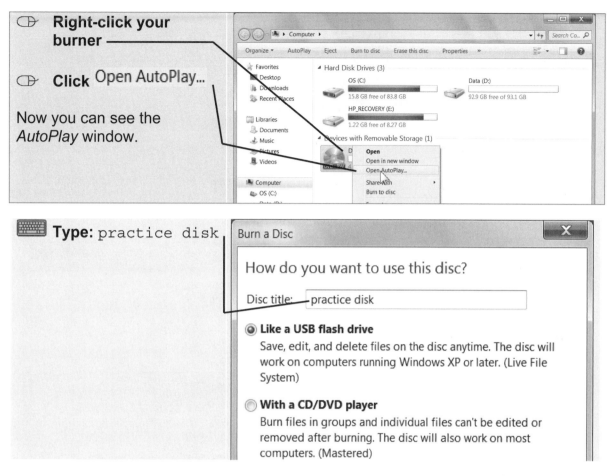

⌨ **Type:** practice disk

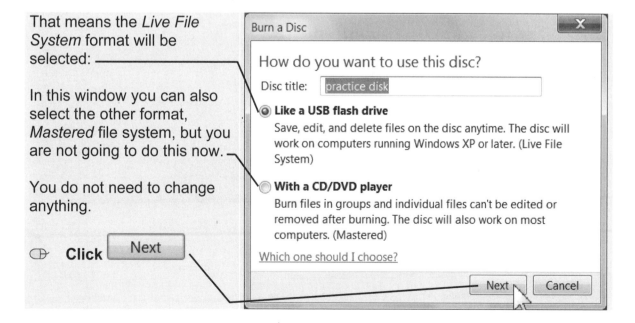

By default, the program will select the option for using the disc 'Like a USB flash drive'.

That means the *Live File System* format will be selected:

In this window you can also select the other format, *Mastered* file system, but you are not going to do this now.

You do not need to change anything.

⊕ **Click** Next

The formatting process is very quick:

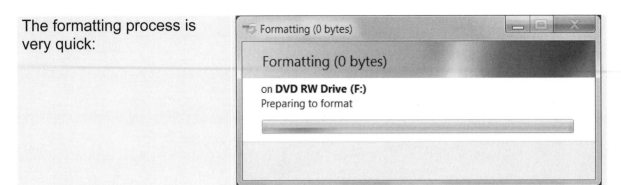

Afterwards, you will see the *AutoPlay* window once again:

☞ **Click**
  Open folder to view files
  using Windows Explorer

Now the folder window of the empty, formatted disc will be displayed. The program used to display the folder windows is called *Windows Explorer*. This program will automatically start up when a folder is opened.

6.4 Creating a Data Disc

Now you can select the files you want to write to the disc:

☞ **Click** Pictures

The *Pictures* library will be opened. A library is a collection of links to different files stored in various locations on your computer.

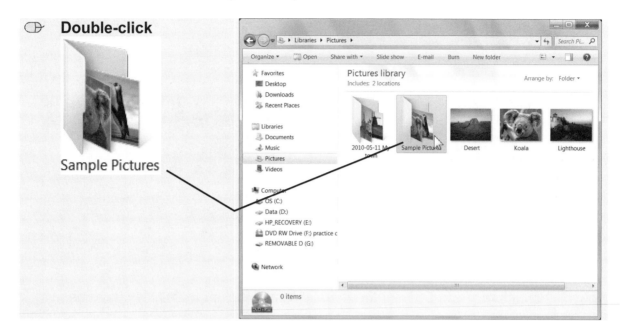

You will see all the pictures in the *Sample Pictures* folder. Here you can select the files you want to copy to the disc:

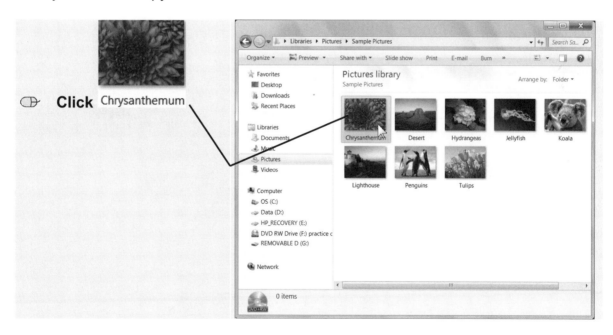

You can select a series of consecutive files by holding the Shift key down while you click the files:

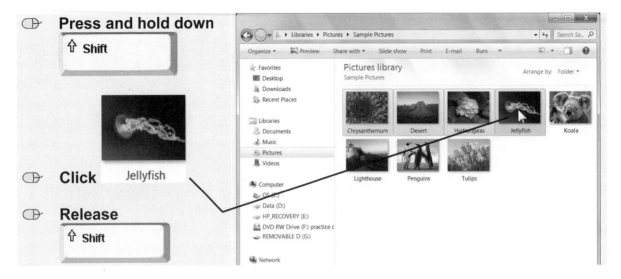

Now all the pictures from *Chrysanthemum* up to and including *Jellyfish* have been selected.

If you do not want to select a consecutive series of files, you can select multiple individual files by holding down the Ctrl key:

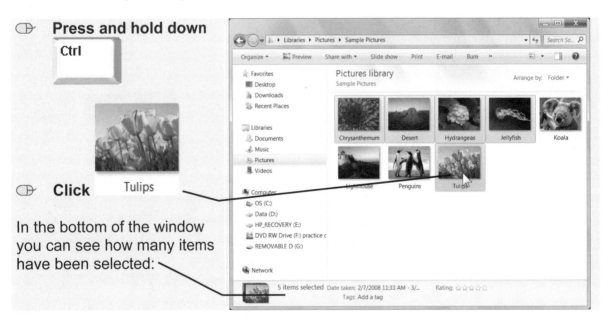

Now you have selected the pictures *Chrysanthemum* up to and including *Jellyfish*, and the *Tulips* picture.

6.5 Burning a Data Disc

The *Live File System* will burn the selected files directly to the disc.

In the right-hand side of the window:

☞ **Click** Burn

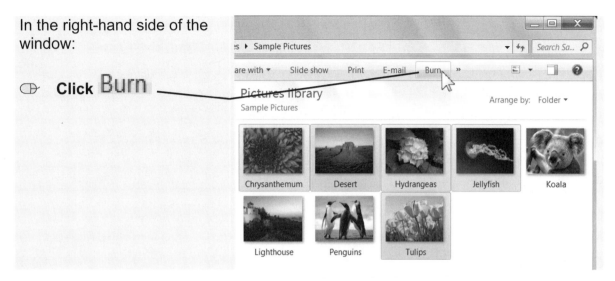

🩹 HELP! I do not see the Burn button

Depending on your computer's screen settings, you may not see the Burn button after you have selected one or more files or folders. If that is the case, you will see a

» button on the toolbar:

☞ **Click** »

Now you will see the Burn option:

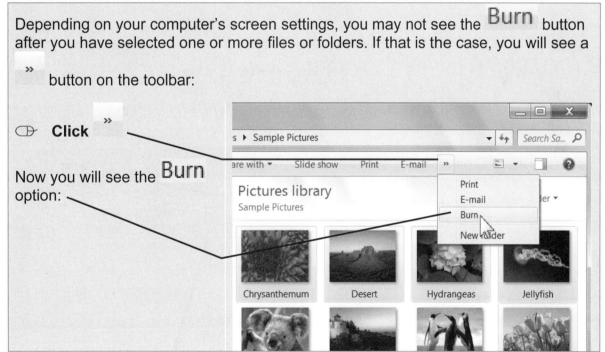

The files will be burned directly to the disc.
You can also burn entire folders in exactly the same way. Just select folders instead of individual files.

During the burn process you will see this window:

Note that here the burn process is called *copying*:

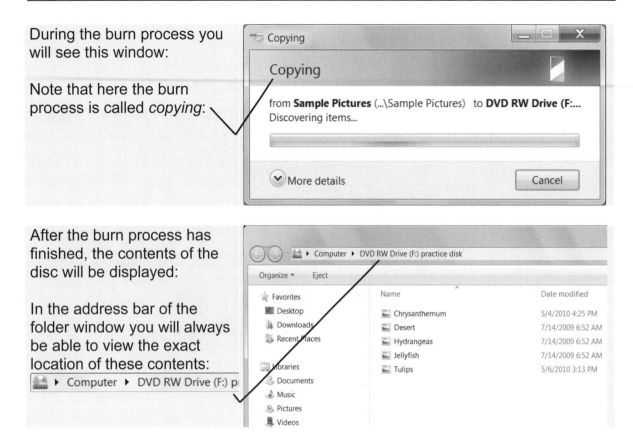

After the burn process has finished, the contents of the disc will be displayed:

In the address bar of the folder window you will always be able to view the exact location of these contents:

6.6 Adding Data To a Live File System Disc

You can always add new data to a disc that has been formatted with the *Live File System*. You do that like this:

Click ╳

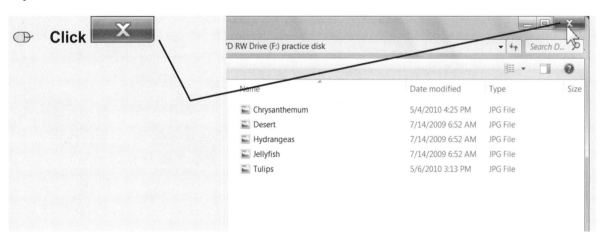

You will see the pictures window:

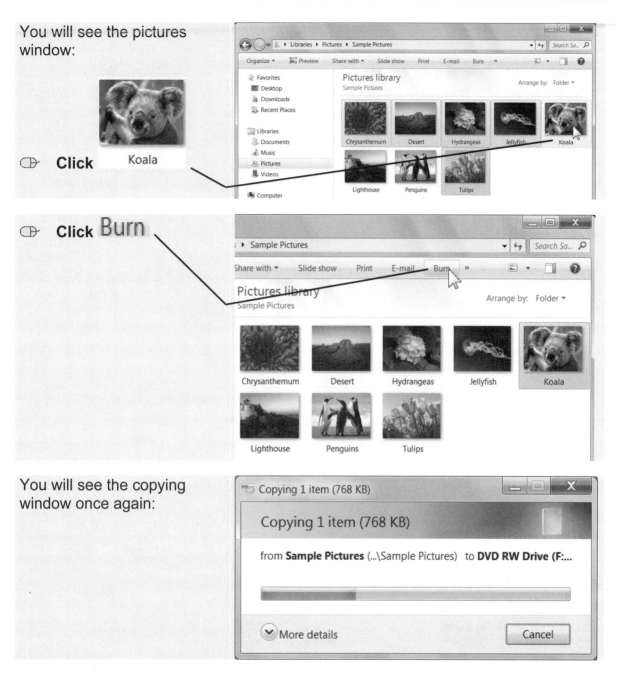

☞ **Click** Koala

☞ **Click** Burn

You will see the copying window once again:

When the burning process has finished, the pictures window will reappear. If you wish, you can add more files to the disc. For now, that will not be necessary. You can close the open windows:

☞ **Close all windows** 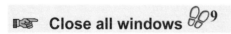⁹

Closing or finishing a disc

If you want to use a rewritable *Live File System* disc in other computers and devices, you will need to close the current burn session and prepare the disc for use in external devices. In *Windows* the disc will automatically close as soon as you press the eject button of the burner drive. Closing a disc may take a few minutes, and will take up 20 megabytes (MB) of disc space. After the session has been closed you will still be able to add new files to the disc, but each subsequent session will need to be closed as well.

Please note: if you are using a recordable disc this will not be possible. This type of disc is suitable for formatting and burning only once.

Closing a session will take up to 20 MB of disc space. Therefore it is recommended to burn as many files as possible in one single session, instead of removing the CD, DVD, or blu-ray disc from the drive each time you have copied a file. The period during which a disc is inserted into the burner without being removed, is called a session.

Some burning programs ask you to *finish* a session instead of closing it. Often the program will not work properly if you do not finish a session. But you will not be able to add files to a disc that has been finished.

6.7 Deleting Data from a Live File System Disc

You can also delete files from a disc that has been formatted using the *Live File System*. Here is how you do that:

☞ **Open the** *Computer* **window** ⚹⁵⁶

⊕ **Double-click your burner**

DVD RW Drive (F:) practice c

4.36 GB free of 4.37 GB

Your computer may use a different letter for the burner drive.

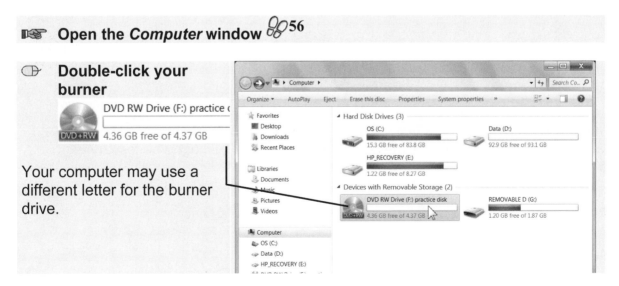

If you want to delete a file from the disc, first you will need to select it:

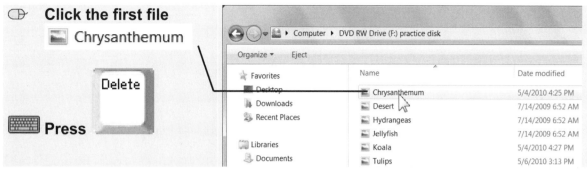

Click the first file

Chrysanthemum

Press Delete

Tip

Deleting multiple files

If you want to delete multiple files at once, you can use the ⇧ **Shift** and **Ctrl** keys to select them, just as in the previous section.

You will need to confirm the deletion:

Click Yes

Now the file will be deleted:

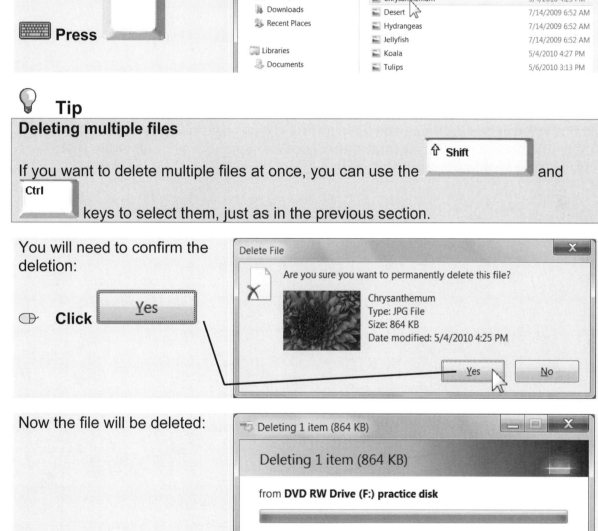

The 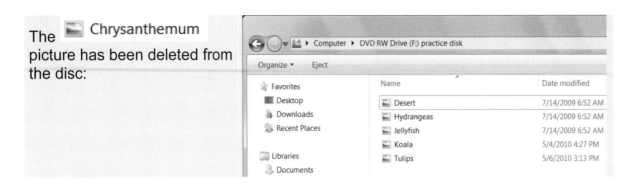 Chrysanthemum picture has been deleted from the disc:

6.8 Erasing a Live File System Rewritable Disc

On a rewritable disc, you can delete all the files at once. Afterwards you can use the empty disc once again, and format it again, for example using the other file system. This is how you erase a rewritable disc:

Click 🖳 Computer

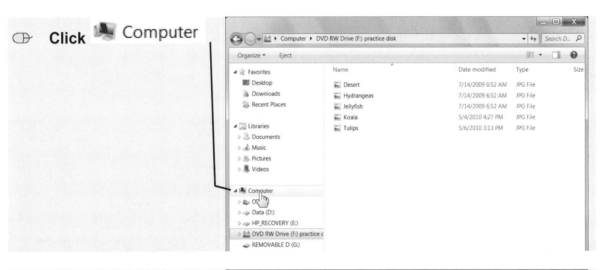

Click your burner

DVD RW Drive (F:) practice dis
DVD+RW 4.36 GB free of 4.37 GB

Click Erase this disc

Please note!

You will not be able to erase a recordable disc in this way. CD recordables (cd-r), DVD recordables (dvd-r / dvd+r), and blu-ray recordables (blu-ray-r) can be formatted only once. If you insert this type of disc into the drive, you will not see the Erase this disc button on the toolbar.

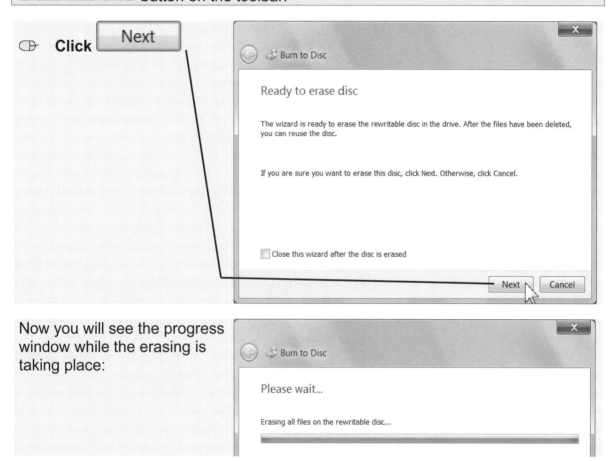

☞ **Click** Next

Now you will see the progress window while the erasing is taking place:

After a while you will see a message that the erasing is done:

At the bottom of the window:

☞ **Click** Finish

Now you will see the *Computer* window.

When you empty the rewritable disc in this manner, the disc will already be formatted for use a second time. You will be able to choose which formatting system you want to use for a new burning session.
Recordable discs do not offer this option. These discs are suited for formatting and burning data one time only.

☞ **Close the *Computer* window** **⁹**

☞ **Remove the disc from the burner**

6.9 The Mastered File System

If you want to use a CD, DVD or blu-ray disc in external devices, such as a DVD or blu-ray player, you will usually need to use the *Mastered* file system. Also, if you want to use the disc in other computers with older operating systems, it is best to select the *Mastered* file system.

➤ Please note!

The *Mastered* file format will first store the files in a temporary folder on your computer before burning them to disc. Make sure you have enough free space on your hard drive, ranging from 650 MB for a CD up to 50 GB for a dual layer blu-ray disc.

☞ **Insert the rewritable disc you have just erased into the burner**

Or, if you do not have this disc:

☞ **Insert a new recordable disc into the burner**

In this example the same rewritable DVD has been used.

You will see this window:

⊕ **Click**

Burn files to disc
using Windows Explorer

Please note: maybe you will see additional options in this window

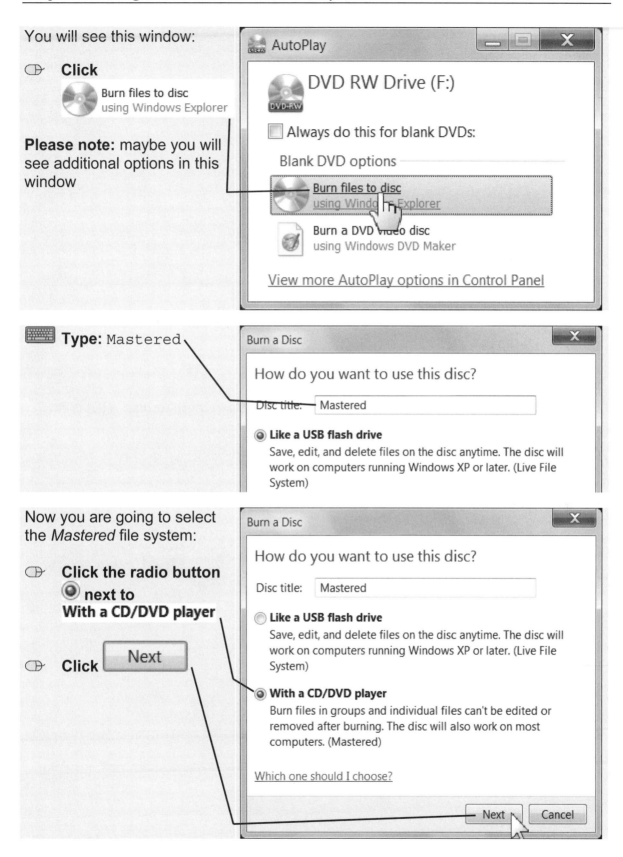

🖮 **Type:** Mastered

Now you are going to select the *Mastered* file system:

⊕ **Click the radio button ◉ next to With a CD/DVD player**

⊕ **Click** Next

You will see directly the contents of the disc:

Currently, the disc does not contain any data.

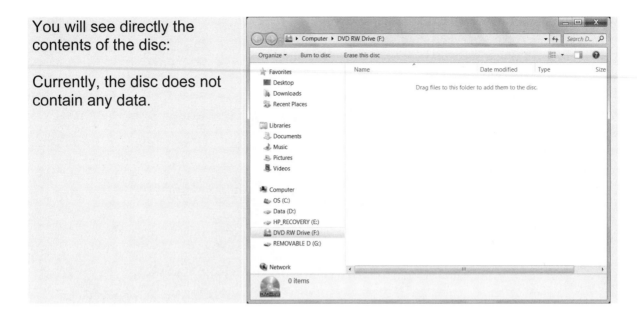

6.10 Adding Files to a Queue

This file system places the files in a queue, before burning them to disc. This is how to add files to the queue:

Click 🔖 Pictures

Double-click

Sample Pictures

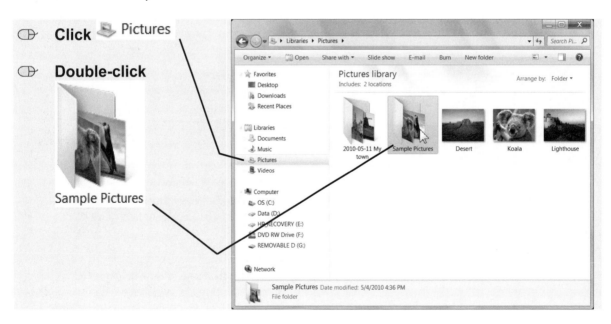

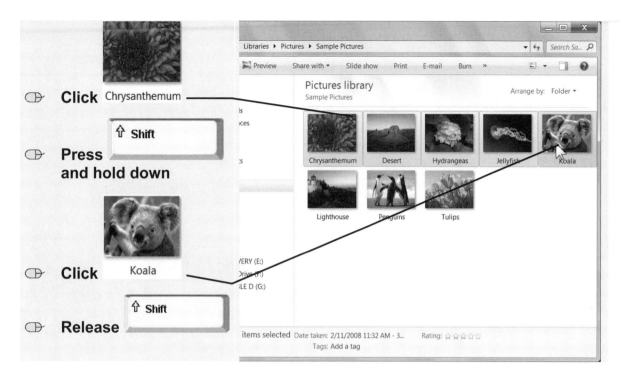

Now all of the consecutive files have been selected.

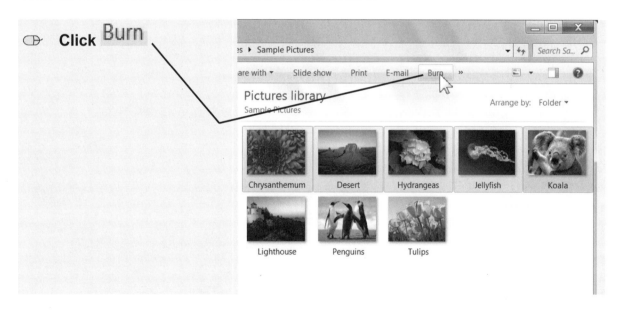

In the *Mastered* file system, the files will not be burned directly, but will be placed in a queue first. All files in this queue will be burned to the disc at once.

You will see the queue in a new window:

You will also see a message saying that you have files waiting to be burned to disc:

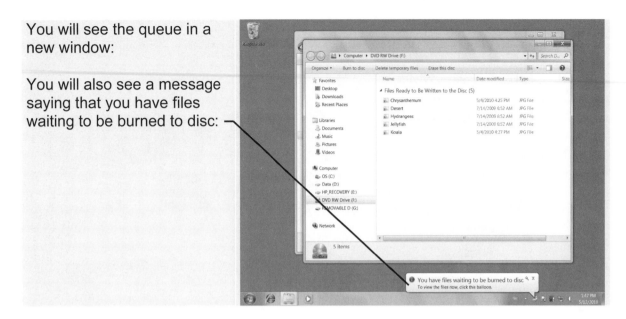

You can always add other files to a queue. First, you are going to minimize the queue window:

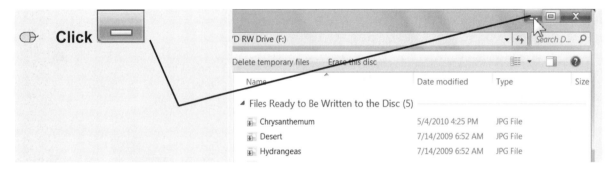

Now you are going to add another file:

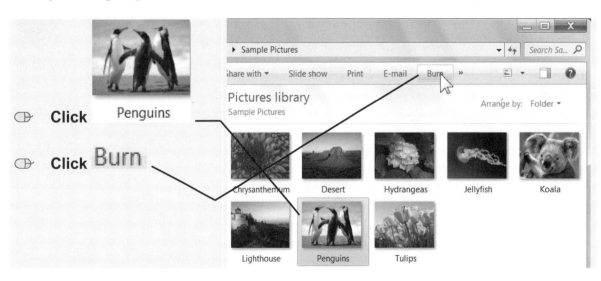

Now you will see the 'files waiting' message again:

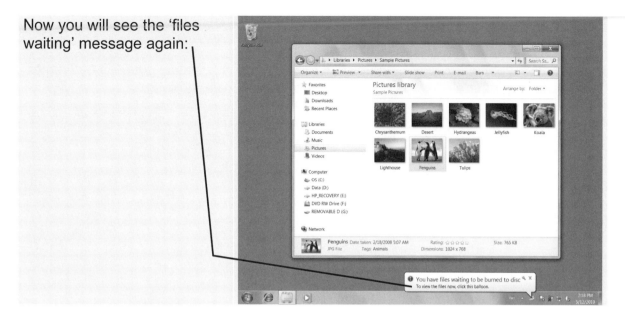

Open the queue window:

On the taskbar:

☞ **Click**

☞ **Click**

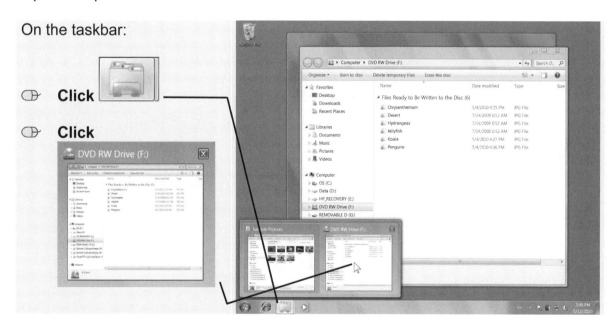

The queue window will reappear.

6.11 Removing Files From the Queue

You can also delete the files in a queue, if for instance you decide you do not want to burn these files after all. This is how you remove a file from a queue:

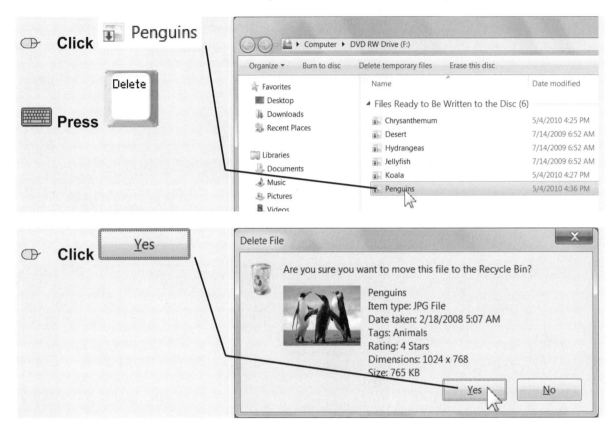

6.12 Burn Files in a Queue to Disc

If you have completed the queue and you are satisfied with your selection, you can start burning the files to disc:

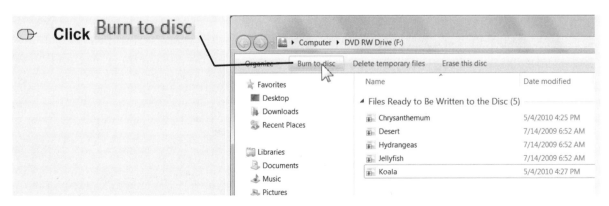

You will see the *Prepare this disc* window:

The recording speed will be automatically selected:

⊕ **Click** Next

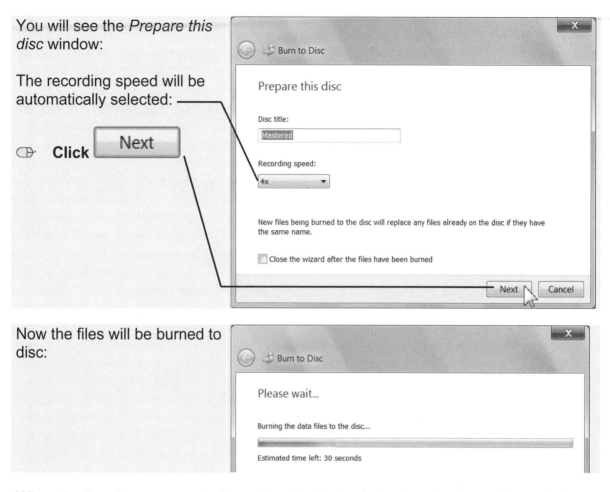

Now the files will be burned to disc:

When the burning process is done, the disc is ejected automatically and you will see this window:

If you wish, you can create another disc using these same files:

For now, that will not be necessary:

⊕ **Click** Finish

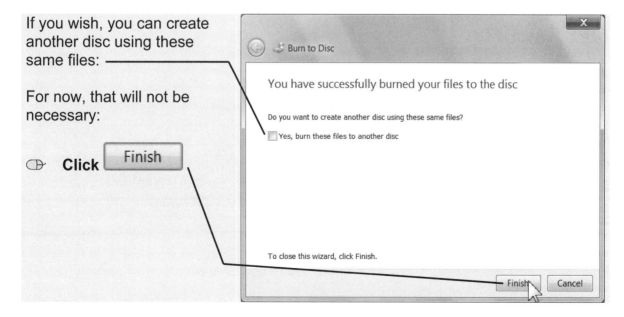

☞ **Remove the disc from your burner**

☞ **Close the *Sample Pictures* window** ℘⁹

Now the pictures have been burned to disc. In the next section you can take a look at these pictures.

6.13 Viewing the Contents of a Disc With Windows Explorer

You are going to check that the files were actually burnt to the disc:

☞ **Insert the dish containing the pictures into your disc drive**

You will see the *AutoPlay* window:

 Click

🗀 Open folder to view files
using Windows Explorer

💡 **Tip**

Option for always using the same program
If you prefer to use *Windows Explorer* when opening a CD, DVD, or blu-ray disc containing pictures, you can select the Always do this for pictures: option.

Windows Explorer will display the contents of the disc:

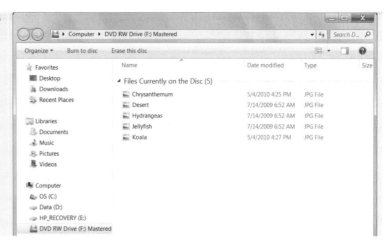

☞ **Close the *Windows Explorer* window** **9**

☞ **Remove the disc from the CD/DVD drive**

6.14 Burn a Windows DVD

Windows 7 has a special program to burn DVDs. *Windows DVD Maker* can create a video DVD of your video files, or a slide show of your pictures in just a few simple steps. You can play a video DVD in your regular DVD player which is connected to your TV set.

Please note!

You cannot use *Windows DVD Maker* to burn blu-ray discs.

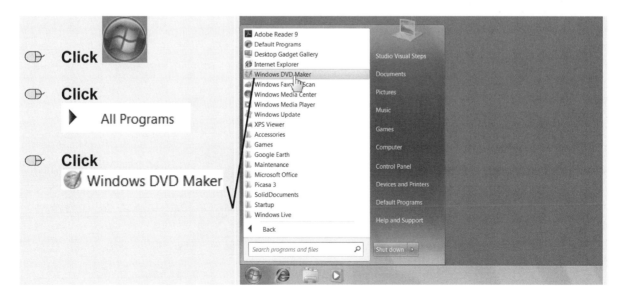

👉 **Click**

👉 **Click**

▶ All Programs

👉 **Click**

  Windows DVD Maker

You will see the introduction window of *Windows DVD Maker*:

☞ **Click**

Choose Photos and Videos

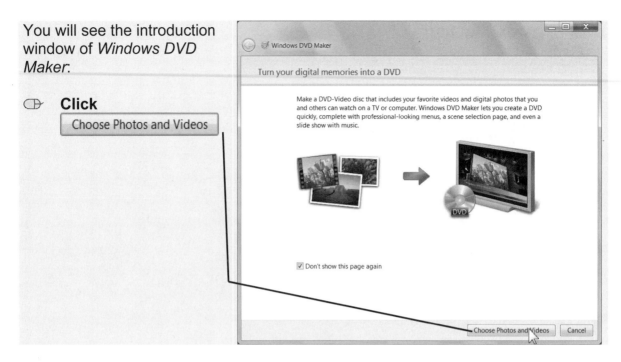

Now you will see the actual *Windows DVD Maker* window. In this window you can add video files and pictures to the video DVD:

☞ **Click** 🗋 Add items

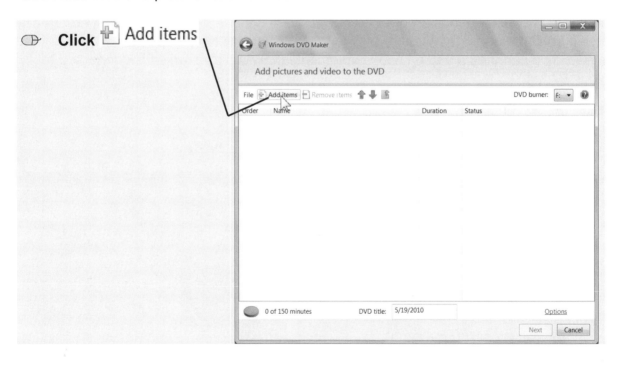

First, you are going to add a video:

⊕ **If necessary, click**
  Videos

⊕ **Double-click**

Sample Videos

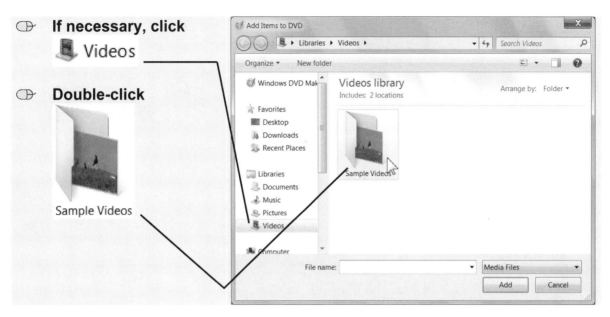

Now you will see the *Windows 7* sample video:

⊕ **Click**   Wildlife

⊕ **Click**   Add

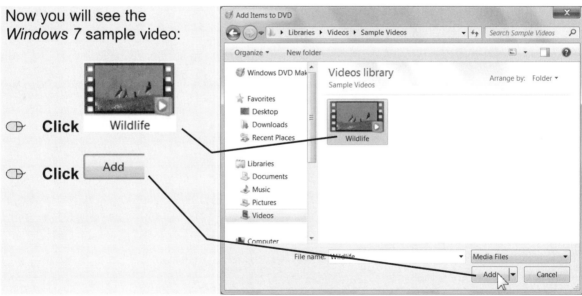

Now the video is included in the list:

You are going to add pictures as well:

⊕ **Click**   Add items

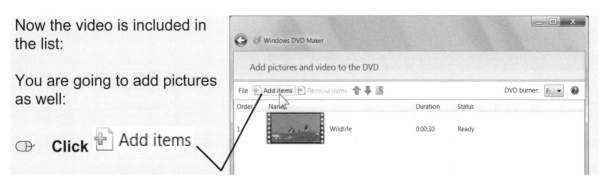

⊕ **Click** ▷ 🖥 Pictures

⊕ **Double-click**

Sample Pictures

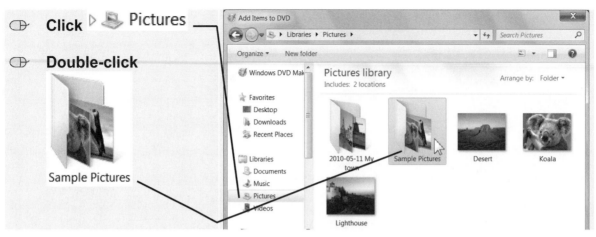

☞ **Select all the sample pictures** 👣58

⊕ **Click** Add

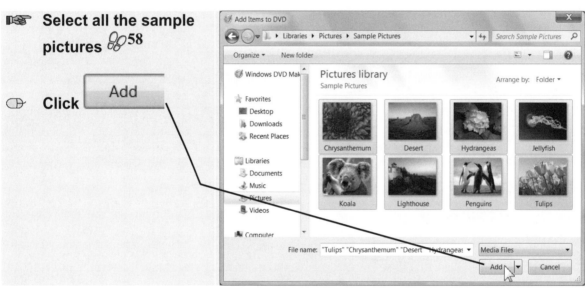

On the DVD, a slide show will be created from these pictures: ──────

You can change the order of play by using the ⬆⬇ buttons:

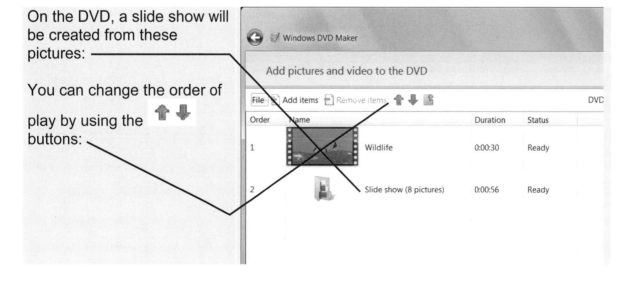

Take a look at the DVD's playing options:

In the bottom right corner of the window:

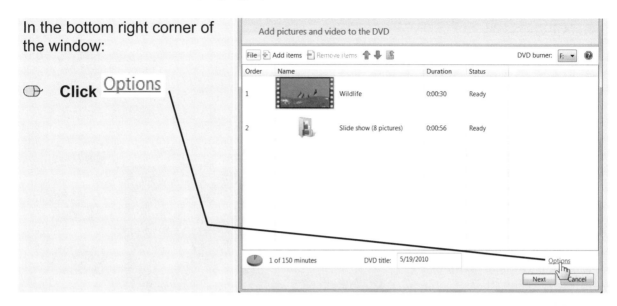

☞ **Click** Options

In this window you can select the settings for playing a DVD:

You can also select the aspect ratio (normal or widescreen): ————————

For playback on North American DVD players you need to select NTSC:————————

For countries using the PAL system, select PAL.

☞ **Click** [OK]

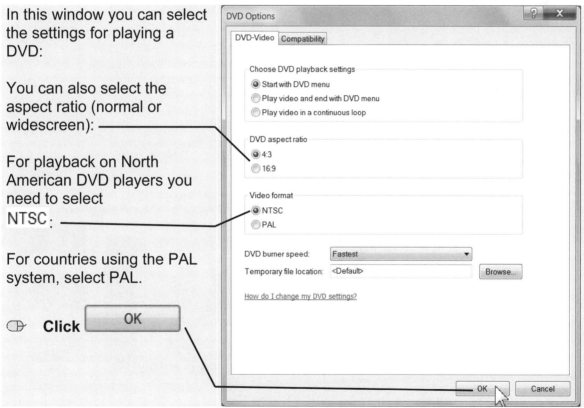

Now you will see the *Windows DVD Maker* window once more:

☞ **Click** [Next]

You will see the wizard's next window. A video DVD will display its contents in a disc menu. The movie DVDs you buy in a store contain the same menus. You can modify the menu yourself.

Use the ▲ Menu text button to modify the text in the menu:

With 🔧 Customize menu you can change the pictures in the menu and add music to the menu:

With 🖼 Slide show you can regulate the speed of the slide show and add music as well.

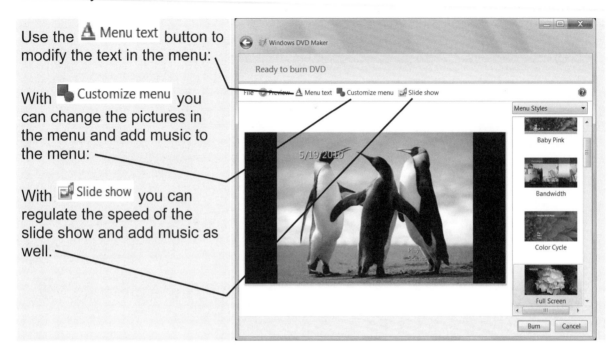

You can also select a different style for the menu:

☞ **Drag the scroll bar downwards**

☞ **Click** Highlights

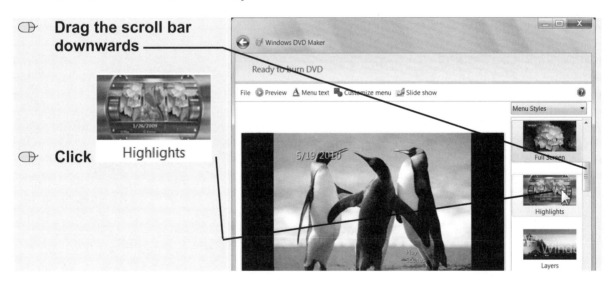

Now you can take a look at a preview of the video DVD.

In the top left of the window:

☞ **Click**  ⏵ Preview

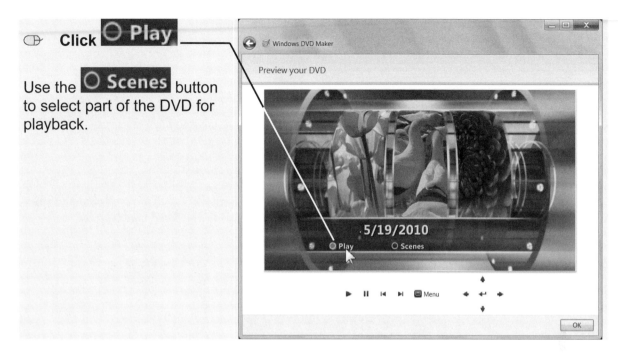

Click ⊖ **Play**

Use the ⊖ **Scenes** button to select part of the DVD for playback.

Now the DVD preview will be played. First, you will see the video and after that you will see the slide show. When you have finished watching the preview:

Click [OK]

If you are satisfied with the results, you can burn the video DVD:

☞ **Insert a blank DVD into the DVD drive**

☞ **If necessary, close the *AutoPlay* window** ⅊[9]

Click [Burn]

First, the files will be encoded, so they will be suitable for playback in a regular DVD player. This process will take a few moments. Afterwards, the DVD will be burned.

If you do not want to burn a DVD right now:

Click [Cancel] **and do not save the project**

When the video DVD has finished burning, the tray of your DVD burner will automatically open.

Click [Close]

☞ **Close the *Windows DVD Maker* window** ✔✔⁹

💡 **Tip**

Saving files in between operations
Do you want to save your project, and continue editing it later on?

☞ Click File , Save

You will see the *Save Project* window:

By File name: :

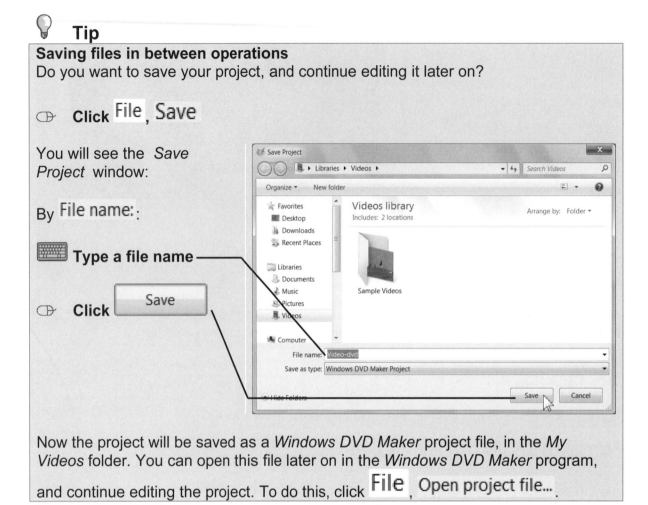

 Type a file name ——

☞ Click [Save]

Now the project will be saved as a *Windows DVD Maker* project file, in the *My Videos* folder. You can open this file later on in the *Windows DVD Maker* program, and continue editing the project. To do this, click File , Open project file... .

💡 **Tip**

Learn more about Windows DVD Maker
In *Windows Help and Support* you will find extensive information and tips regarding the *Windows DVD Maker* program. Just type the program name (*Windows DVD Maker)* in the search box, and you will see all relevant topics.

In this chapter you have learned various methods for burning files to a disc. In the next few exercises you can practice these operations.

6.15 Exercises

Have you forgotten how to do something? Then you can use the number behind the footsteps to look up the description in *Appendix B How Do I Do That Again?*

Exercise: Live File System

In this exercise you are going to burn files to a CD or a DVD which is formatted with the *Live File System*.

☞ Insert a new or an older blank disc into the burner.

☞ Click  .

☞ Format the disc using *Live File System*. $\wp\wp$**57**

☞ Click the *Music* folder.

☞ Double-click the *Sample Music* folder.

☞ Select two files. $\wp\wp$**58**

☞ Burn the files to disc. $\wp\wp$**59**

☞ Delete one of the files. $\wp\wp$**60**

☞ Delete all the files on the disc (this will only be possible if you are using a rewritable disc). $\wp\wp$**61**

☞ Close the window. $\wp\wp$**9**

☞ Remove the disc from the burner.

Exercise: Mastered

In this exercise you are going to burn files to a CD or a DVD which is formatted with the *Mastered* file system.

☞ Insert a new or an older blank disc into the burner.

☞ Click 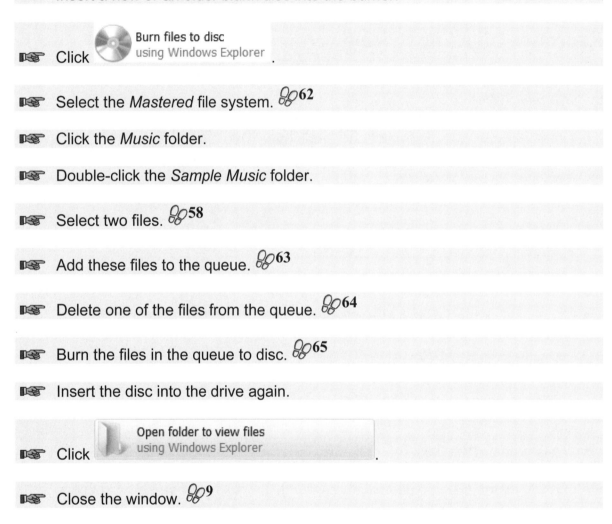 **Burn files to disc** using Windows Explorer .

☞ Select the *Mastered* file system. $\mathscr{B}^{62}$

☞ Click the *Music* folder.

☞ Double-click the *Sample Music* folder.

☞ Select two files. $\mathscr{B}^{58}$

☞ Add these files to the queue. $\mathscr{B}^{63}$

☞ Delete one of the files from the queue. $\mathscr{B}^{64}$

☞ Burn the files in the queue to disc. $\mathscr{B}^{65}$

☞ Insert the disc into the drive again.

☞ Click **Open folder to view files** using Windows Explorer .

☞ Close the window. $\mathscr{B}^{9}$

☞ Remove the disc from the burner.

6.16 Background Information

Dictionary	
Burner/writer	A device which copies files to recordable CDs, DVDs or blu-ray discs.
Close a disc	The process that enables you to use a CD, DVD, or blu-ray disc in another computer or device. As long as you have free space on the disc, additional files can be added to the disc after it is closed. The closing process will take up approximately 20 MB per session.
Data	All documents, photos, videos, and music files are data files stored on your computer.
Disc menu	The menu on a video DVD, where you can select the video or slide show you want to play.
Finalize a disc	The process that occurs after files are burned (copied) to a CD, DVD, or blu-ray disc. After a disc is finalized, it is ready to be played in another computer or device, but you can no longer add files to it.
Formatting	Before you can burn files to a CD, DVD, or blu-ray disc, the disc must first be prepared using a process called formatting. The disc will be prepared for use in *Windows 7*.
Live File System	A file storage system that can be used to create CDs, DVDs, and blu-ray discs. Discs formatted with *Live File System* allow you to copy files to the disc at any time, instead of copying (burning) them all at once. This system can be used on *Windows 7, Windows Vista* and *Windows XP* computers. This system may not be compatible with other devices.
Mastered format	A file system used to create CDs and DVDs. Discs created using the *Mastered* format are more likely to be compatible with older computers, but an additional step is required to burn the collection of files to the disc. Blu-ray discs can only be played on specific blu-ray players. Check the player's manual to find out about this.
Queue	Overview of the files that are waiting to be burned to a CD, DVD, or blu-ray disc, using the *Mastered* file format.

- Continue reading on the next page -

Quick format	Quick format is a formatting option that creates a new file table on a hard disk but does not fully overwrite or erase the disk. A quick format is much faster than a normal format, which fully erases any existing data on the hard disk.
Video DVD	A DVD which is suitable for playing videos. Such a DVD can be played on the DVD player that is connected to your TV set, for example.
Windows DVD Maker	The program that enables you to burn video DVDs, suitable for playback in a regular DVD player.
Windows Explorer	The program that is used to display the folder window.

Source: Windows Help and Support

How does a burner operate
The data on a CD, DVD, or blu-ray disc is recorded in digital form, that is, in a series of 1's and 0's. These 1's and 0's are represented by millions of tiny bumps and flat areas on the disc's reflective surface. The bumps and flats are arranged in a continuous track. When the disc is played, the player will rotate the disc and pass a laser beam over the disc's reflective surface. The light that is reflected will be picked up by an optical sensor. When the beam passes over a bump or a spot, the light is bounced away from the optical sensor. On the basis of this information, the sensor will or will not pass on an electrical current to the computer. The computer will process this information and translate it to a format you can use.

A factory-made disc will contain information in the form of tiny pits. Your computer's burner will use pits (CD/DVD/blu-ray recordables) or opaque spots (CD/DVD rewritables). To do this, the laser beam heats up the recording surface. As a result of this process, the translucent material on the surface of a rewritable disc will acquire opaque spots, which can also be erased by heating them once more. When a rewritable disc is burned with new information, the old information will be deleted at the same time. This process will take up more time than the single burn process. For a disc to be read correctly, it is important that the pits or spots are spaced evenly, when they are burned to the disc. That is why you need to select the burn speed before the process starts, and why you cannot adjust the speed during the burn process.

If any interruptions occur during the burn process, the disc will be rendered useless. Such an interruption may occur if the constant stream of information that is copied to the burner is disturbed. The introduction of the *burnproof* technology for burners has made sure that the burning process will continue in the correct way, even if the stream of information to the burner has temporarily been interrupted.

Choosing between Live File System or Mastered

Your choice between these two methods will depend on the purpose for which you want to use the CD, DVD, or blu-ray discs you are going to burn.

Live File System discs:

- Allow you to directly copy (burn) files to the disc.
- Are useful if you want to leave the disc in the burner and copy a few files once in a while.
- Are useful because recording data is quicker than on *Mastered* discs.
- Allow you to delete individual files, or re-format the disc if you want to free up space, that is, if you use a rewritable disc, such as a cd-rw, dvd-rw, dvd-ram, or blu-ray-re.
- Will have to be closed* before they can be used on another computer.
- Are only compatible with *Windows XP*, *Windows Vista*, and *Windows 7*.

Mastered-discs:

- Allow you to drag files to the disc, and burn them to disc all at once.
- Are useful if you want to burn a large collection of files, such as a music CD.
- Are compatible with older computers and devices, like CD, DVD, and blu-ray players.
- Require a larger amount of disk capacity (just as much space as on the disc you want to burn).

* Before you will be able to use a disc formatted with *Live File System* (like a cd-r, dvd-r, dvd+r, or blu-ray-r) in other computers and devices, you will need to close the current session and prepare the disc for use. In *Windows* the disc is closed by default, as soon as the eject button of the drive is pressed. The closing process may take a few minutes and needs about 20 megabyte (MB) of disk space. At the bottom right of your screen you will see this message:

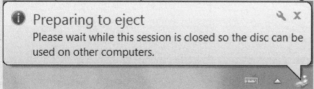

After you have closed a write session, you will still be able to add additional files to the disc. If you want to use the disc on another computer, you will need to close each new session.

Please note: some programs will compel you to finalize the disc, instead of closing the session. You will not be able to add other files to a disc that has been finalized.

Source: Windows Help and Support

Types of CDs and DVDs

By now there exist many different types of CDs and DVDs. Here is a brief overview of the most important characteristics:

Type	Properties	Cap.	Compatible with
CD ROM	Read-only.	650 MB	Most computers and devices (CD and DVD players).
DVD ROM	Read-only.	4,7 GB	Most computers and devices (DVD players).
CD-R	Rewritable multiple times. Data cannot be deleted.	650 MB Or 700 MB	After it has been closed: most computers and devices (CD and DVD players).
DVD-R or DVD+R	Rewritable multiple times. Data cannot be deleted.	4,7 GB	After it has been closed: most computers and devices (DVD players).
CD-RW	Rewritable multiple times. Data can be deleted.	650 MB	Many, but not all computers and devices. In particular, older devices may cause problems.
DVD-RW or DVD+RW	Rewritable multiple times. Data can be deleted.	4,7 GB	Many, but not all computers and devices. In particular, older devices may cause problems.
Dual layer DVD, Dvd DL	DVD with double storage capacity.	8,5 GB	Only suitable for the newest devices. Not yet supported by all software programs.
Blu-ray-r	Rewritable multiple times. Data cannot be deleted.	25 GB	Only suitable for the newest devices. Not yet supported by all software programs.
Blu-ray-re	Rewritable multiple times. Data can be deleted.	25 GB	Only suitable for the newest devices. Not yet supported by all software programs.
Dual layer Blu-ray	Blu-ray disc with double storage capacity.	50 GB	Only suitable for the newest devices. Not yet supported by all software programs.

Notes:
- r stands for recordable. Data can be written to disc, but cannot be erased. rw stands for rewritable. Data can be written to disc multiple times, and can also be erased.
- The + and – versions of a DVD indicate a different type of DVD. Most devices will be able to use both types of discs. The technical specifications of your equipment will state which type of disc can be used.

Burn speed

In the product specifications of a burner you will always see numbers, like '4x', '16x', or '48x'. The 'x' indicates the number of times with which the speed increases. For instance, '4x' indicates that this burner burns the data to disc with a speed that is four times faster than the basic speed. This basic speed is 150 kB per second for CD burners, and 1.13 MB per second for DVD burners. Actually, the process will take a while longer, because the burner needs time to start up, initialize and finalize the disc. This means the burning process will always take up more time than is needed for the actual burning of the data.

Burners that can work with rewritable discs will present you with three or four different numbers. These numbers indicate the read speed, the write speed for recordable discs, and the write speed for rewritable discs. These speeds may vary according to the type of disc, for example for a CD, DVD, DVD-dl (dual layer), or a blu-ray disc. By comparing these numbers you can roughly compare the speed of various burners.

The write speed for burning data also depends on the maximum write speed of the CD you are using. This speed may vary for each type and brand of CD. The CD package contains information on the speed of the CD. If the maximum speed of the CD is lower than the burner's speed, the CD will be burned at a lower speed.

Writing audio or video CDs, DVDs, and blu-ray discs

If you want to play music and movies in a CD, DVD, or blu-ray player, the discs will need to be formatted in a specific way. It is recommended to use programs that are suitable for working with images and sounds. These programs allow you to create discs that can be played in regular CD, DVD, or blu-ray players.

For example, *Windows DVD Maker* lets you create a video DVD of all your pictures and/or video files. With *Windows Media Player* you can burn audio CDs for music files.

6.17 Tips

 Tip

Data stream to burner
During the disc burning process, it is important that the information stream to the burner is not interrupted. If this stream is interrupted, this may result in a burn failure. The new *burnproof* burners automatically repair this problem. In the burner's manual you can look up the specifications and find out whether your burner is burn proof.

Are you having problems with the burn process in *Windows 7*?
Here are a number of things that may help:

- close all other programs;
- disable the screen saver;
- disconnect the Internet connection (temporarily);
- disable anti-virus programs and other programs that scan your computer for viruses (temporarily);
- make sure that there is enough space on your hard drive;
- make sure that the recordable discs and the burner itself are clean;
- try to use a lower burn speed (see the *Tip* on *Lower Burn Speed*);
- try to use a different brand of recordable discs;
- try defragmenting the hard disk.

 Tip

UPS (Uninterruptible Power Supply)
A power surge (voltage peaks) may disrupt your computer and therefore your burner's operations. Even a second's blinking of the lights may indicate a power fluctuation. You can prevent this by not using any heavy equipment yourself, during the burn process. But sometimes the power fluctuations are due to outside influences. In that case it may be worthwhile to buy a UPS (uninterruptable power supply) unit.

A UPS is a device that is placed between your computer and the regular input power source; this device contains a battery that will allow the computer to operate for a while, after the power has been interrupted. Usually UPS equipment also provides protection in case of short-lived power surges or interruptions.

Tip

Lower Burn Speed
When you are using a disc that is formatted with the *Mastered* file system, you will be able to select the burn speed. Normally, you will want to burn at the highest speed. But if the discs are not burned properly and the process keeps failing, you can also select a lower speed. This is how you select the burn speed:

Click

Click the desired speed

Your burner may display different speeds.

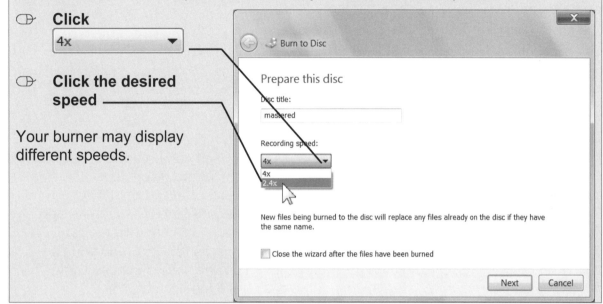

 Tip

Regularly check important discs
Contrary to general opinion, the data on a disc will not be preserved forever. The outcome of various tests suggests that the data may be useless in a matter of years.

Therefore, it is recommended to store important data on high quality discs. Among other things, this quality depends on:
• the manufacturing process
• the type of burner that is used
• the burn method (multiple sessions, or all at once)
• the way in which a disc is stored and treated
• the type of disc

Because more expensive discs are not necessarily better discs, it is a good idea to check out the various websites that offer disc tests, preferably conducted by independent organizations such as consumer associations, computer magazines, etc.

As time goes by, you will probably be storing more and more important data onto discs. It is recommended that you check your discs regularly. This will minimize the chance of not being able to view your video and photo collection in a few years' time.

Tip

Mark your CDs, DVDs, and blu-ray discs

Are you familiar with this? You are absolutely sure that you have saved your holiday photos on a disc, but which disc was it? If you create back-ups and copies on a regular basis, you will quickly have gathered a large collection of discs. That is why it is very important to mark these discs and write down their content. There are several methods for this:

- If your discs are kept in their original package, you can just write down the contents on the package. This is recommended for music CDs/DVDs, because you will also be able to write down all the track titles. However, discs that come in a box are more expensive than unpackaged discs, or discs on a spindle, and they take up more space.
- You write down the contents on the disc itself, using a special pen or marker. Only use a special marker, because other types of pens can damage the surface of the disc. Make sure you write on the printable side of the disc, that is, the side where the brand and type of disc is printed. You will not have a lot of writing space. Tip: just write down a number, and keep a record of these numbers and their contents in a different location (on your computer, or a handwritten list).
- You can buy special disc labels. These labels are the correct size and you can stick them on a disc without damaging the disc. You will need a special *center tool* to center the label in the middle of the disc. If the label is not exactly centered, the disc may become unbalanced and will not play properly. You can write on the labels with a pen, or print them from your computer.
- Modern burners use the *lightscribe* technology, which allows you to print text on the special discs that are used with this technology. These discs have a special coating, which can be written by the burner's laser beam. First, you burn your data on one side, and then you turn over the disc and print the label on the other side.

Also, there exist special programs that will let you burn your photo or music collection, and create an index of the contents at the same time. You can use various search options to retrieve the information on a disc. But even then, you will need to identify the correct disc by its name or number.

Tip

Drag files to a disc
If you want to burn files to a disc that is formatted with the *Live File System*, you can also drag the files to the burner. This may come in useful with programs that do not have a *Burn* button, such as *Paint,* for example.

☞ **Click the file**

Or:

☞ **Select the files**

☞ **Drag the file(s) to the burner**

Make sure that you have identified the correct burner, before you release the mouse button:

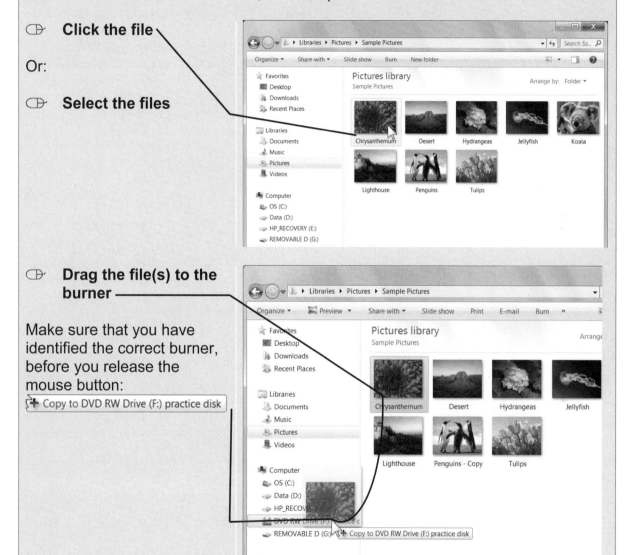

If the burner does not contain a disc, you will see a message asking you to insert a disc.

- Continue reading on the next page -

Now you will see that the files are being copied to the disc.

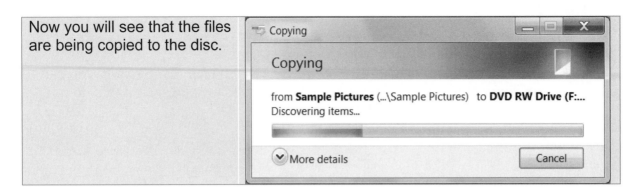

7. Interesting Programs and Handy Features in Windows 7

Windows 7 contains many interesting programs and handy features.

For instance, you can use the *Sticky Notes* program to place memos on your desktop. You needn't worry about forgetting important appointments anymore. The *Snipping Tool* lets you create screenshots quickly and easily. This comes in handy when you want to explain a specific program option or feature to someone else.

You're probably already familiar with the *Calculator* from previous *Windows* editions. Along with its basic arithmetic function, the *Calculator* now includes scientific and statistical functions as well. You can also use it to convert measurements. Furthermore, *Windows 7* comes with several other useful features. Some of these features have already been discussed in **Windows 7 for Seniors** (ISBN 978 90 5905 126 3). To be on the safe side, we will briefly go over these features again in this chapter.

A *Jump List* lets you see at a glance which files were recently open in a particular program. If you click one of the files, it will immediately open in that program. The *Aero Peek* feature lets you flip through all the windows that are currently open. With *Aero Snap* you can display two windows of the same size next to each other. *Aero Shake* will help you minimize or maximize windows very quickly. Finally, *Aero Flip 3D* will display all open windows in a three dimensional view. This way you can quickly find the window you are looking for.

In this chapter you will also learn more about the games included in *Windows 7*.

In this chapter you will learn how to work with:

- *Sticky Notes*;
- the *Snipping Tool*;
- the *Calculator*;
- Jump Lists;
- *Aero Peek, Aero Shake* and *Aero Snap*;
- *Aero Flip 3D*;
- the *Windows* games.

7.1 Sticky Notes

The *Sticky Notes* program lets you keep important information at your fingertips. You can create yellow-colored memos that get 'stuck' onto your desktop:

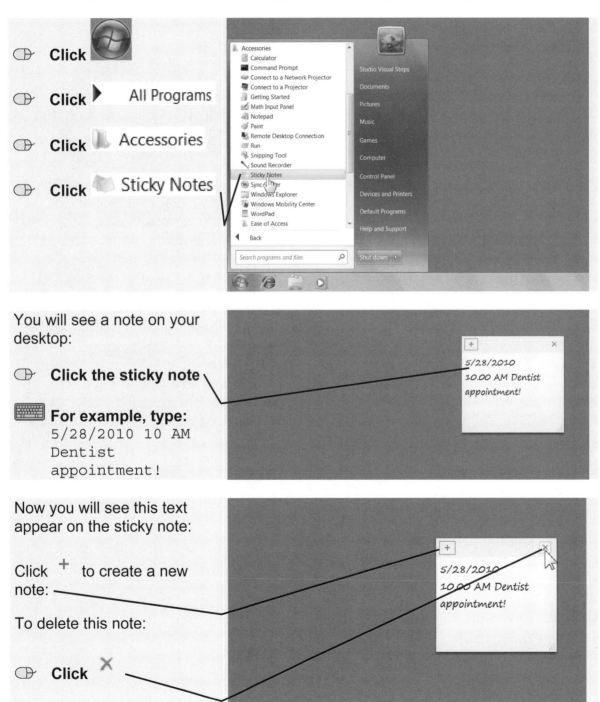

☞ **Click**

☞ **Click** ▶ All Programs

☞ **Click** Accessories

☞ **Click** Sticky Notes

You will see a note on your desktop:

☞ **Click the sticky note**

⌨ **For example, type:**
5/28/2010 10 AM
Dentist
appointment!

Now you will see this text appear on the sticky note:

Click + to create a new note:

To delete this note:

☞ **Click** ✕

⊕ **Click** `Yes`

7.2 Snipping Tool

Windows 7 contains a handy tool for making screenshots (capture screens) of any object on your screen. The *Snipping Tool* is located in the *Accessories* folder:

⊕ **Click** , ▶ All Programs , Accessories , Snipping Tool

By New :

⊕ **Click**

You can select a free-form snip, a rectangular snip, a window snip, or a full-screen snip. Just try a rectangular snip:

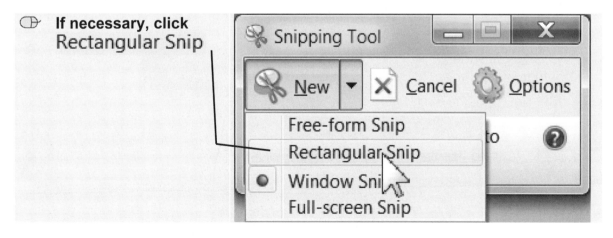

⊕ **If necessary, click Rectangular Snip**

Now you can draw a rectangular shape around the object you want to snip, the *Recycle Bin*, for instance:

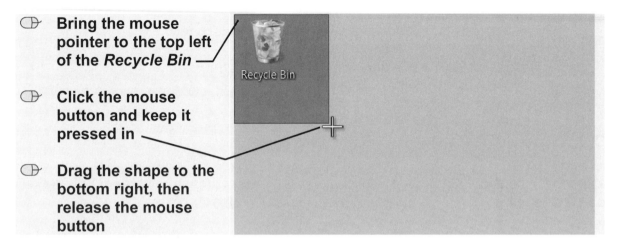

- ☞ **Bring the mouse pointer to the top left of the *Recycle Bin***
- ☞ **Click the mouse button and keep it pressed in**
- ☞ **Drag the shape to the bottom right, then release the mouse button**

The captured shape now appears in the mark-up window of the *Snipping Tool*.

You can use the pen or the highlighter to add text or a drawing to this snip.

Click to delete the text or drawing you have added.

Click to save the snip.

Click to copy the snip and paste it into another program.

Click to send this snip by e-mail.

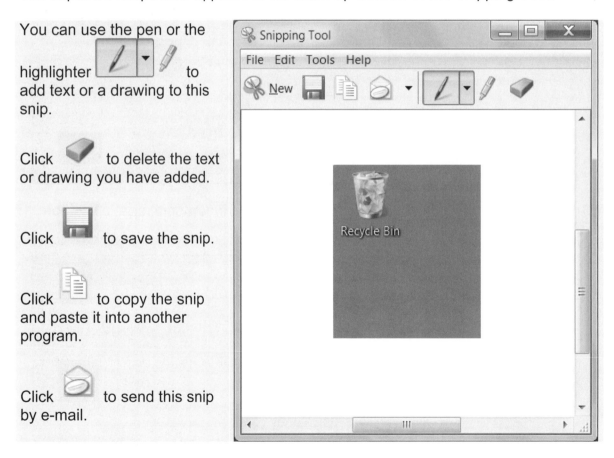

In *Windows Help and Support* you can find more information about this useful program. You can go there by clicking the "Help" button in the mark-up window.

☞ **Close the *Snipping Tool* window and do not save the changes** ✍⁹

7.3 Calculator

If you have worked with *Windows* before, you may already be familiar with the *Calculator* program. This program can be used to perform simple calculations. In *Windows 7* this program offers more advanced functions. Now you can use it to perform scientific and statistical calculations and convert measurements.

☞ **Click** 🪟 , ▶ All Programs , 📁 Accessories , 🖩 Calculator

Now you will see the *Calculator*:

In the standard mode you can perform simple calculations.

Click the calculator buttons to enter the numbers:

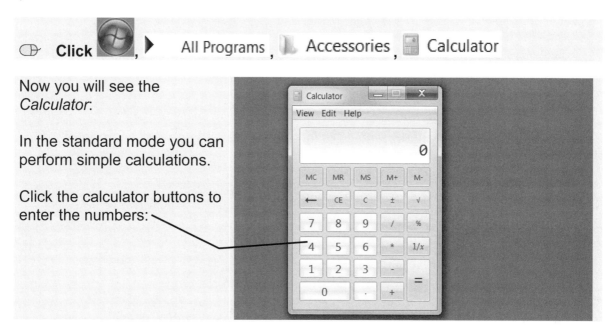

You can select additional modes:

☞ **Click View**

You will see the other functions listed here:

☞ **Click Scientific**

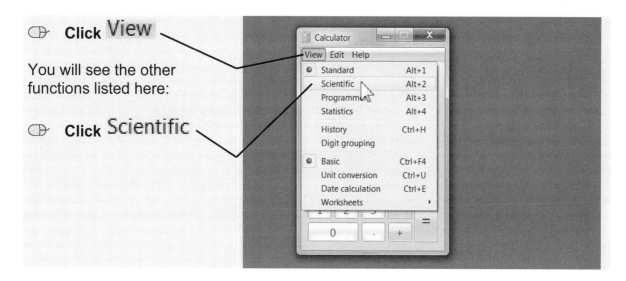

Now you will see the
Calculator's scientific mode:

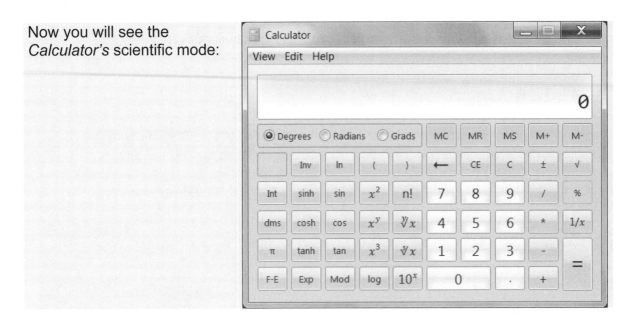

You can also convert measurements. For instance, you can convert a temperature in Fahrenheit to one in Celsius:

☞ **Click** View

The menu displays all the
other modes:

☞ **Click**
Unit conversion

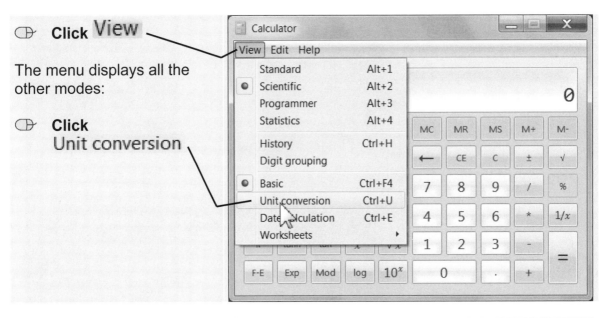

The *Calculator* becomes
much bigger:

☞ **Click** Angle

Now you will see a menu with various units that can be converted:

☞ **Click** Temperature

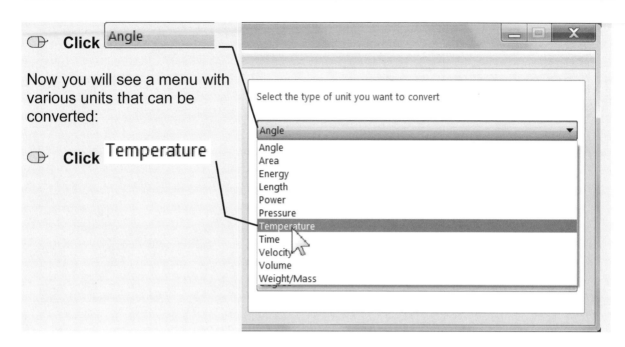

You are going to convert a temperature value from Fahrenheit to Celsius:

By From :

☞ **Click** Enter value

⌨ **Type:** 78

☞ **Click** Degrees Celsius

☞ **Click** Degrees Fahrenheit

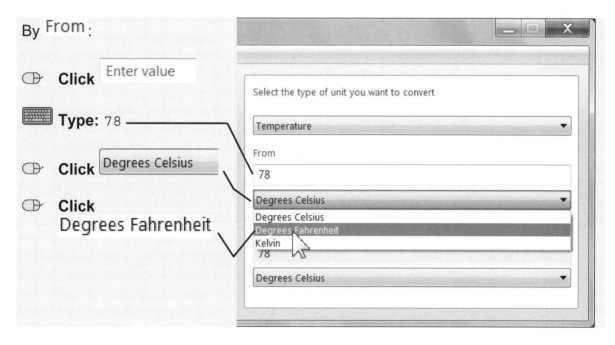

You will see the result right away: ————

78 degrees Fahrenheit is a little over 25 degrees Celsius.

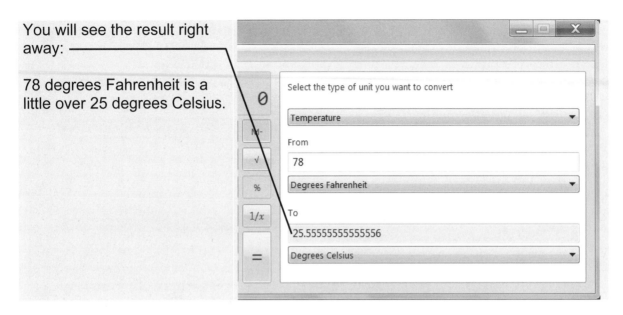

This is how you return to the standard view of the *Calculator*:

⊕ **Click** **View** ————

⊕ **Click** **Standard** ———

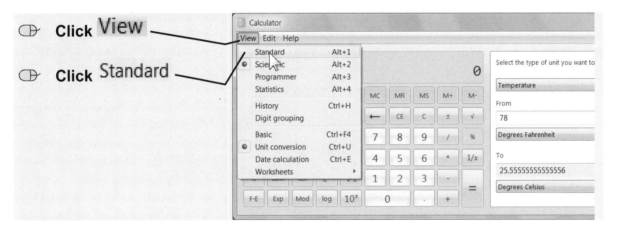

You can close the unit conversion window:

⊕ **Click** **View** ————

⊕ **Click** **Basic** ——

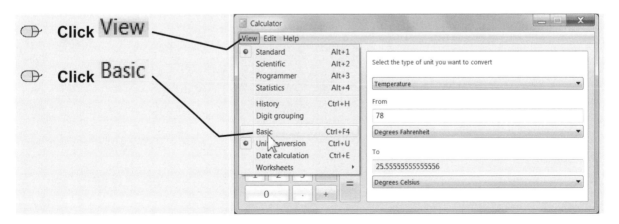

Now you will see the familiar *Calculator* window once again. If you want to learn more about using this updated *Calculator*:

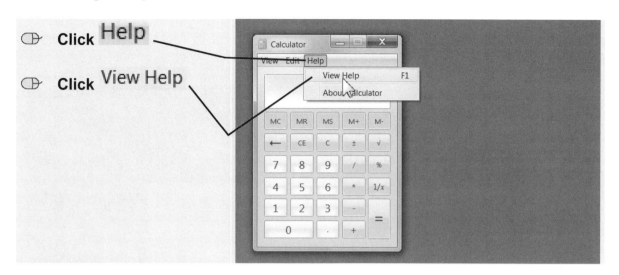

☞ **Click** Help

☞ **Click** View Help

You will see the page with helpful information about the *Calculator*:

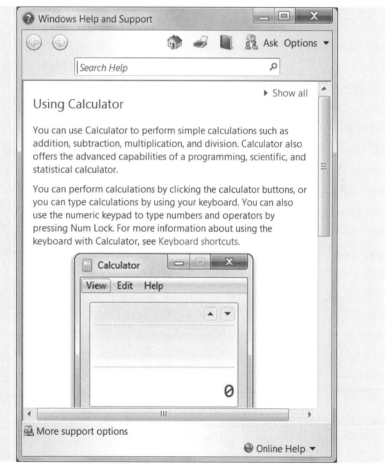

You can leave the windows open for a bit.

7.4 Jump Lists

In *Windows 7* you can quickly see which files and programs you last used. All this information is recorded in a *Jump List*. Take a look now at the Jump List for *Windows Media Player*.

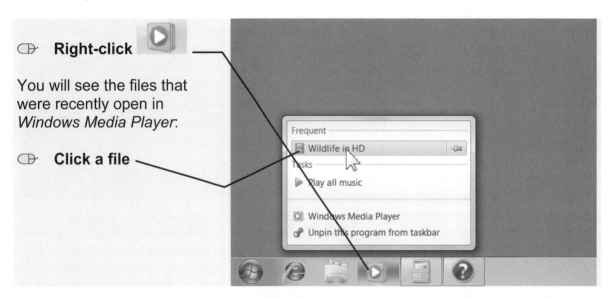

☞ **Right-click**

You will see the files that were recently open in *Windows Media Player*:

☞ **Click a file**

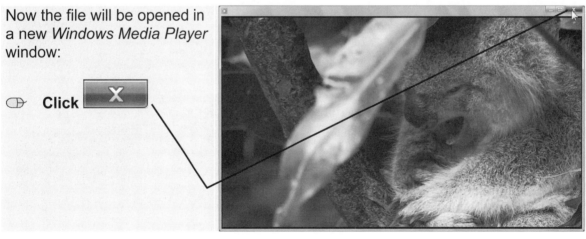

Now the file will be opened in a new *Windows Media Player* window:

☞ **Click**

When you want to find a specific file quickly, you can pin it to the Jump List. You do that like this:

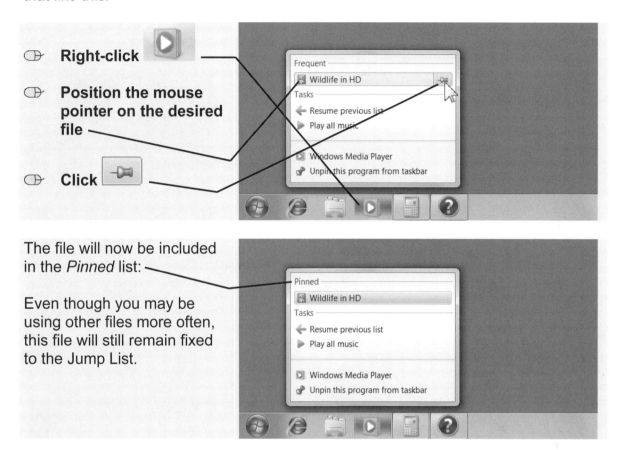

⊕ **Right-click**

⊕ **Position the mouse pointer on the desired file**

⊕ **Click**

The file will now be included in the *Pinned* list:

Even though you may be using other files more often, this file will still remain fixed to the Jump List.

You can always remove a file from the *Pinned* list whenever you want to:

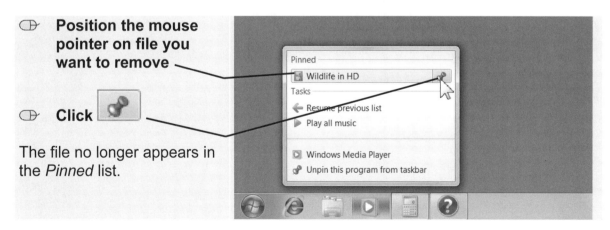

⊕ **Position the mouse pointer on file you want to remove**

⊕ **Click**

The file no longer appears in the *Pinned* list.

To close the Jump List:

⊕ **Click a spot somewhere off the Jump List**

Tip

Other programs
Many other programs use Jump Lists as well.
WordPad, for example, will display a list of files that were recently open.

Internet Explorer displays a
list of the websites you
recently visited:

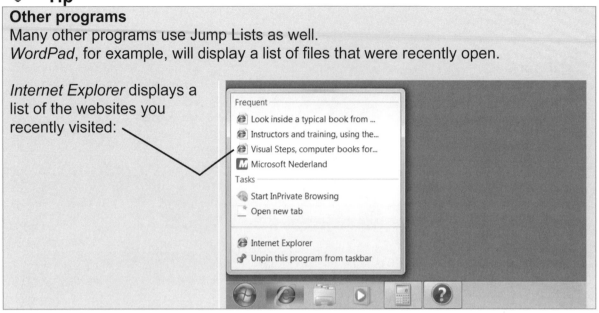

Tip

Jump List in the Start menu
In the Start menu you can also use Jump Lists:

All programs with the ▶
icon, use a Jump List:

☞ **Place the mouse
pointer on a program**

The Jump List appears on
the right side of the Start
menu:

☞ **Click a file**

Now the file will be opened in
the corresponding program.

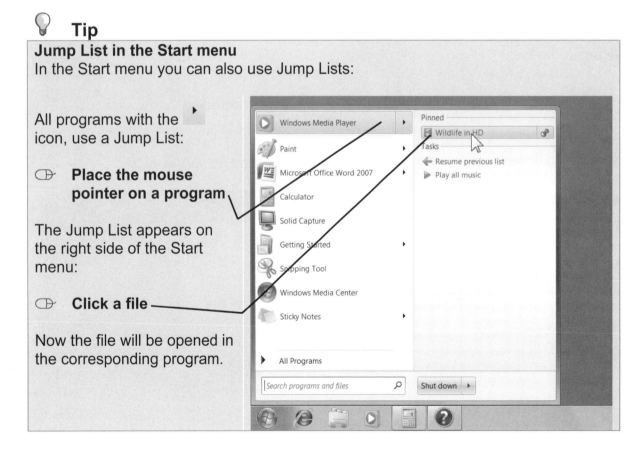

7.5 Aero Peek

Aero Peek is one of the useful new features in *Windows 7*. This feature allows you to see ('peek') through all the open windows on your screen. Just try it yourself:

☞ **Open *Internet Explorer*** 👣**66**

Now the *Internet Explorer* window lays on top of the other windows:

In this example you see the Visual Steps website, **www.visualsteps.com**

Look down in the bottom right corner of your screen:

👈 **Place the mouse**

pointer on

All open windows will now become transparent. You will only see their contours on the desktop:

Please note: If the windows are maximized, the contours cannot be seen.

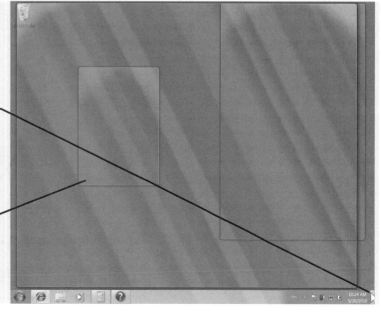

When you move the mouse pointer away, the windows are visible again:

⊕ **Slide the mouse
   pointer up a bit** ——

Now you will see the top
window once more:

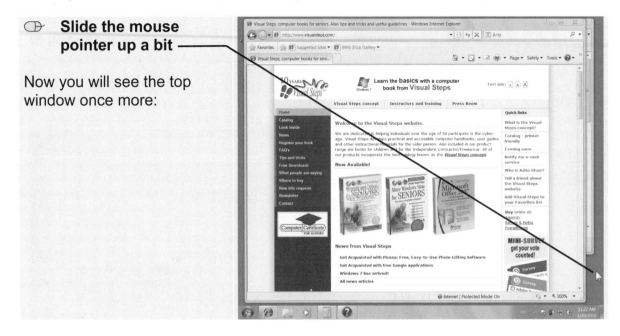

You can also use this button in the following way:

⊕ **Click** ——

Now all open windows will be
minimized and you will see
the desktop:

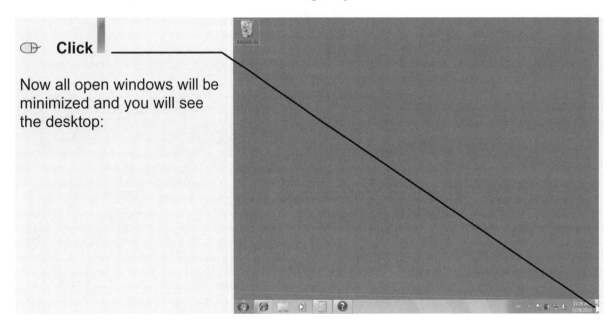

If you want to see the *Internet Explorer* window, on the taskbar:

⊕ **Click**

Aero Peek will also let you quickly view a preview window:

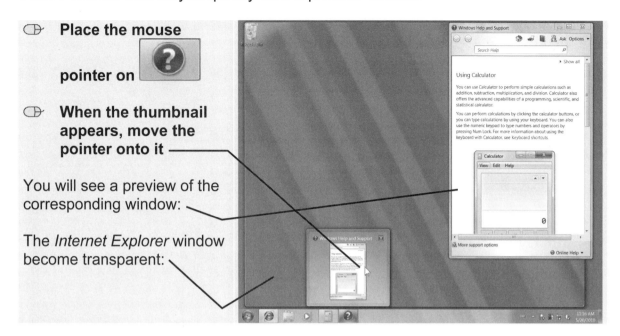

☞ **Place the mouse pointer on**

☞ **When the thumbnail appears, move the pointer onto it**

You will see a preview of the corresponding window:

The *Internet Explorer* window become transparent:

In this way, you can quickly see if this is the window you want to open. If you want to open this window:

☞ **Just click the thumbnail**

In this example you do not need to open the window:

☞ **Move the mouse pointer away from the thumbnail**

Now the thumbnail and the preview window will disappear.

7.6 Aero Shake

Aero Shake lets you quickly maximize or minimize all open windows, except the window you want to focus on. You can do this by shaking this window.

First, you are going to maximize the *Windows Help and Support* window:

On the taskbar:

☞ **Click**

☞ **Open the *Calculator*** 🦶**68**

Now the open windows will lay one on top of the other.

⊕ **Move the pointer to the title bar of the *Calculator* window**

⊕ **Click the mouse button and keep it pressed in**

⊕ **Shake the window quickly back and forth**

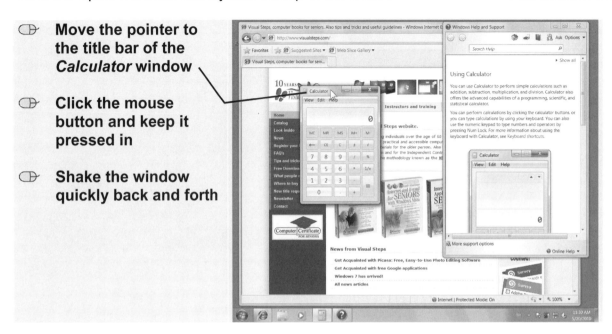

The window you have just shaken will be the only window that stays open. The other windows disappear. To bring them back in view again, simply repeat the previous action:

⊕ **Move the pointer to the title bar of the *Calculator* window**

⊕ **Click the mouse button and keep it pressed in**

⊕ **Shake the window quickly back and forth**

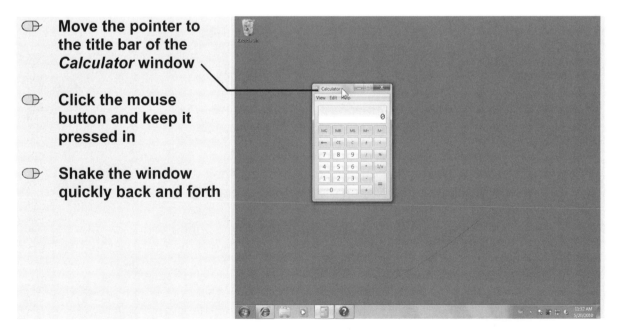

All the windows are visible again:

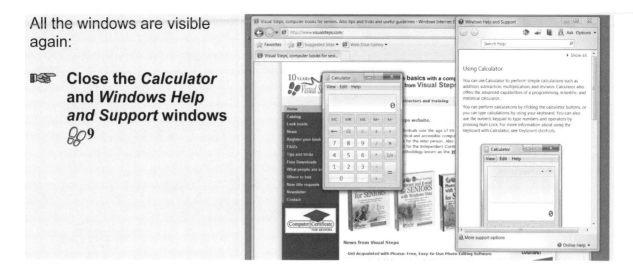

☞ **Close the *Calculator* and *Windows Help and Support* windows** 𝄞⁹

7.7 Use Aero Snap to Quickly Maximize Windows

In **Windows 7 for SENIORS** (ISBN 978 90 5905 126 3) you learned how to maximize a window with the  button. In *Windows 7* there is also another way to do this by using the *Aero Snap* feature.

If the *Internet Explorer* window is already maximized to the fullest:

⊕ **Click** [image]

This is how you maximize the window:

⊕ **Drag the window as far as possible to the top of your screen**

As soon as you see a larger, transparent window:

⊕ **Release the mouse button**

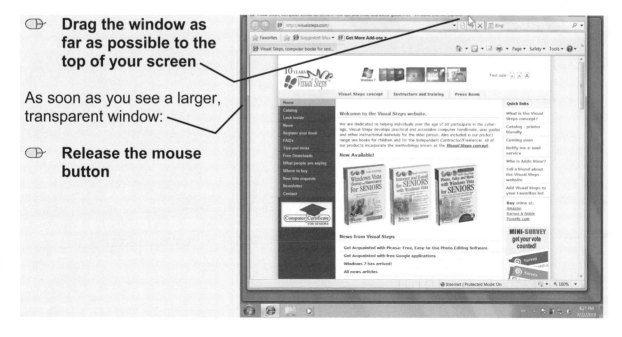

Now the window is fully
maximized:

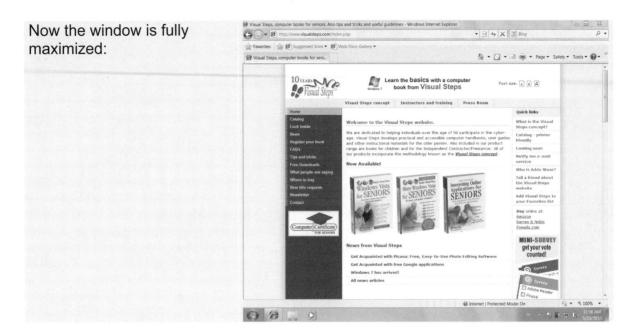

To minimize the window back to its previous size:

⊕➤ **Click and drag the
        window down a bit**

The window will become
smaller again:

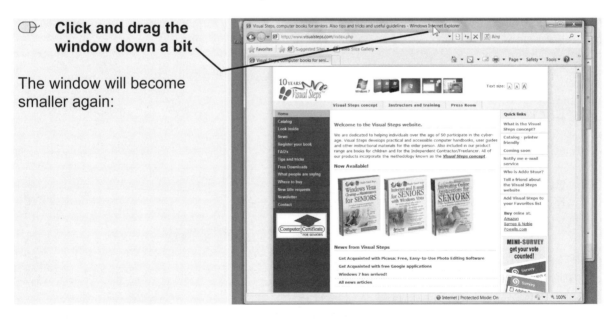

7.8 Align Windows With Aero Snap

With *Aero Snap* you can also resize two open windows and display them side by
side. First you need to open an additional window:

☞ **Open the *Pictures* library** 🦶²⁸

☞ **Drag the *Pictures* window as far to the right as possible**

As soon as you see a larger, transparent window:

☞ **Release the mouse button**

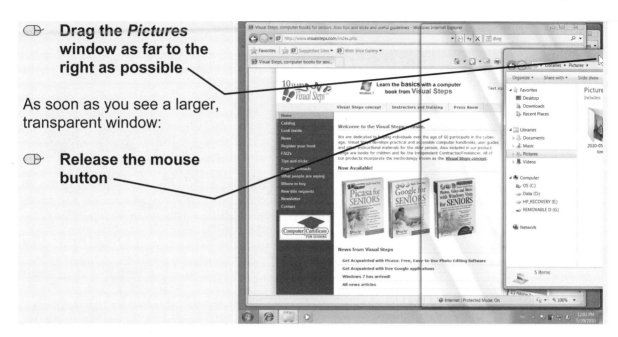

Now the *Pictures* window will take up half of your screen:

On the other half of your screen, you can still see the *Internet Explorer* window:

☞ **Drag the *Internet Explorer* window as far as possible to the left**

As soon as you see a larger, transparent window:

☞ **Release the mouse button**

Now both windows have the same size:

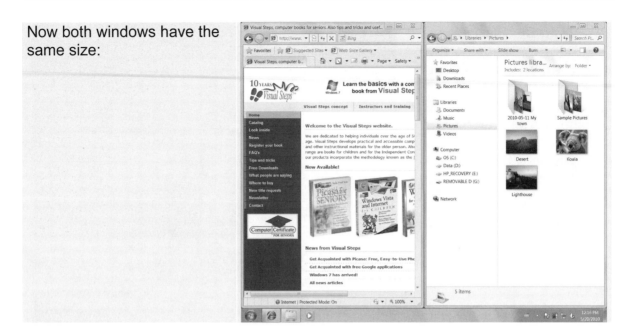

To resize the windows once more:

 **Drag both windows downwards a bit**

Then you can drag the windows to the middle of your screen again or use the minimize and maximize buttons as desired.

7.9 Aero Flip 3D

If you have previously worked with *Windows Vista*, you will already be familiar with the *Aero Flip 3D* feature. This feature has also been included in *Windows 7*, but you've got to dig a little bit to find it.

☞ **Open the *Control Panel*** 🦶[17]

At this point, there are three windows open. *Aero Flip 3D* lets you quickly display previews of all open windows, without clicking the buttons on the taskbar. This can be very useful when you have a lot of windows open. You can open *Aero Flip 3D* with the following key combination:

⌨ **Simultaneously press** `Ctrl` , `⊞` **and** `⇥ Tab`

Aero Flip 3D will display the open windows in the form of a 'three-dimensional stack':

To select the window you want to use:

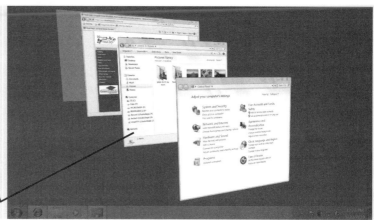

☞ **Click one of the windows in the stack**

You can flip through the stack of windows by using the scroll wheel of your mouse, or the arrow keys.

☞ **Close all windows** ⚇⁹

7.10 Games

Windows 7 comes with a number of built-in games. Your computer may not contain all of these games. This is how you open the games window:

☞ **Click** ⊕ , Games

🩹 **HELP! I do not see** Games **in the list**

If Games is not listed in the Start menu, you can find it in another way.

☞ **Click** ⊕ , ▶ All Programs , 📁 Games

Now you will see Games listed in the Start menu.

You will see the games window:

Some of these games are played on the Internet against adversaries from all over the world:

Internet Backgammon
Microsoft Corporation

Backgammon is a classic two-person board game that is played with pieces. You have won if you are the first to move all your pieces around and off the board.

Internet Checkers
Microsoft Corporation

The popular *Checkers* game can also be played online against other players. If your opponent has run out of pieces or moves, you have won.

Internet Spades
Microsoft Corporation

Spades was invented in the United States in the 1930's and is a very popular card game. You need a partner to play this game. *Spades* is a game where you have to win rounds. Your team has won if you have won 500 points or if your opponents have reached 200 negative points.

Source: Windows Help and Support

In *Windows Help and Support* you can find extensive rules for these games.

For example, start a game of checkers:

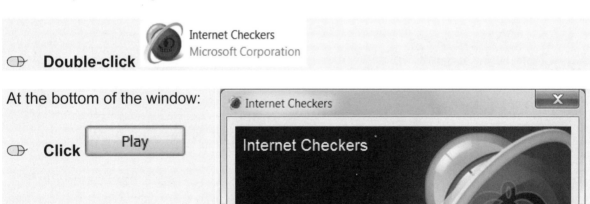

☞ **Double-click**   Internet Checkers
                      Microsoft Corporation

At the bottom of the window:

☞ **Click** Play

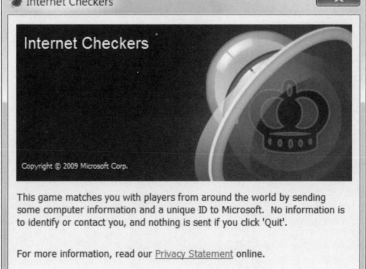

Now the Internet connection will start up and you will be linked to an opponent.

You can move your checkers by dragging them:

You can also chat with your opponent. Use the

(Select a message to send)

button to open a menu with various messages you can send: ⎯

At the top right of the window you will see the buttons you can use to resign or call it a draw: ⎯

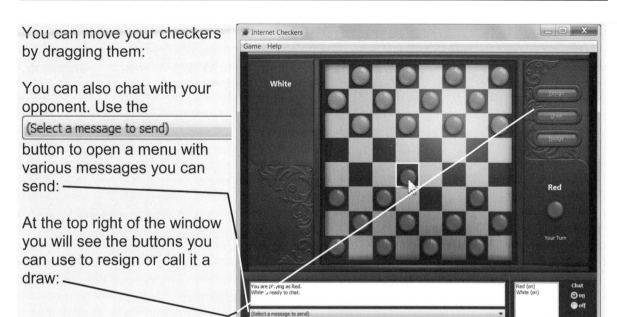

☞ **Close the *Internet Checkers* window** **9**

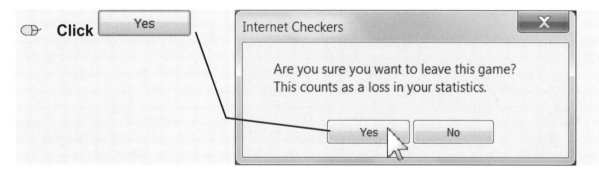

Here is a brief overview of the other games:

Hearts
Microsoft Corporation

Hearts is a popular and fast-paced card game for four players. In the Windows version, all three of your opponents are played by the computer.

Minesweeper
Microsoft Corporation

Minesweeper is a deceptively simple test of memory and reasoning and one of the most popular Windows games of all time. The goal: find the empty squares and avoid the mines.

- Continue reading on the next page -

Purble Place
Microsoft Corporation

Purble Place is actually three games in one: *Comfy Cakes*, *Purble Shop* and *Purble Pairs*.
These games help teach children memory, pattern recognition and reasoning skills.

Spider Solitaire
Microsoft Corporation

Spider Solitaire is a popular variant of solitaire using two decks of cards. The object is to remove all the cards from the table in the fewest number of moves. You do this by building columns of cards of the same suit in descending order from king to ace.

Chess Titans
Microsoft Corporation

Chess Titans brings the classic strategy game to life with three-dimensional graphics and animation. You can select three difficulty levels: beginner, intermediate, advanced.

FreeCell
Microsoft Corporation

FreeCell is a form of solitaire played with a single deck. Create four stacks of 13 cards, one per suit in each of the four home cells. Each stack must be built from the low card (ace) to the high (king).
The key to victory lays in the four free cells in the corner of the table - hence the name!

Mahjong Titans
Microsoft Corporation

Mahjong Titans is a solitaire game played with colorful tiles instead of cards. In this classic game you have to remove all tiles from the board by clicking matching pairs of tiles.

Solitaire
Microsoft Corporation

Solitaire is the classic, single player solitaire game. The object is to build four stacks of cards, one for each suit, in ascending order from ace to king.

Source: Windows Help and Support

You are bound to become much attached to one or more of these games. Just try playing some of them. If you want to learn more about the rules of these games, you can look them up in *Windows Help and Support*.

☞ **Close the *Games* window** ✌⁹

In this chapter you have been introduced to some of the interesting programs and handy features in *Windows 7*. In the following exercises you can practice some of the operations once more.

7.11 Exercises

Have you forgotten how to do something? Then you can use the number next to the footsteps to look up the description in *Appendix B How Do I Do That Again?*

Exercise: Snipping

In this exercise you are going to use various capture methods with the *Snipping Tool*.

☞ Open the *Calculator*. ℰℰ**68**

☞ Open the *Snipping Tool*. ℰℰ**69**

☞ Select the *Free-form Snip*. ℰℰ**70**

☞ Keep the mouse button pressed in while you draw a shape around the *Calculator* window.

☞ Click ✂ <u>New</u> .

☞ Select the *Window Snip*. ℰℰ**71**

☞ Point to the *Calculator* window. When you see a red frame, click the mouse.

☞ Close the *Snipping Tool*, do not save the changes. ℰℰ**9**

Exercise: Calculator

In this exercise you are going to take a look at the various views of the *Calculator*.

☞ Select the *Unit conversion* view. ℰℰ**72**

☞ Select the *Scientific* view. ℰℰ**73**

☞ Close the *Unit conversion* view. ^{74}

☞ Select the *Standard* view. ^{75}

☞ Close the *Calculator* window. ^{9}

Exercise: Aero Peek and Aero Snap

In this exercise you are going to practice some of the *Aero Peek* and *Aero Snap* operations.

☞ Open *Internet Explorer*. ^{66}

☞ Open the *Pictures* library. ^{28}

☞ Open the *Control Panel*. ^{17}

☞ Take a look at the desktop preview with *Aero Peek*. ^{76}

☞ Use *Aero Snap* to maximize the *Control Panel* window. ^{77}

☞ Take a look at the *Pictures* library preview with *Aero Peek*. ^{78}

☞ Minimize the *Control Panel* window to its original size. ^{79}

☞ Put the *Control Panel* and *Picture* library windows next to each other with *Aero Snap*. ^{80}

☞ Restore the windows to their original size. ^{79}

☞ Drag the windows back to the middle of the screen.

☞ Close all windows. ^{9}

Exercise: Checkers

In this exercise you are going to play checkers on the Internet.

☞ Open the *Games* window. 🦶**81**

☞ Open the checkers game. 🦶**82**

☞ Play the whole match.

☞ Close all windows. 🦶**9**

7.12 Background Information

Dictionary	
Aero Flip 3D	You can use *Aero Flip 3D* to quickly preview all of your open windows without clicking the taskbar. *Aero Flip 3D* displays your open windows in a three-dimensional stack. You can flip through the windows by means of the arrow keys or the scroll wheel of your mouse.
Aero Peek	Use this feature to quickly preview the desktop or a minimized window without minimizing all your other windows.
Aero Shake	By shaking one window you can quickly minimize all open windows on the desktop except the one you want to focus on.
Aero Snap	Method to arrange and resize windows on the desktop with a simple mouse movement, by dragging them to the top or side of the screen.
Jump List	A list of recently opened files which can be opened with a button on the taskbar or from the Start menu.
Screenshot	A capture of the objects you see in your window, created by using the *Snipping Tool*. Also called a *snip*.
Snip	A part of an object on the window, created with the *Snipping Tool*. Also called a *screenshot*.
Snipping Tool	Program that captures (snips) any object on the screen.
Sticky Note	A yellow memo that you can use to write notes and lists, and stick it on your desktop.

Source: Windows Help and Support

8. Windows Explorer, Libraries and Folder Windows

In the *Windows Explorer* window you can view the contents of your computer. This window lets you work with your folders, libraries and files.

Windows 7 is the first edition of *Windows* that uses libraries. Libraries have been added to the program to let you search for and manage your files more quickly and easily.

A library looks a lot like a regular folder. The main difference is that a folder actually contains files. A library does not contain the actual files; in other words your files are not *stored* in a library. A library offers an *aggregate view* of your folders and files as a single collection even though they may actually reside in a number of different folder locations, even across different systems. A library allows you to quickly and easily view your files all in one place.

Libraries are also displayed on external hard drives as long as they are connected to your computer. To this end, *Windows* uses folder locations that are linked to the library.

A library will help you more easily find files of a specific type, for instance pictures. The greatest advantage of the libraries is that you can search for files much quicker in *Windows 7* than in previous editions of *Windows*.

In this chapter you will learn how to:

- open a library;
- create a new library;
- select the properties for a library;
- add folder locations to a library;
- use the search box;
- filter search results;
- search outside a library;
- save a search operation;
- look up a previously saved search operation and execute this search;
- delete a file from a library;
- delete a folder from a library;
- delete a library.

8.1 Opening a Library

In *Chapter 5 Photos, Music and Videos* you were introduced to the *Pictures* library, one of the default libraries in *Windows 7*. There are three other default libraries. Open *Windows Explorer* and take a look at the default libraries:

On the taskbar:

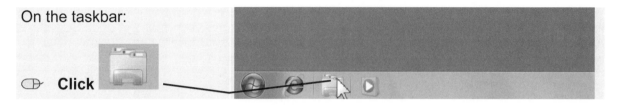

☞ **Click**

Windows Explorer is the program *Windows* uses to display the folder window. Now the *Libraries* folder window will be opened:

You will see the four default libraries:

The four default libraries are: *Pictures, Documents, Music*, and *Videos*. Their names speak for themselves.

A library is similar to a folder, but it does not contain the actual files. Unlike a folder, a Library gathers files that are stored in several locations into a single view. This is a subtle, but important difference. Libraries do not actually store a user's files, they only monitor folders that contain files, and let the user access and arrange these items in different ways.

You will need to distinguish the libraries apart from personal folders that have similar names, such as *My Pictures*. Personal folders *do* contain original files.

Open the *Pictures* library:

Now you can view the
contents of the *Pictures*
library:

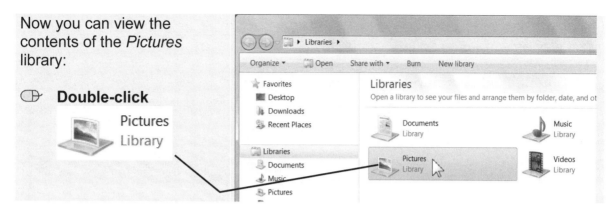

☞ **Double-click**

      Pictures
      Library

The *Pictures* library will be opened:

The physical contents of this
library are stored in two
different locations on your
computer:

☞ **Double-click**

      Sample Pictures

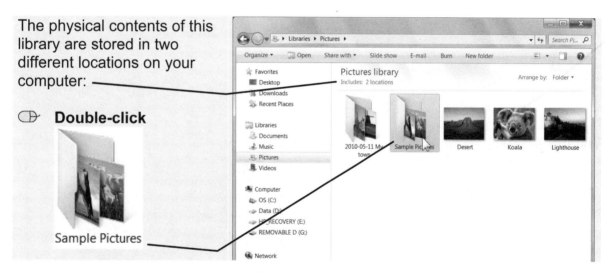

You will see the contents of
the *Sample Pictures* folder:

When you are working with a library, it will appear as if you are using regular folders and files. In essence, this is also true. In *Chapter 5 Photos, Music and Videos* you have been able to see that you can use the folders and files in a library in much the same way as you would do in a regular folder. You can copy, move, and open them:

Double-click a picture

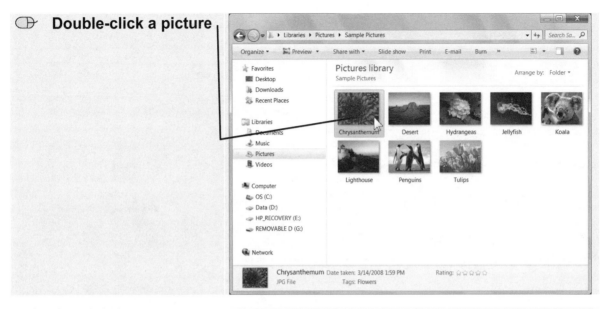

The picture will be opened:

Click

In *Windows 7* you can use folders and files in two different ways. In separate folders, or in folders that are collected in a library.
Libraries offer the possibility of managing and organizing your files as a collection, even though they are stored in different locations. For example, all your pictures, music files, video files or documents.

8.2 Creating a New Library

In the **Windows 7 for SENIORS** book (ISBN 978 90 5905 126 3) you learned how to add an extra library yourself. We will briefly go over that again:

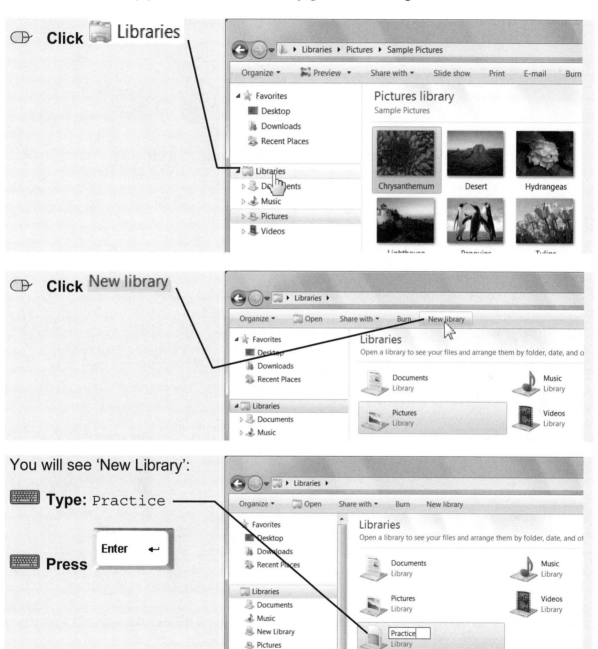

Click <img> Libraries

Click New library

You will see 'New Library':

Type: Practice

Press Enter ↵

Now you have created a new library:

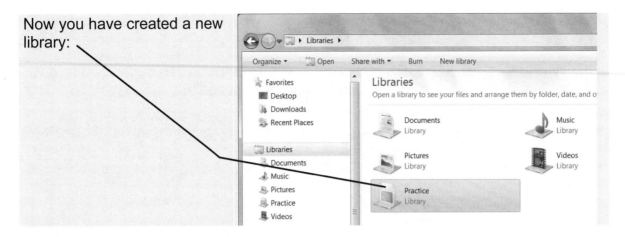

You can use this library to manage various files on your computer.

8.3 Select the Properties for a Library

You can start adding folder locations to this library right away, but it is a good idea to select some properties for this library first.
For instance, you can optimize this library for a specific file type:

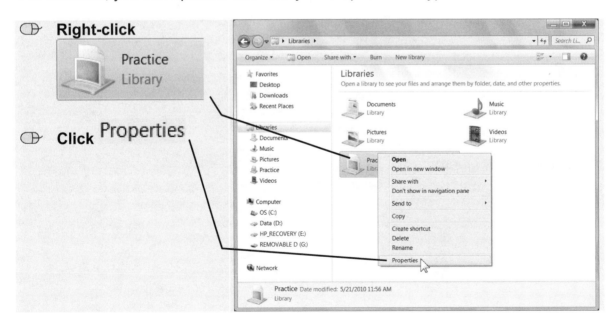

You will see the *Practice Properties* window:

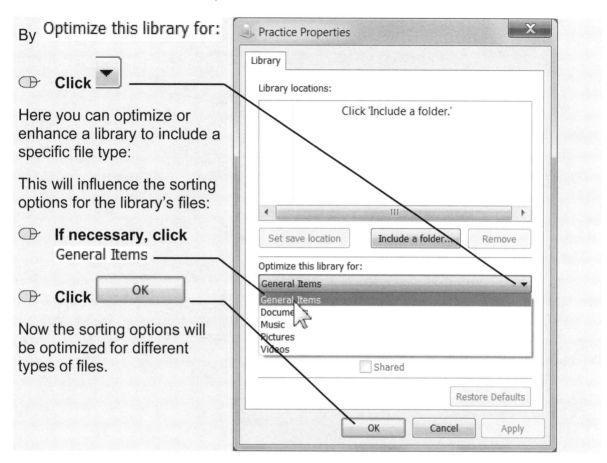

By Optimize this library for:

⊕ **Click** ▼

Here you can optimize or enhance a library to include a specific file type:

This will influence the sorting options for the library's files:

⊕ **If necessary, click** General Items

⊕ **Click** [OK]

Now the sorting options will be optimized for different types of files.

8.4 Adding Folder Locations To a Library

If you want to display files in a library, you will need to add the folder location which contains the files to the library. This means that a reference to this folder will be added to the library. The actual folder will not be moved to the library.
To practice this, first you will need to create two new folders. Then you will add a number of pictures to these new folders:

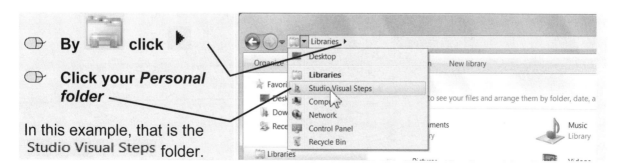

⊕ **By** 🖥 **click** ▶

⊕ **Click your *Personal folder***

In this example, that is the Studio Visual Steps folder.

Double-click

My Pictures

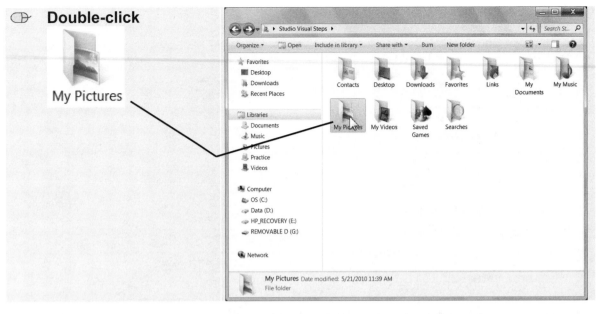

Click New folder

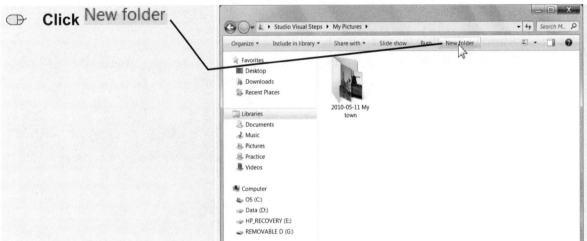

You can type a name for the new folder right away:

Type: Holiday photos

Press Enter ⏎

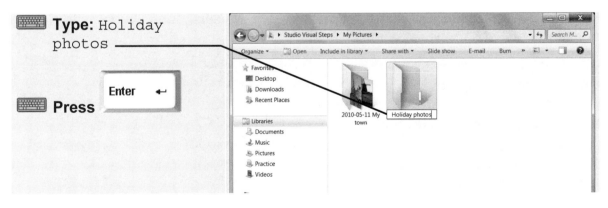

Now you are going to add two pictures to the *Holiday photos* folder. First, you will need to open the *Sample Pictures* folder:

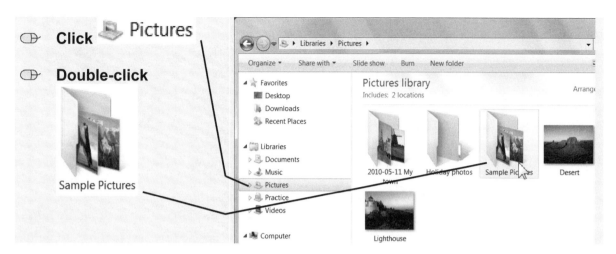

Now you will see the sample pictures once again. You are going to select two pictures:

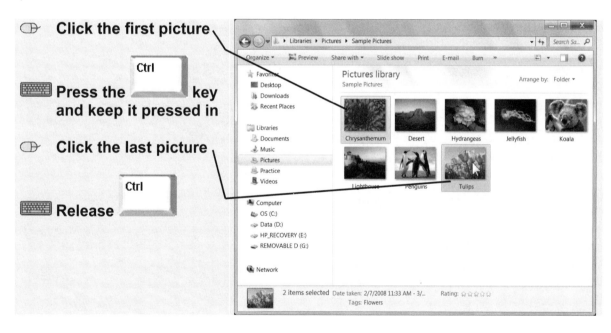

Both photos are now selected.

👆 **Right-click one of the selected pictures**

👆 **Click Copy**

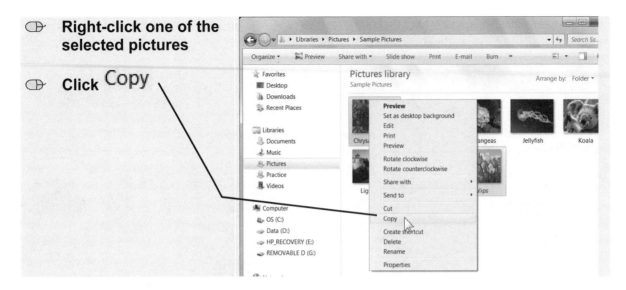

Open the *Holiday photos* folder:

👆 **Click 🖼 Pictures**

👆 **Double-click**

Holiday photos

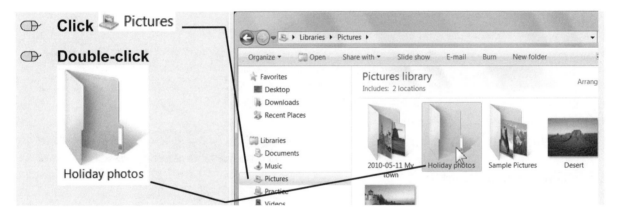

The *Holiday photos* folder is still empty:

👆 **Right-click a spot in the empty window**

👆 **Click Paste**

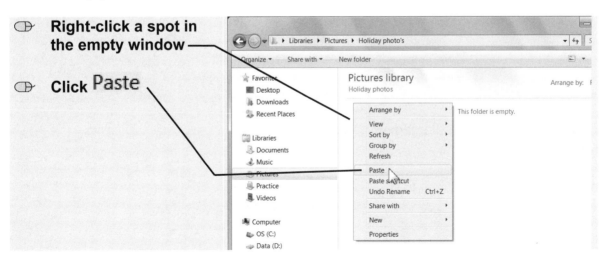

Now both pictures have been added to the *Holiday photos* folder. Since the names of these pictures are the same as the original picture files, it is a good idea to rename the copies:

☞ **Click the picture's name twice**

⌨ **Type:** Picture 1

☞ **Press** Enter ↵

☞ **Rename the second picture as well. Call it** *Picture 2* ᐟᐟ92

Next, you will create a new folder in the *My Documents* folder:

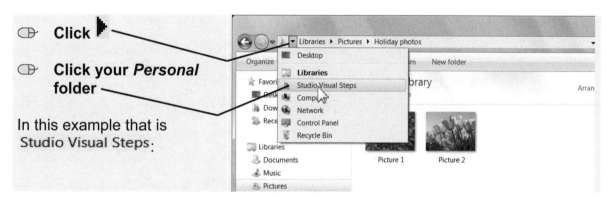

☞ **Click** ▶

☞ **Click your *Personal* folder**

In this example that is Studio Visual Steps:

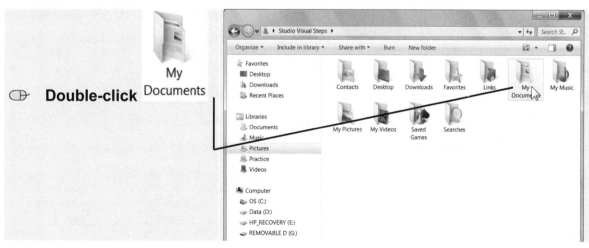

☞ **Double-click** My Documents

☞ **Create a new folder** ᐟᐟ84

You can type a name for the new folder right away:

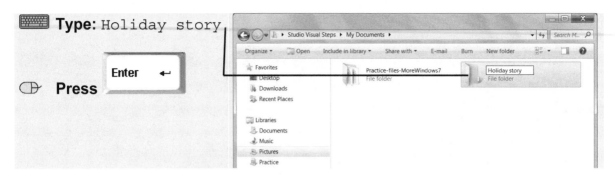

Type: Holiday story

Press | Enter ↵ |

Now you are going to add these two new folder locations to the *Practice* library:

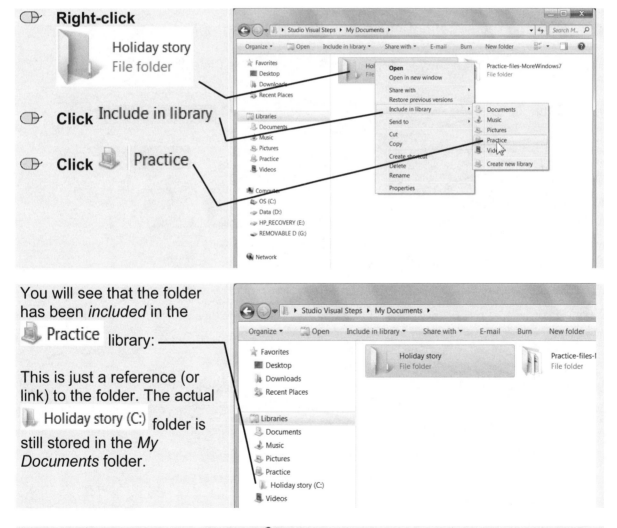

Right-click

       Holiday story
       File folder

Click Include in library

Click Practice

You will see that the folder has been *included* in the Practice library:

This is just a reference (or link) to the folder. The actual Holiday story (C:) folder is still stored in the *My Documents* folder.

☞ **Open the** My Pictures **folder** ⏍85

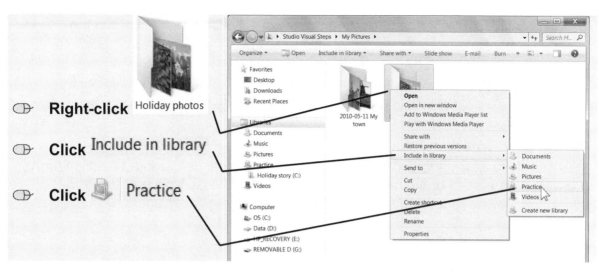

☞ **Right-click** Holiday photos

☞ **Click** Include in library

☞ **Click** Practice

Now both of the new folder locations are included in the Practice library: ————

You can view the folders in the *Practice* library:

☞ **Click** ◢ Practice

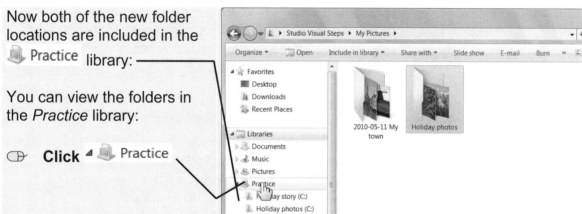

You will see the contents of the ◢ Practice library: ——

You cannot view the actual folders you have just added to the ◢ Practice library. You will only see the files in these folders.

For each file you will see the corresponding folder name (its actual physical location):

Since the *Holiday story* folder has no content, you will see (Empty) next to the folder name:

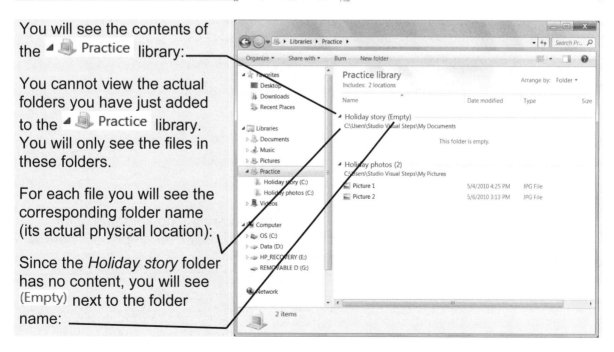

If you add a file to one of these practice folders, it will also be displayed in the *Practice* library.

Please note!

You can include up to fifty folders in a library.

Please note!

If you decide to move a folder after you have included this folder in a specific library, you will not be able to open this folder in that library. The reference to this folder will be lost. You will need to include this folder in the library all over again.

Tip

External storage devices
You can also include folders in a library when these folders are located on external devices, such as external hard drives, or other computers connected to the network. These folders will only be displayed when the external device is connected to the computer.

8.5 Using the Search Box

If you have previously used other *Windows* editions, you will discover that in *Windows 7* the search options are greatly improved. Searches are executed much faster, largely due to indexing techniques that are also used in libraries.

In the top right corner of the window you see a search box:

When you type something in the search box, it will search the folder or library that is currently open.

In this example, it is the *Practice* library:

The quickest way to search is to search through the libraries. The contents of the libraries have already been indexed and references to the files are in place. There is no need to look them up again on the hard drive.

Please note!

It sometimes takes a while before folders that were recently added to a library become visible in a search index.

⊕ **Click** 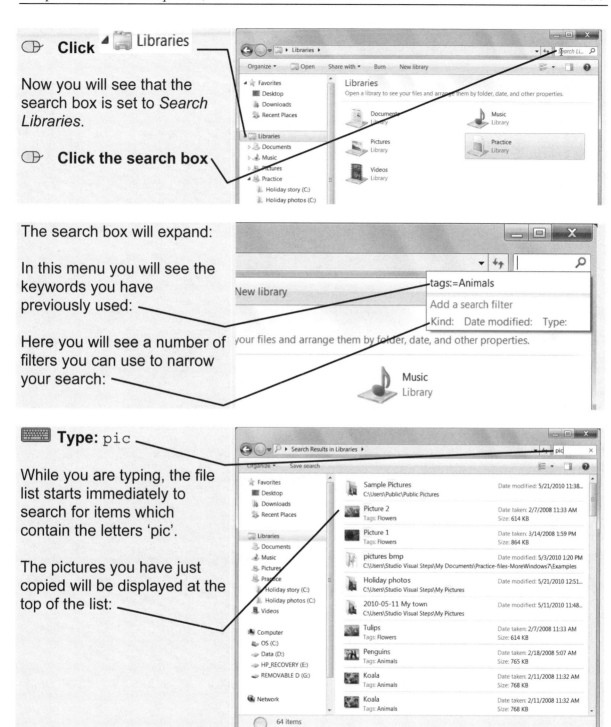 **Libraries**

Now you will see that the search box is set to *Search Libraries*.

⊕ **Click the search box**

The search box will expand:

In this menu you will see the keywords you have previously used: —

Here you will see a number of filters you can use to narrow your search: —

⌨ **Type:** pic —

While you are typing, the file list starts immediately to search for items which contain the letters 'pic'.

The pictures you have just copied will be displayed at the top of the list: —

 Please note!

Your own screen may display more or less files. This will not affect the operations in this chapter.

8.6 Using a Search Filter

If your search results are too extensive, you can narrow them down a bit by using a search filter. The first step is to delete the text in the search box:

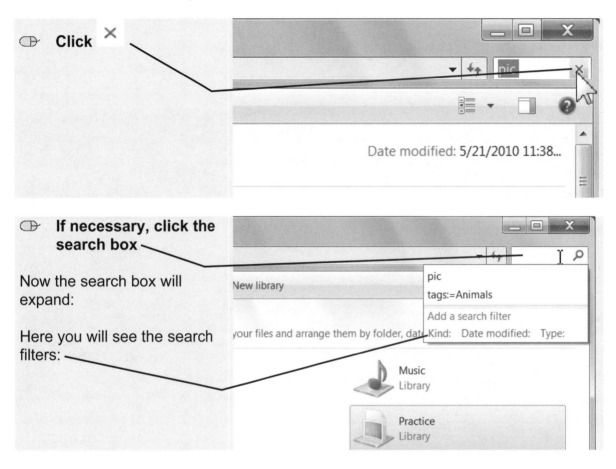

Click ✕

If necessary, click the search box

Now the search box will expand:

Here you will see the search filters:

You can use the following search filters:

Kind: the search results will only contain files of a certain kind. For example, e-mail files, documents or folders.

Date modified: the search results will only contain files that have been modified on a certain date or before or after a certain date.

Type: the search results will only contain files of a specific file type. For example, JPG files or WMV files.

👆 **Click** Date modified:

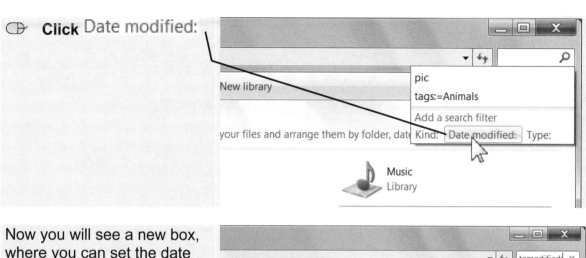

Now you will see a new box, where you can set the date filter:

Use the calendar to set the exact date:

You can also select one of the extra options:

👆 **Click** A long time ago

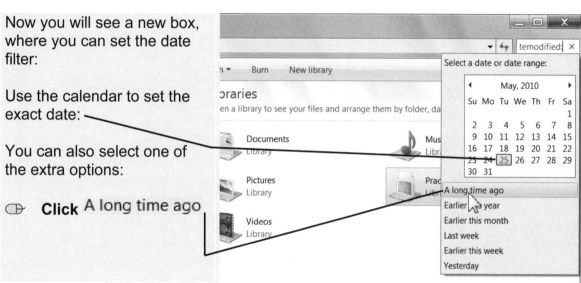

⌨ **Type:** picture

In this example you will see quite a large number of search results:

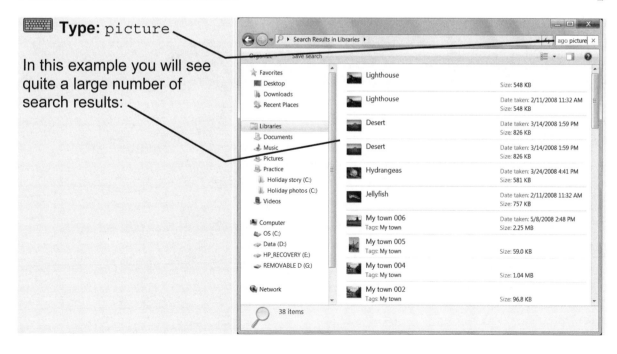

You can also search by *Type*:

⊙ **Click the search box**

⊙ **Click** Type:

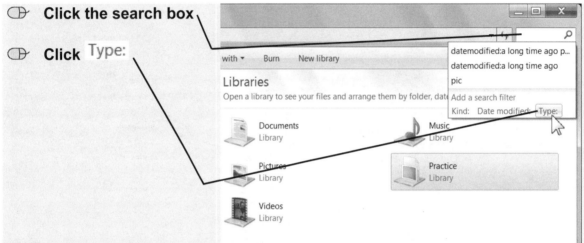

You will see a separate menu, where you can select the file type:

⊙ **Click** .jpg

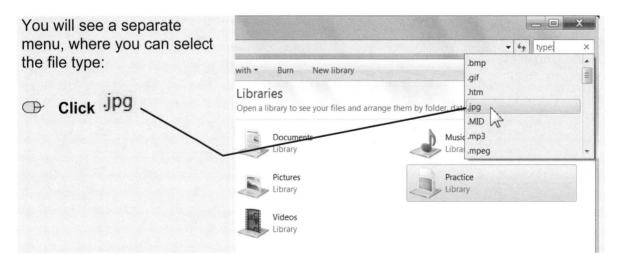

Now the search results will only display JPG files:

The search results on your own screen may be displayed in a different order.

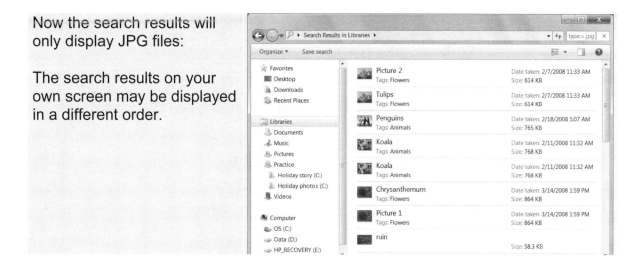

8.7 Search Outside the Library

You will often search for files that are included in one of the libraries. But you do not need to limit your search to the libraries. You can also search all of the folders on your computer. In that case the search operation will take longer, because you will not be searching indexed files.

If you have not found what you were looking for in the library search, you can immediately continue searching elsewhere:

☞ **Drag the scroll bar downwards**

You will find new search options in Search again in:

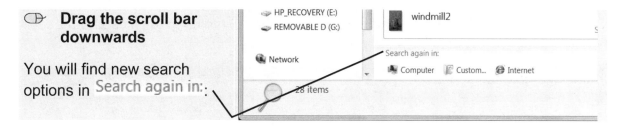

A new search can be started in:

Computer: search all files on the computer.
Custom: search a custom scope.
Internet: use *Internet Explorer* to search the Internet.

☞ **Click 📁 Custom...**

You will see the *Choose Search Location* window:

By 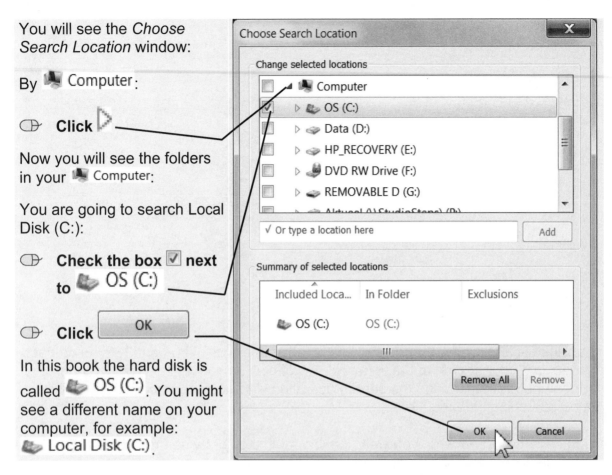 Computer:

⊞ **Click** ▷

Now you will see the folders in your 🖳 Computer:

You are going to search Local Disk (C:):

⊞ **Check the box** ☑ **next to** 💾 OS (C:)

⊞ **Click** OK

In this book the hard disk is called 💾 OS (C:). You might see a different name on your computer, for example: 💾 Local Disk (C:).

Now *Windows 7* will search the entire Local Disk (C:) for files of the JPG file type. This may take a while because the hard drive usually contains many files and these files are not always indexed:

In this example the search result has produced a large number of files:

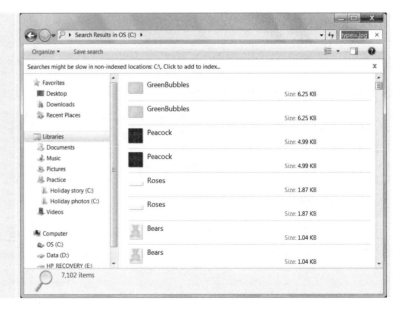

💡 Tip

Search in a folder window
You can also directly search a specific folder in the folder window:

👉 **Click the folder** ⎯⎯⎯

👉 **Click the search box** ⎯

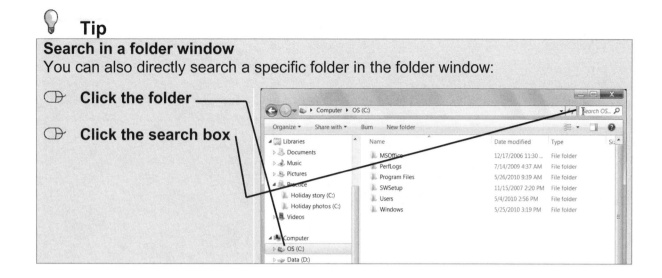

8.8 Filtering Search Results With Column Headers

If your search operation has produced a long list of files, you can filter these results by sorting with *column headers*. For instance, you can filter all image files from your search results:

👉 **Click** 🗂 **Libraries**

👉 **Click the search box**

Do the same search operation from the previous example:

👉 **Click** type:=.jpg

Set the folder window to the *Details* view:

By 📧 :

👉 **Click** ▾

👉 **Click** 📧 **Details**

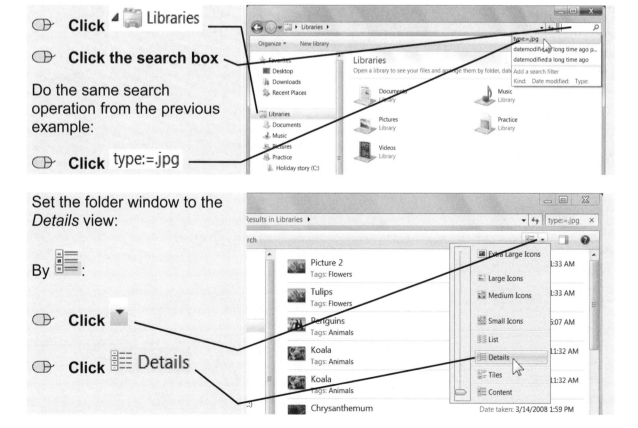

Now the window displays the
details of the files:

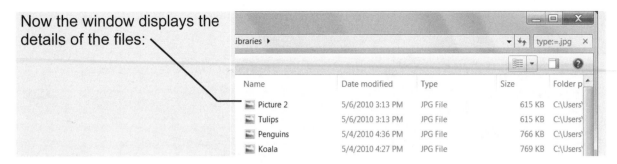

You can filter (or sort) the files by their file name, for example. To do this, you will
need to use the column header called Name:

By Name :

⊕ **Click** ▼

⊕ **Check the box** ☑ **by**
   📦 **A – H**

🠖 Please note!

If your computer contains a lot of photo files, or different kinds of files, your list
options may look different from the example in this book. The photo's and files on
your computer can influence the view of the list options in your window.

⊕ **Click the empty part**
   under the search
   results

Now the selection menu will
be closed.

You will see the filtered
search results which will
contain only file names
beginning with the letters A
through H:

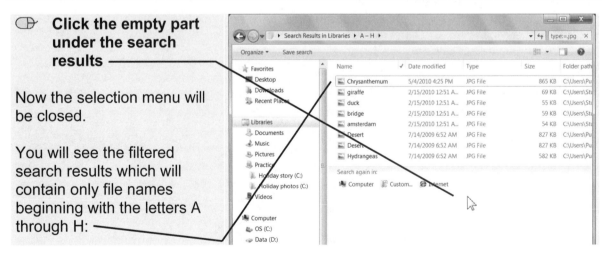

Tip

Additional Filter options
You can sort the search results further by using the following column headers:

- **Name**: you can choose between various first letters, such as A-H, I-P, and Q-Z.
- **Date modified**: here you can select a specific date.
- **Type**: here you can select a specific file type.
- **Size**: here you can select various file sizes.
- **Folder path**: if the search results contain files from different subfolders, you can specify which folder(s) you want to include in the search results.

8.9 Saving a Search Operation

Windows 7 lets you save a search operation. This means that when you want to search your files later on you won't have to enter your search criteria all over again:

Click **Save search**

Now you will see a window where you can enter a name for this search operation:

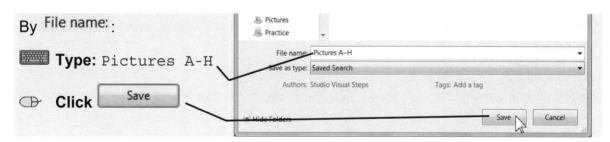

By **File name:** :

⌨ **Type:** Pictures A-H

Click **Save**

Now the search operation has been added to the *Searches* subfolder in your *Personal folder*. The search operation will automatically be executed once more and the address bar in this example will look like this:

8.10 Execute a Saved Search Operation

Your search operation has been saved in the *Searches* subfolder. Here is how to find it. In the address bar next to the name of your *Personal folder*:

 Click Searches

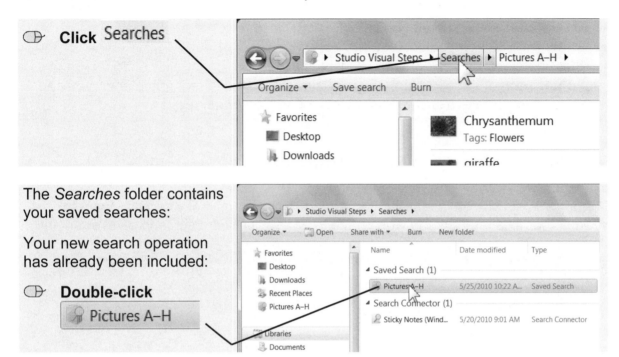

The *Searches* folder contains your saved searches:

Your new search operation has already been included:

 Double-click
   🔍 Pictures A–H

🖐 Please note!

You can execute a saved search anytime you want to. But, if in the mean time you have added or deleted files or folders which match the search criteria, the search results will be different.

Here you will see the search results once more. Since you have not added or deleted any files, the search results will still be the same:

💡 **Tip**

The search box in the Start menu
The folder window is not the only place where you can execute a search.

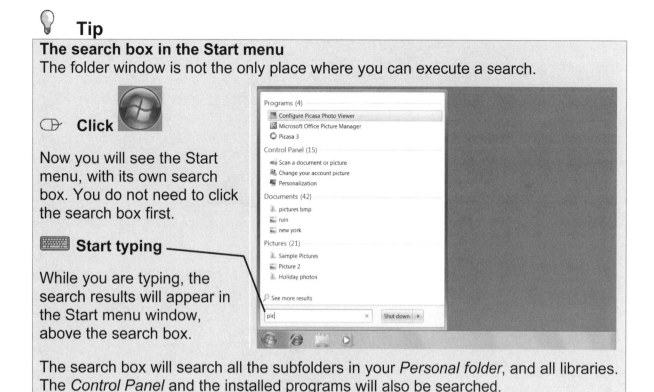

👆☞ **Click**

Now you will see the Start menu, with its own search box. You do not need to click the search box first.

⌨ **Start typing**

While you are typing, the search results will appear in the Start menu window, above the search box.

The search box will search all the subfolders in your *Personal folder*, and all libraries. The *Control Panel* and the installed programs will also be searched.

8.11 Deleting a File From a Library

If you delete a file from a library window, the file will also be physically deleted from the folder where it is stored:

👆☞ **Click** 🖳 Practice

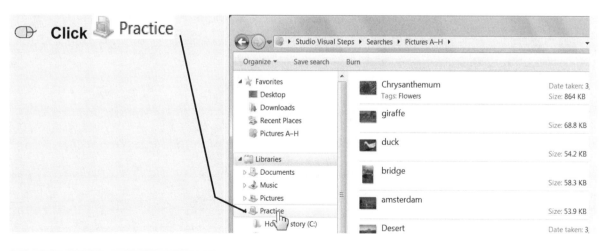

☞ **Select the** 🔲 **Large Icons** **view for this folder window** 👣⁸⁶

Click Picture 1

Press Delete

Windows 7 will ask you if you want to move the file to the *Recycle Bin*:

Click Yes

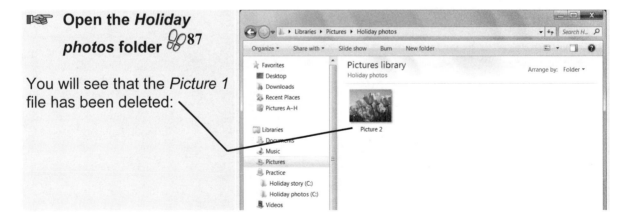

Now the *Picture 1* file has been removed from the *Holiday photos* folder as well:

☞ **Open the *Holiday photos* folder** ℔87

You will see that the *Picture 1* file has been deleted:

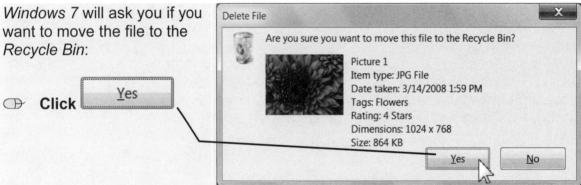

8.12 Deleting a Folder From a Library

When you no longer want a specific folder to be displayed in a library, you can remove the reference to this folder. The folder will still remain stored in its original location on your computer.

Click Practice

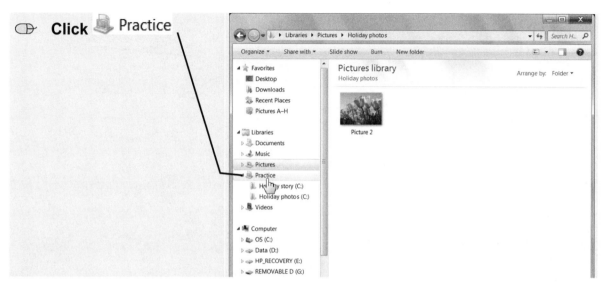

Click 2 locations

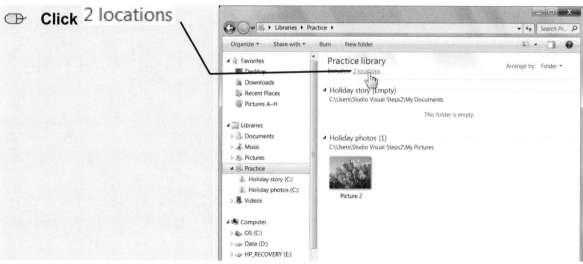

Now you will see the *Practice Library Locations* window:

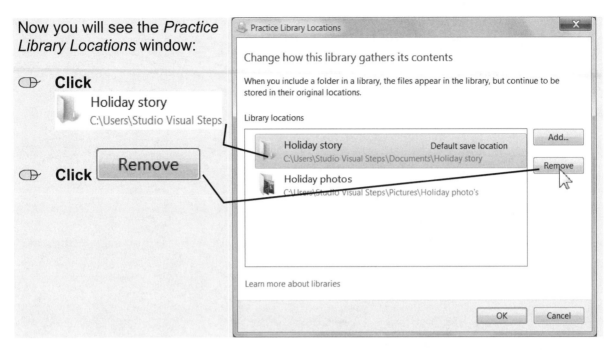

⊕ **Click**

    📁 Holiday story
      C:\Users\Studio Visual Steps

⊕ **Click** **Remove**

You will see that the folder has been removed from the library:

The actual folder is still stored on the hard drive.

In the bottom of the window:

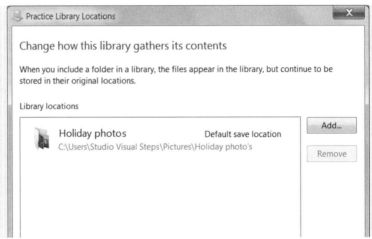

⊕ **Click**  **OK**

You will see that this library only contains the *Holiday photos* folder:

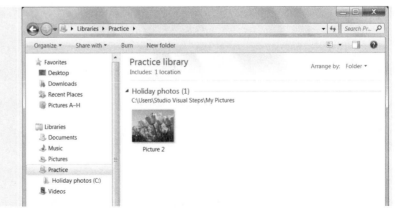

8.13 Deleting a Library

If you no longer want to use a library, you can delete the entire library. The files and folders that are displayed in the library will not be deleted and will still be stored in their original location on your computer's hard drive:

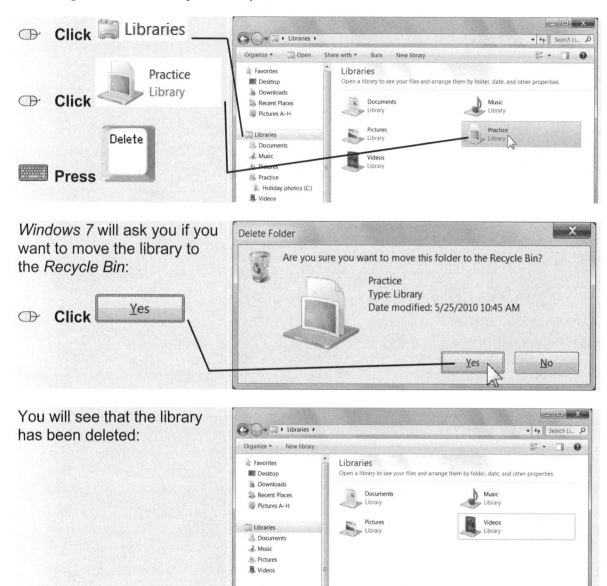

⊘➤ **Click** 🗐 **Libraries**

⊘➤ **Click** Practice Library

⌨ **Press** Delete

Windows 7 will ask you if you want to move the library to the *Recycle Bin*:

⊘➤ **Click** Yes

You will see that the library has been deleted:

👉 **Close the *Libraries* window** 👣⁹

In this chapter you have learned how to take advantage of the new library feature in *Windows 7* making it easier and quicker to work with files and folders. In the following exercises you can practice all the operations we have discussed in this chapter.

8.14 Exercises

Have you forgotten how to do something? Then you can use the number next to the footsteps to look up the description in *Appendix B How Do I Do That Again?*

Exercise: Libraries

In this exercise you are going to include a new folder in a new library.

☞ Open *Windows Explorer.* $\mathcal{QQ}$**88**

☞ Create a new library and call it *Practice library.* $\mathcal{QQ}$**89**

☞ Open the *My Pictures* folder. $\mathcal{QQ}$**85**

☞ Create a new folder and call it *Practice folder.* $\mathcal{QQ}$**84**

☞ Open the *Sample Pictures* folder. $\mathcal{QQ}$**90**

☞ Select the *Koala* and *Penguins* pictures. $\mathcal{QQ}$**58**

☞ Copy these pictures to the *Practice folder* folder. $\mathcal{QQ}$**91**

☞ Enter the names for these pictures and call them *exercise 1* and *exercise 2.* $\mathcal{QQ}$**92**

☞ Open the *My Pictures* folder. $\mathcal{QQ}$**85**

☞ Add the *Practice folder* to the *Practice library* library. $\mathcal{QQ}$**93**

☞ Close all open windows. $\mathcal{QQ}$**9**

Exercise: Search

In this exercise you are going to search the folder window in different ways.

☞ Open *Windows Explorer*. 𝄚**88**

☞ Click the search box and type: `prac`

☞ Delete the text in the search box. 𝄚**94**

☞ Use the *Type* search filter and filter for jpg type files. 𝄚**95**

☞ Change the folder window view; select the *Details* view. 𝄚**86**

☞ Filter the search results for files that begin with the letters *I-P* in the *Name* column. 𝄚**96**

Exercise: Delete

In this exercise you are going to delete the new folder and the new library.

☞ Open the *Practice library*. 𝄚**97**

☞ Delete the file called *Exercise 1*. 𝄚**98**

☞ Delete the *Practice folder* folder from the *Practice library* library. 𝄚**99**

☞ Delete the library called *Practice library*. 𝄚**100**

☞ Open the *My Pictures* folder. 𝄚**85**

☞ Delete the folder called *Practice folder*. 𝄚**101**

☞ Delete the *Holiday photos* folder. 𝄚**101**

☞ Close all open windows. 𝄚**9**

8.15 Background Information

Dictionary	
Column headers	The headers that appear at the top of the columns in the *Details* view of the folder window. For instance, *Name*, *Type*, or *Size*.
Indexing	Saves the location and properties of the files and folders on your computer's hard drive. This helps to speed up search operations for these files and folders later on.
Library	In some ways, a library is similar to a folder. However, unlike a folder, a library does not contain the actual files but only has references to these files. A library gathers and displays files that are stored in several locations on the computer. This way, you can easily find, organize and manage files of the same file type, such as pictures.
Search	A search operation, looking for a name or specific file properties. A search can be saved and executed later on.
Search box	The box where you can enter keywords to search for folders and files. It is located in the folder window.
Search filter	A feature in Windows 7 that allows searching for files by specific properties.
Windows Explorer	The program that displays the folder window.

Source: Windows Help and Support

9. System Management and Computer Maintenance

Just as a house or a car need regular maintenance, so does your computer. You will occasionally want to buy new software and remove old programs you no longer use. In this chapter you will be able to practice removing and installing software programs, by using the *Adobe Reader* program as an example. You can use this program to open PDF files. You will also learn how to install a new, fun gadget onto your desktop.

Your computer's hard drive is the central location where you store your files. Now and then, you need to clean up your hard drive. For this purpose you can use the *Disk Cleanup* and *Disk Defragmenter* tools.

The *Disk Cleanup* tool removes unnecessary files from your hard drive.

The *Disk Defragmenter* enhances your computer's performance. In the course of time, your computer's hard drive becomes disorganized and there is a buildup of many fragmented files. You may notice this as your computer seems to operate slower and slower. This means it is time to defragment your hard drive. All files and parts of files will be organized and reordered in a new sequence. Your hard drive can then find your files easier and faster, and your computer will work more efficiently.

At the end of this chapter you can read how to deal with unexpected computer problems. *Windows 7* contains a number of useful troubleshooters to help you solve these problems. And if you ever find yourself in the situation where *Windows 7* no longer seems to work correctly at all, you can use the *System Restore* program.

In this chapter you will learn how to:

- delete (uninstall) programs;
- install programs;
- clean up your hard drive;
- defragment your hard drive;
- solve frequently occurring problems;
- use the troubleshooters;
- create a system restore point;
- use the *System Restore* tool.

9.1 Uninstall a Program

As time goes by, your computer will eventually contain programs you no longer use. You can easily remove these programs yourself. When you install a program, an uninstall program is usually installed at the same time. This uninstall program will delete all program files and the program name from the Start menu. You can see how this works by deleting the *Adobe Reader* program from your computer.

Please note!

You can safely remove *Adobe Reader* from your computer, even if you use this program regularly. You can install the most recent edition of *Adobe Reader* later on. If you do not have *Adobe Reader* installed on your computer, you can just read through the following section. This will give you a general guideline of how to delete a program when that becomes necessary later on.

This is how you delete a program:

☞ **Open the *Control Panel*** ⅋ℓ⁷¹⁷

Here you will see the *Control Panel*:

At Programs :

CD▸ **Click**
Uninstall a program

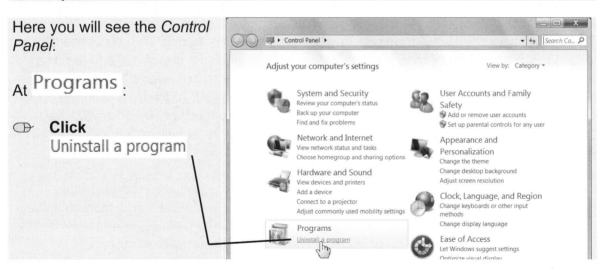

You will see a list of programs that you can delete. You are going to select Adobe Reader, edition 7, 8, or 9. In this example, edition 9.1 will be deleted.

Please note!

If your computer contains a different *Adobe Reader* edition, you can still delete this program in exactly the same way.

First, you need to select the program.

☞ **Click**

📄 Adobe Reader 9.1

Now you can remove the program.

☞ **Click** Uninstall

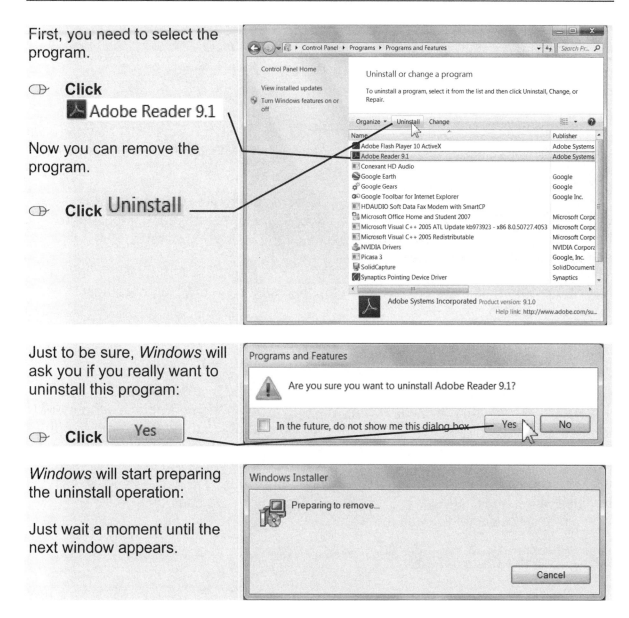

Just to be sure, *Windows* will ask you if you really want to uninstall this program:

☞ **Click** Yes

Programs and Features

⚠ Are you sure you want to uninstall Adobe Reader 9.1?

☐ In the future, do not show me this dialog box   Yes   No

Windows will start preparing the uninstall operation:

Just wait a moment until the next window appears.

Windows Installer

Preparing to remove...

Cancel

Now the screen will turn dark. You will see the *User Account Control* window and you will need to give permission to continue:

☞ **Click** Yes

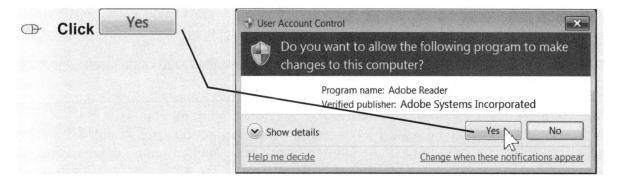

User Account Control

Do you want to allow the following program to make changes to this computer?

Program name: Adobe Reader
Verified publisher: Adobe Systems Incorporated

⌄ Show details   Yes   No

Help me decide   Change when these notifications appear

The green color of the
progress bar increases as the
uninstall operation nears
completion:

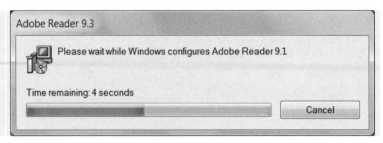

 Please note!

Adobe Reader 9 does not require you to reboot the computer after the program is
uninstalled. It will however, sometimes be necessary to restart your computer after
having uninstalled a program. If you see a message telling you to reboot the
computer, go ahead and do so.

Now the program has been removed. In the next section you will practice how to
install a program.

 Tip

Do you want to uninstall another program?
Always follow the procedure as described in this section. Simply deleting the
program icon from your desktop or removing the program name from the Start menu
will not be enough. If you do that, you only delete part of the program. Some of the
files will still remain stored on your hard drive.
Never delete individual files from the program folders on your hard drive. By doing
this, you will often delete only part of the program and many unnecessary files will
remain behind and clutter up your computer. Moreover, you can easily make a
mistake and accidentally delete the wrong files.

 **Close the *Control Panel* **$\mathcal{B}\mathcal{G}^9$

9.2 Install a Program

If you want to use a program on your computer, you first need to install it. This means
that all the files will be copied to the correct folder on your computer's hard drive. The
program will be included in the program list and a program icon (optional) will be
placed on your desktop.
All these operations are executed by an *install program*. This kind of program is also
called a *setup* program.

Many software programs will start up by themselves as soon as you insert the
software CD into the CD drive. In some cases you will need to start the install
program yourself, for instance if you want to install programs you have downloaded
from the Internet.

Usually, an install program can be identified by the following names:

- **setup**   (setup.exe);
- **instal**   (instal.exe);
- **install**   (install.exe);
- **eightlettername**   (eightlettername.exe).

You will see the full program name between parentheses. The .exe extension indicates that this is an executable program. If you want to start an install program, you first need to look for a program with one of the names listed above.

Some programs do not come with a specific install program. The entire program and the install software will be compressed into a single file. This is the case for the *Adobe Reader* program, which you will be downloading and installing in the next section.

9.3 Installing Adobe Reader

The following exercise lets you practice with the most recent edition of *Adobe Reader*. You can download this program from the *Adobe* website. As of the writing of this book, the most recent edition was version 9.

 HELP! I see a different edition

Do you see a different edition of *Adobe Reader*? Go to the website that accompanies this book and take a look at the News page. This web page will contain information about any recent updates to *Adobe Reader*.

☞ **Open** *Internet Explorer* ⚇⁶⁶

☞ **Go to the website get.adobe.com/reader** ⚇⁶⁷

Now you will see the *Adobe* website:

☞ **Uncheck the box** ✓ **next to**
    Free Google Toolbar (option

Uncheck the box ✓ next to any other programs that may also be installed. The only program you need for this exercise is *Adobe Reader*.

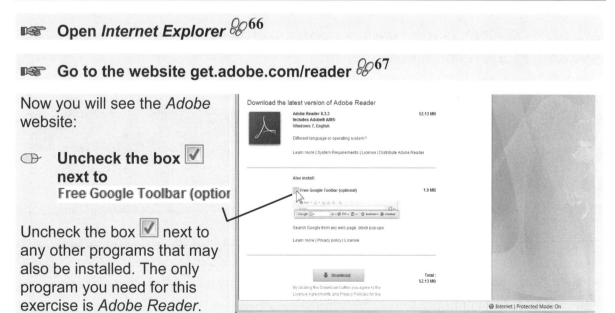

⊕ **If necessary, drag the**
    scroll bar downwards

⊕ **Click**

    ⬇ **Download**

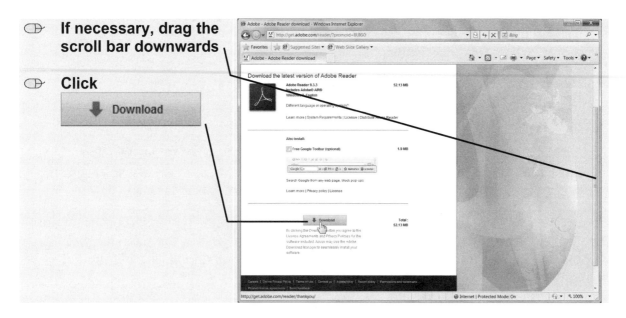

If you want to download this program, you will need to use the *Adobe Download Manager*. You can install this program by clicking the information bar in the window below:

⊕ **Click**

    ⑦ This website wants to insta

⊕ **Click**

    Install This Add-on for All I

Now the screen will turn dark. You will see the *User Account Control* window and you will be asked to give permission to continue.

⊕ **Click**   Yes

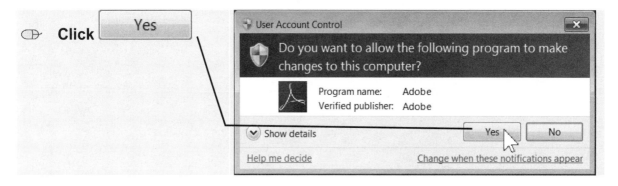

The *Adobe Download Manager* window will appear. The download and installation process is indicated by the green bar:

Next, you will see this window:

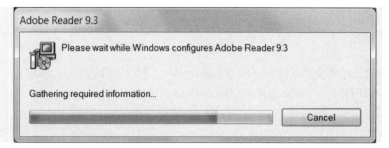

When the installation has finished, you can close the *Adobe Download Manager*:

Click

Close Download Mana

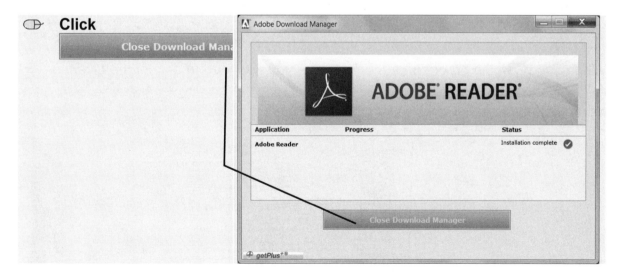

Now the installation is complete. In the next section, you can get acquainted with the *Adobe Reader* program.

☞ **Close all open windows** 👣⁹

9.4 Open Adobe Reader

Adobe Reader is a useful, free program for viewing PDF documents. The abbreviation PDF stands for *Portable Document File*. This file format is used by many businesses, organizations, educational institutions and government entities as a means of providing information for you to download from their websites. For example, a wide variety of manufacturers offer instruction manuals for their products as a PDF download.

 Please note!

In order to work through this chapter, you will need to download the folder with practice files from the website that goes with this book. You can read how to do this in *Appendix A Download Practice Files* at the back of this book.

The folder with the practice files also contains a number of PDF documents. You will be opening one of these documents shortly.

When *Adobe Reader 9* was installed, a shortcut was added to your desktop. You can use this shortcut to open the program:

☞ **Double-click**

When you open the program for the first time, you will need to accept the *License Agreement* (you only need to do this once):

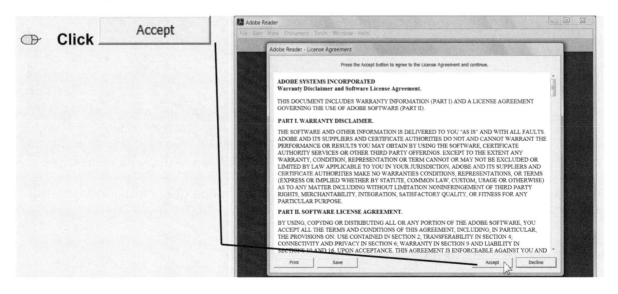

☞ **Click** `Accept`

9.5 Opening a PDF File

Now you will see the *Adobe Reader* window:

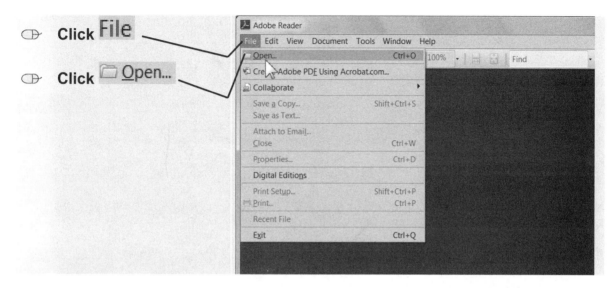

☞ **Click** File

☞ **Click** 📁 Open...

In the *Practice-files-MoreWindows7* folder you will see several PDF files. You can find this folder in the *Documents* library:

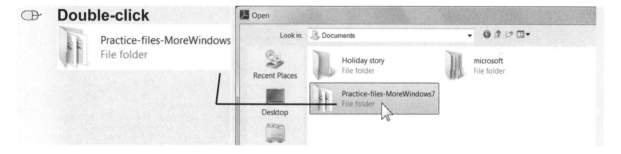

☞ **Double-click**

Practice-files-MoreWindows
File folder

In the *Examples* folder you will find a folder containing PDF documents:

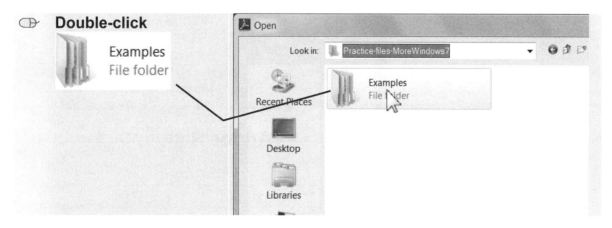

☞ **Double-click**

Examples
File folder

Double-click

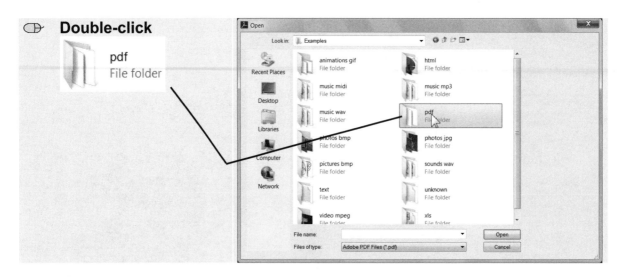

Now you are going to select the guide that will show you how to work with *Adobe Reader 9*:

Click 🔲 Adobe Reader 9

Click [Open]

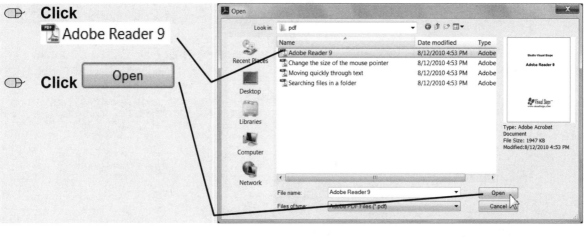

The document will appear in a new window:

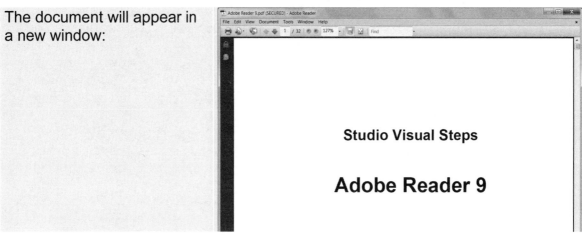

If you do not have any previous experience with *Adobe Reader 9*, you can work through this guide. This will be easier if you print the document. You can do that in *Adobe Reader 9*:

☞ Check if your printer is turned on

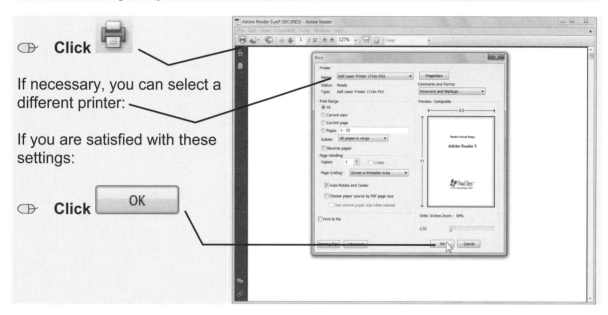

⊙ **Click**

If necessary, you can select a different printer:

If you are satisfied with these settings:

⊙ **Click** OK

Now the document will be printed. You can use this guide to practice working with *Adobe Reader 9* and quickly learn its main features.

☞ Close all open windows ⁹

💡 Tip

PDF tips on the website
On the **www.visualsteps.com/tips** website you will find additional tips in PDF format. These tips are constantly revised, and new topics are added regularly. You can select a topic that interests you and open the documents in *Adobe Reader*. This way, you can easily expand your knowledge.

This service is available to the subscribers of the free Visual Steps Newsletter that is distributed in regular intervals by e-mail. If you have not yet subscribed to the newsletter, why not give it try? You will receive the latest news about each new Visual Steps title, new free PDF guides and more. There are no strings attached. When you enter your e-mail address, you will receive a confirmation e-mail to activate your subscription. After you have activated your subscription, you will have access to all free downloads available on the website.

- Continue reading on the next page -

If you already have a subscription, you can enter your e-mail address here:

If you do not yet have a subscription, just enter your e-mail address here:

On the website you can select tips on various topics. If you are looking for a specific tip, you can also enter a keyword.

If you want to open a PDF tip, click **Download**.

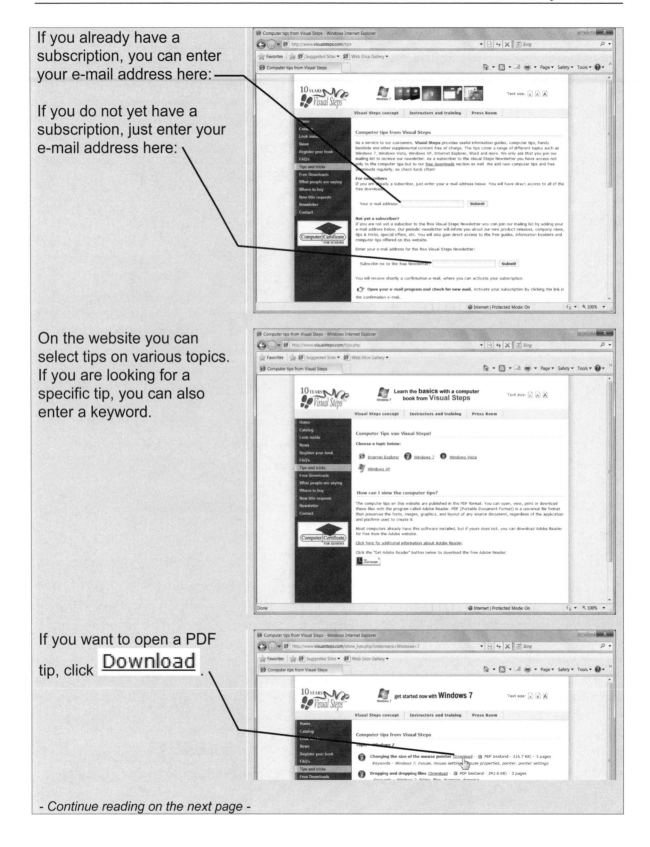

- Continue reading on the next page -

The tip will open automatically in the *Adobe Reader* window. If you want, you can also print the tip.

You can download as many tips as desired.

Tip

Free PDF guides

There are other free downloadable PDF files available on the Visual Steps website. They cover a wide range of different subjects. The practice files folder also contains PDF files. You have already seen one of these: the *Adobe Reader 9* guide.

On the **www.visualsteps.com/info_downloads** web page you will find handy information guides, instructional booklets and overviews. You can download these PDF files in the same way as the PDF tips.

Here are a few examples:

- *A Short Guide to Windows Internet Explorer 8;*
- *Plan Your Trip with Google Maps;*
- *How to Search more effectively with Google;*
- *Subscribing to RSS feeds.*

9.6 Install the Visual Steps Alarm Gadget

When you began the installation procedure for *Adobe Reader*, you were first asked to download the *Adobe Download Manager*. Other programs may also require plugins such as this. Most of the time, an installation procedure will walk you through various windows where you can enter your preferences. However, some installations work differently. For instance, notice the difference when you want to install a gadget on your desktop. Gadgets are small programs with special features, especially suited for your desktop.

On the website accompanying this book, you will find the *Visual Steps Alarm Clock* gadget:

☞ **Open *Internet Explorer*** 𝒪𝒪⁶⁶

☞ **Open the www.visualsteps.com/morewin7 website** 𝒪𝒪⁶⁷

You will see this web page:

👆 Click **Practice files**

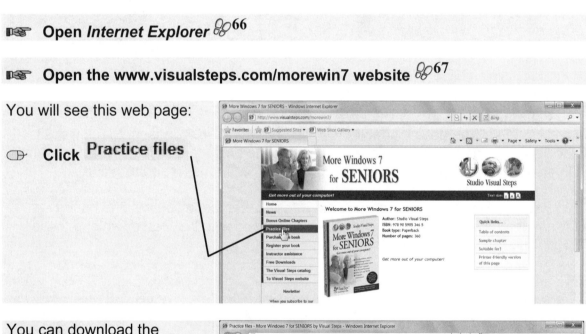

You can download the program:

👆 **Right-click**
Download the Alarm Clock ga

👆 Click **Save Target As...**

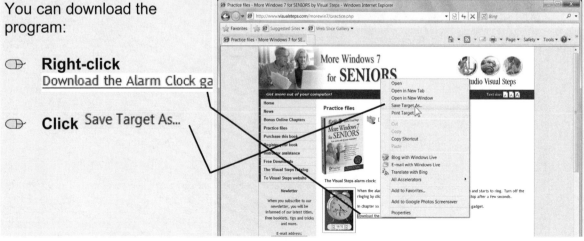

Now you need to add an extension to the name of the alarm clock:

☞ **Click** Downloads

☞ **Click twice next to** Visual Steps Alarmclock

⌨ **Type:** .gadget

Now the full name is
Visual Steps Alarmclock.gadget

Be sure not to forget the "."
(dot) before the word gadget!

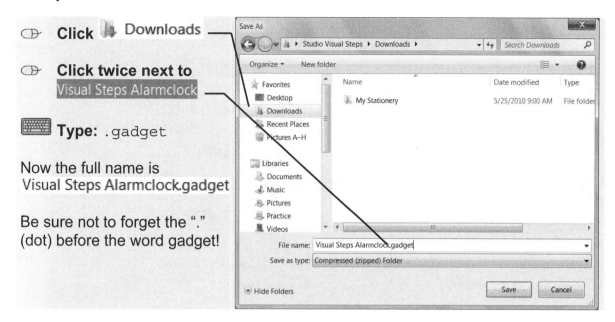

Now you select the file type:

☞ **Click**
Compressed (zipped) Folder

☞ **Click** All Files

Now you can save the alarm clock:

☞ **Click** Save

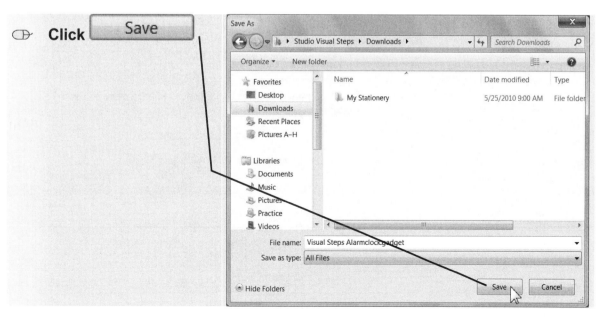

You can open the folder where the gadget is stored right away:

⊕ **Click** `Open Folder`

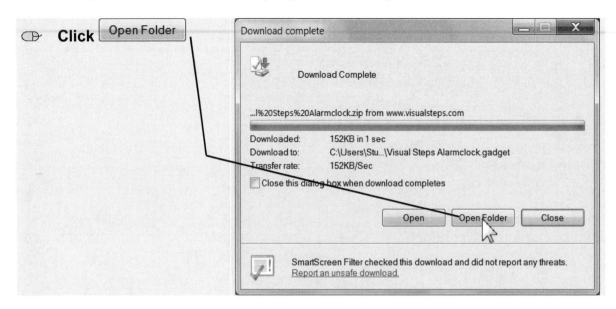

Now you can install the alarm clock:

⊕ **Double-click**
    🖼 Visual Steps Alarmclock

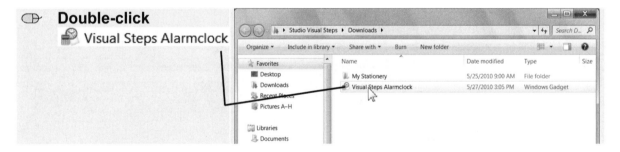

You will see a security warning:

⊕ **Click** `Install`

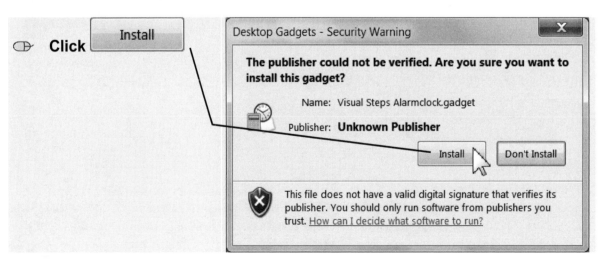

During the installation procedure, you will not be asked to enter any preferences.

☞ **Close all open windows** ⬬⁹

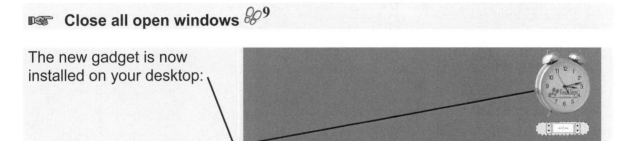

The new gadget is now installed on your desktop:

You have seen how easy it is to install a gadget. You can start using the *Visual Steps Alarm Clock* gadget right away. The alarm clock will register the correct time, and you can set a time for when the alarm should go off.

You can set the alarm with the [⬛] bar below the alarm clock. Use the arrows [⬛] to set the hours and minutes.
The alarm will go off at the appointed time. If you want to hear the alarm:

☞ **Check to make sure your computer's speakers are turned on**

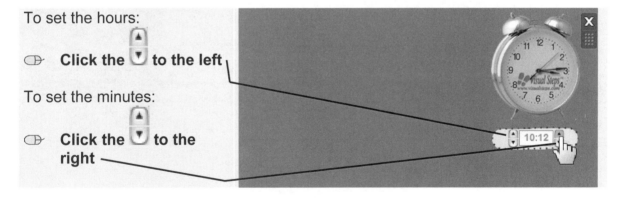

To set the hours:

☞ **Click the [⬛] to the left**

To set the minutes:

☞ **Click the [⬛] to the right**

If you keep the mouse button pressed in, the hours and minutes will change very quickly. By clicking an arrow repeatedly, the set time will change hour by hour, or minute by minute. For example, try to set a time that is just a few minutes later than the current time.

The alarm clock will go off at the time you have set. It will start to shake and move up and down. The hands of the clock will start turning very fast. You will also hear the sound of the alarm bell.

After about ten seconds this will stop by itself. You can also stop the alarm manually like this:

☞ **Click the alarm clock, somewhere in the middle**

The sound and the animation will immediately stop.

You can use the *Visual Steps Alarm Clock* as a way of protecting yourself against RSI. Have you ever experienced problems with your wrists or fingers after working on your computer for a long time? If you set the alarm clock one or two hours ahead every now and then, you will be reminded to take a break.

💡 **Tip**

Cancel the alarm
Do you want to cancel the alarm, after you have already set it? It is easy to do, just:

☞ **Click** 10:12

The set time will disappear and you will see once again.

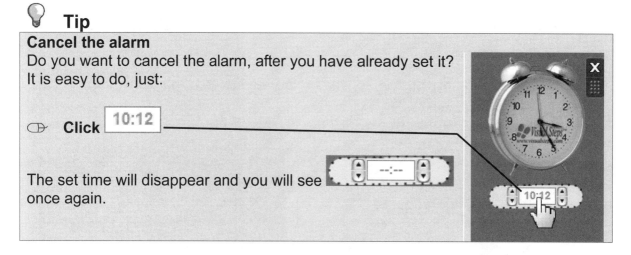

When the alarm is not activated, you can use it to go to the Visual Steps website:

☞ **Click the middle of the alarm clock**

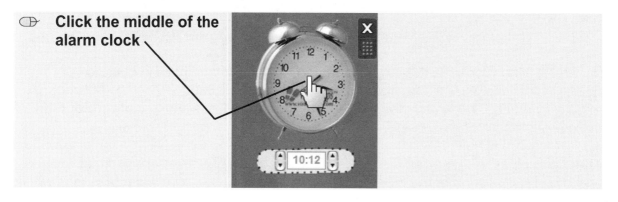

Internet Explorer will open automatically and you are connected to the internet.

You will see the home page of the Visual Steps website **www.visualsteps.com**:

Click the ▆Tips and tricks▆ button to open the web page with the free tips:

Click the ▆Free Downloads▆ button to open the web page with the free computer guides:

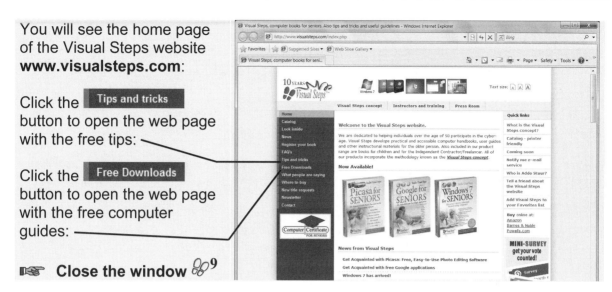

 Close the window ✃⁹

💡 **Tip**

Delete a gadget
If you no longer want the alarm clock, you can always delete it. In section *1.13 Using Gadgets* you can read how to remove a gadget from your desktop.

9.7 Cleaning Up Your Hard Drive

If you use your computer frequently, you gradually build up files on your hard drive. When you surf the Internet for example, temporary files are added to your computer. This helps to make surfing more efficient but over time it can also clutter up your hard drive and your computer may start to get sluggish. This is why it's a good idea every now and then to clean up your hard drive. You can easily check how much capacity you have left on your hard drive:

☞ **Open the *Computer* window** ✃⁵⁶

You will see the window showing the components of your computer:

The amount of free disk space available and the capacity of your computer's C drive is indicated by a blue bar and by the text below the bar:

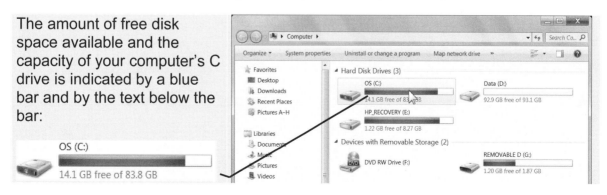

Please note!

In this book the hard disk is called OS (C:) . You might see a different name on your computer, for example: Local Disk (C:) .

 HELP! My window looks different

If your window shows a different arrangement of the icons, you can change the File and Folder view to match the illustration above. In the upper right corner of your window:

By 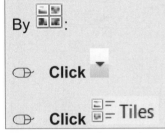 :

☞ **Click** ▼

☞ **Click** ⊟ Tiles

♀ **Tip**

10% free space
The rule of thumb is that your hard drive needs to have at least 10% extra free disk space available, but preferably more than that. From experience, we know that a computer performs slower when the hard drive is full and problems may occur with certain programs. This is caused in part by the large number of software programs that use the hard drive for temporary data storage. If there is not enough available disk space, these programs get 'constricted' and will not perform correctly.

There is also another way to view the amount of available free disk space:

☞ **Right-click**
     OS (C:)
     14.1 GB free of 83.8 GB

☞ **Click** Properties

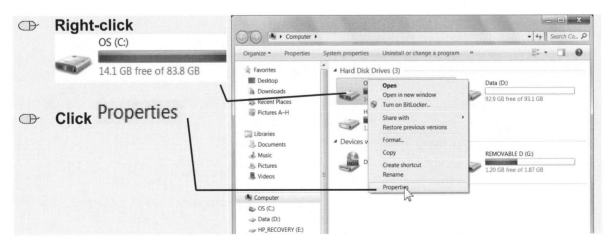

Now the *Properties* window of *Local disk (C:)* will be opened.

In the pie chart you will see the amount of free and used disk space:————

Windows has a special program to clean up your hard disk. This is how you open it:

☞ **Click** Disk Cleanup

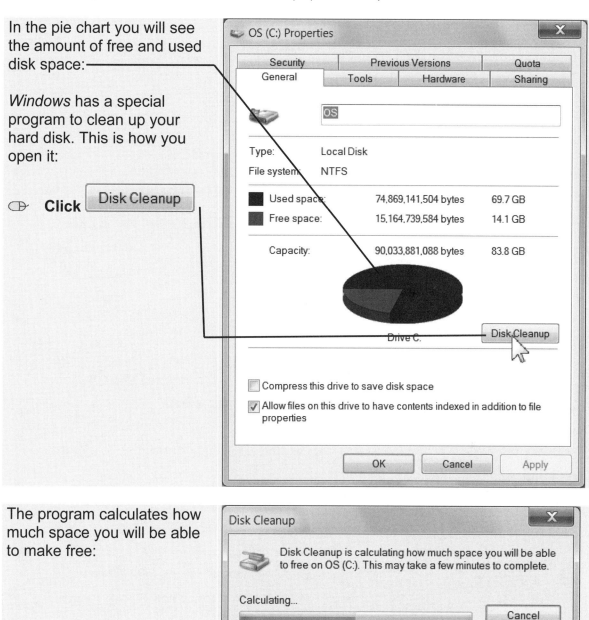

The program calculates how much space you will be able to make free:

In this window you can select the type of files you want to delete to free up space:

For instance, you can empty the *Recycle Bin*:

☞ **Drag the scroll bar down until you see** **Recycle Bin**

☞ **Check the box ☑ next to** **Recycle Bin**

Please note: make sure that the other boxes are not checked.

☞ **Click** | OK |

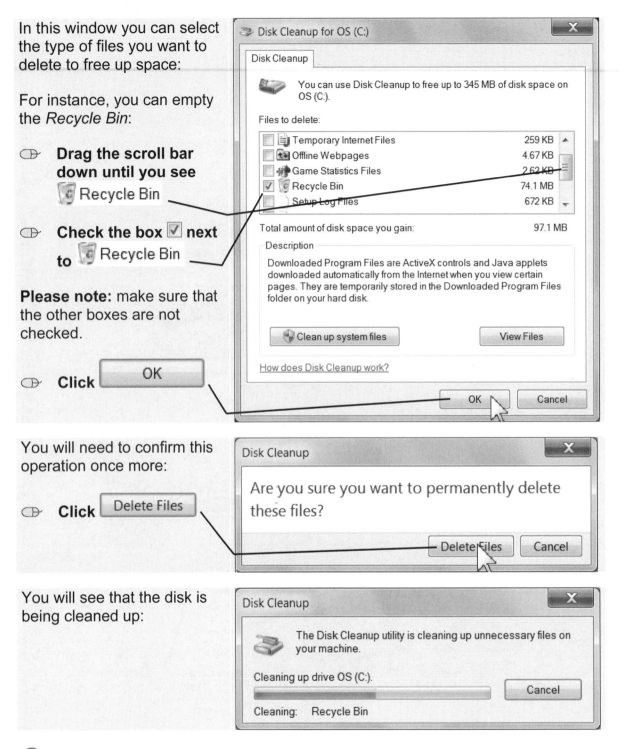

You will need to confirm this operation once more:

☞ **Click** | Delete Files |

Disk Cleanup

Are you sure you want to permanently delete these files?

| Delete Files | | Cancel |

You will see that the disk is being cleaned up:

Disk Cleanup

The Disk Cleanup utility is cleaning up unnecessary files on your machine.

Cleaning up drive OS (C:).

| Cancel |

Cleaning: Recycle Bin

💡 **Tip**

Unnecessary programs
Is your hard drive getting full? You can always decide to remove programs you no longer use. In this chapter you have already learned how to do this.

9.8 Defragmenting Your Hard Drive

After a while, your computer's hard drive will become more and more cluttered and disorganized, and it will contain lots of loose file fragments. You will notice this yourself when your computer starts to perform slower and slower. This means it's time to *defrag* your hard drive. All files and file fragments will be realigned and re-organized so that your computer can retrieve them quickly and easily.

This is how you start the defragmentation:

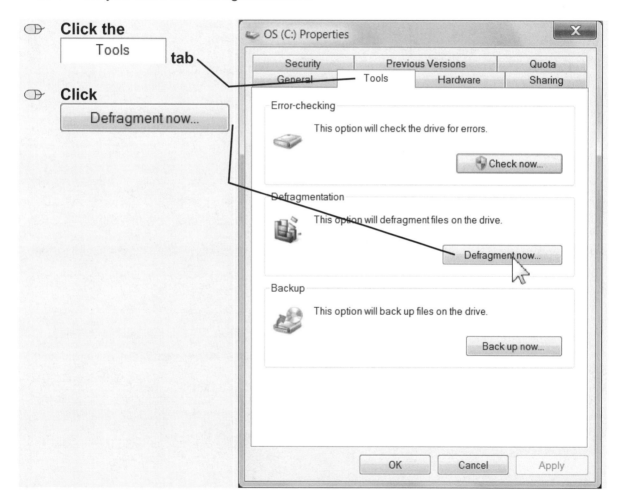

Now you will see the *Disk Defragmenter* window. First, you are going to let the program analyze your disk drive (C:):

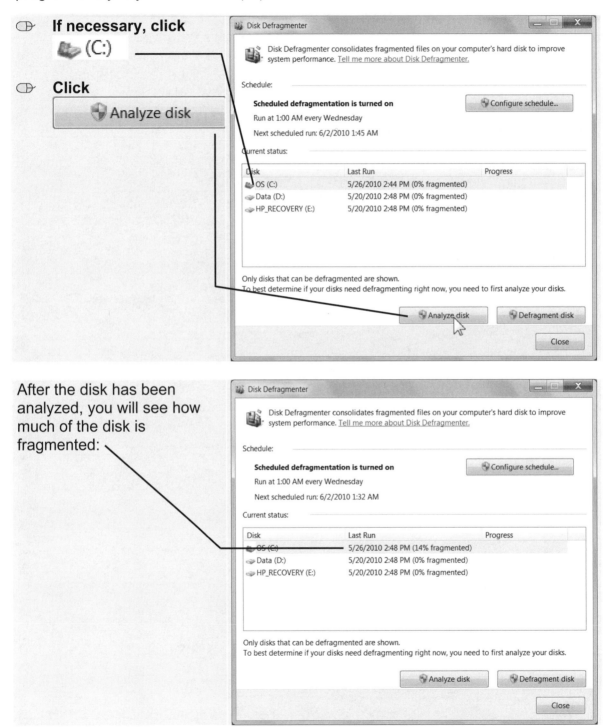

☞ **If necessary, click**

   🖳 (C:)

☞ **Click**

   🛡 Analyze disk

After the disk has been analyzed, you will see how much of the disk is fragmented:

If the disk is more than ten percent fragmented, it is recommended that you run the defragment.

Usually, the disk defragmentation operation will be scheduled to run on a weekly basis: ────

You can also start up the operation yourself:

☞ **Click**

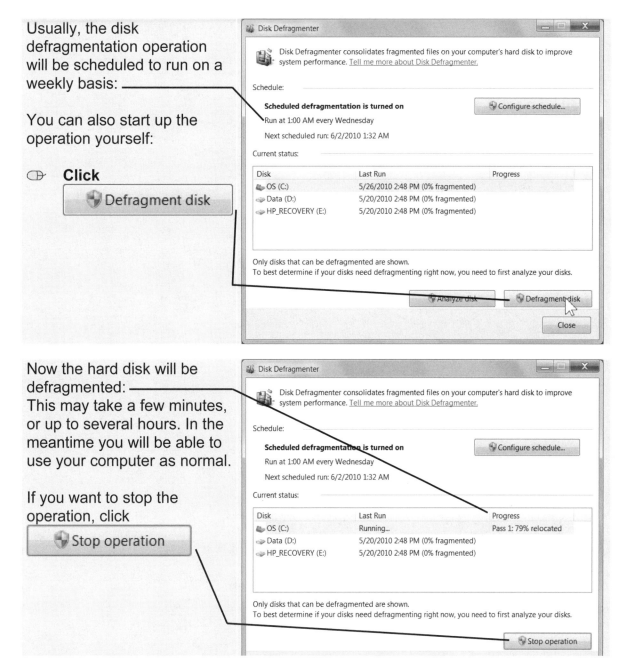

Now the hard disk will be defragmented: ────
This may take a few minutes, or up to several hours. In the meantime you will be able to use your computer as normal.

If you want to stop the operation, click

After the disk has been defragmented, you can close the window:

At the bottom of the window:

☞ **Click**

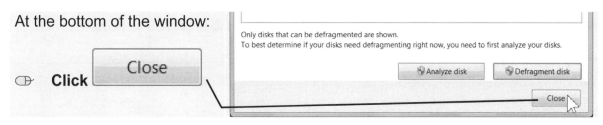

☞ **Close all windows** ✇⁹

💡 **Tip**

The system tools
You can also start the various maintenance programs in the following way:

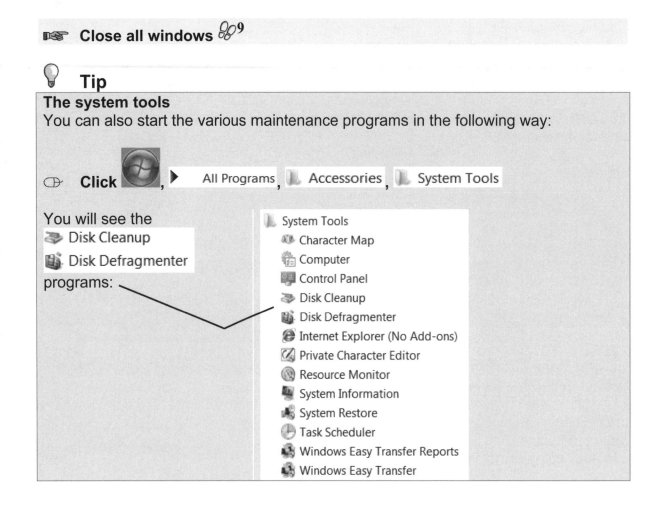

⊕ **Click** 🪟 , ▶ All Programs , ▮ Accessories , ▮ System Tools

You will see the
⟱ Disk Cleanup
🗗 Disk Defragmenter
programs:

9.9 Frequently Occurring Problems

 HELP! A program does not perform well

Is one of your programs not working very well?
Does the program get stuck for some reason, or it refuses to start up?
Always try these steps first:
☞ Turn the computer off, wait a few minutes, and then restart the computer.

That did not help?
☞ Install the program once more. In this way, all the files will be 'refreshed'.

That did not help?
☞ First, uninstall the program, and then re-install it again.

-Continue reading on the next page -

That did not help?

☞ Check the software manufacturer's website for a solution to your problem. Sometimes you will be able to download and install an update for your software which will solve the problem.

That did not help?

☞ Contact the software manufacturer's help desk (by telephone or e-mail). It is important that you can describe the problem well. If you contact them by phone, make sure you are sitting at your computer and that the computer is turned on. In this way, you can try out the solution right away.

 HELP! One of the computer's components does not work

Does an external device, such as a printer, not work properly?

☞ Start the troubleshooter for printers. Follow the instructions in the windows. In the next section you can read how to open and use the troubleshooters.

That did not help?

☞ Re-install the software for this external device. All files will be refreshed.

That did not help?

☞ Close *Windows* and unplug the device from your computer. Restart your computer without connection to the device and then close *Windows*. Then reconnect the device to your computer and start up *Windows* once more. The device will be recognized as a 'new' device and all the settings will be renewed.

That did not help?

☞ Check the software manufacturer's website for a solution to your problem. Sometimes you will be able to download and install an update or patch for your software which will solve the problem.

That did not help?

☞ Contact the manufacturer's helpdesk.

HELP! A program gets stuck or freezes

Does a program suddenly stop functioning? Then you can use this emergency procedure to close the program:

Simultaneously press the `Ctrl`, `Alt` **and** `Delete` **keys**

Now your screen will turn blue and you will see a number of options.

☞ **Click** *Start Windows Task Manager*

After a while you will see the *Windows Task Manager* window. Here you will see a list of currently running applications (programs). Somewhere in that list you will find the program that has jammed. Usually the status will be *Not responding*.

☞ **Click the program that is not responding**

☞ **Click** `End Task`

Usually, you will need to wait a few moments, while *Windows* tries to close the program.

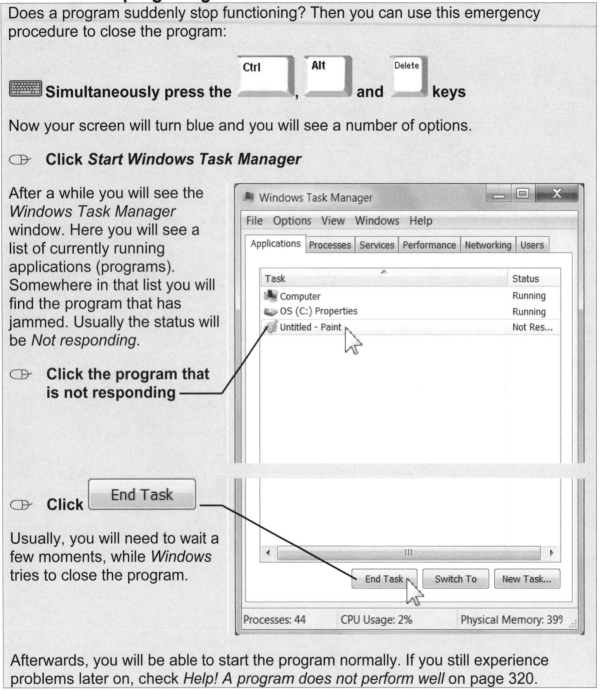

Afterwards, you will be able to start the program normally. If you still experience problems later on, check *Help! A program does not perform well* on page 320.

9.10 Troubleshooters

The *Find and fix problems* section in *Windows 7* contains various features that will automatically solve a number of common computer problems. For instance, problems with your network connection, with the Internet connection, hardware and device problems, or software compatibility problems.

Troubleshooters cannot solve all problems. But, they are designed as an emergency tool and will often save you a lot of time and trouble. This is how you open the *Find and fix problems* window:

☞ **Open the *Control Panel* ** 𝒪𝒪**17**

⊂⊃ **Click**
Find and fix problems

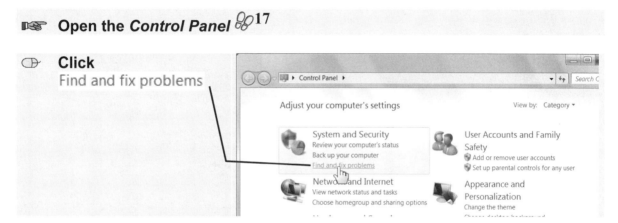

Now you will see the various tasks for which *Windows 7* contains troubleshooters:

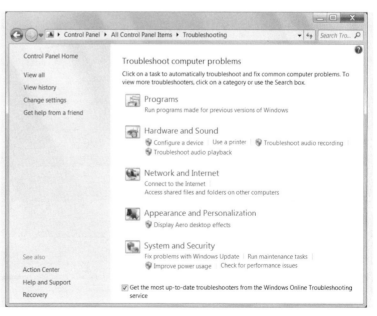

Just take a look at the troubleshooter for your printer, for example. You can also do this if your printer works properly.

☞ **Click** Use a printer

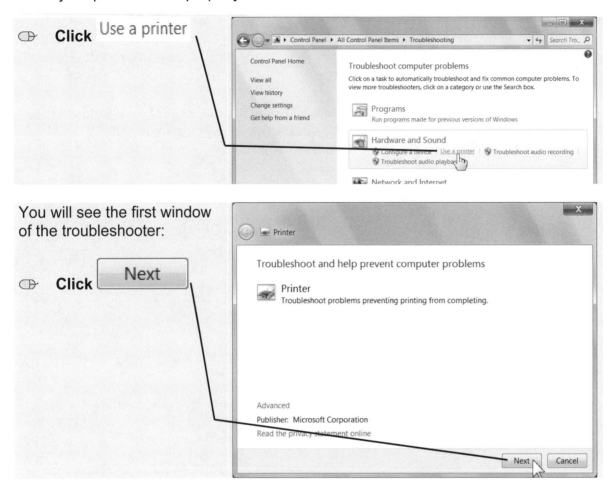

You will see the first window of the troubleshooter:

☞ **Click** Next

Now you will need to select the printer that is not working properly:

☞ **Click your printer**

☞ **Click** Next

Now the troubleshooter will check the printer, the printer connection and the driver:

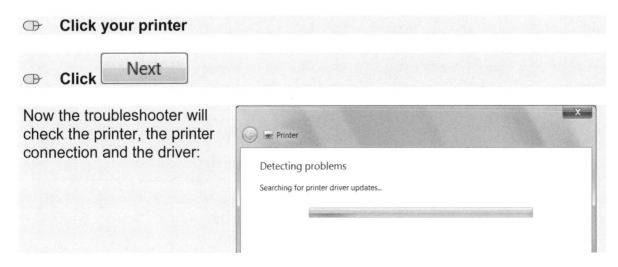

If your printer does not present any problems, nothing will be found. But if you are experiencing problems, you will now receive instructions for solving the problem, in various consecutive windows.

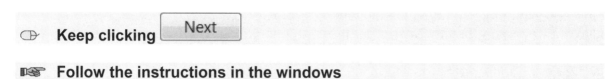

☞ **Keep clicking** | Next |

🖝 **Follow the instructions in the windows**

Now, the problem should be solved.

After the troubleshooter has finished, you can close the window:

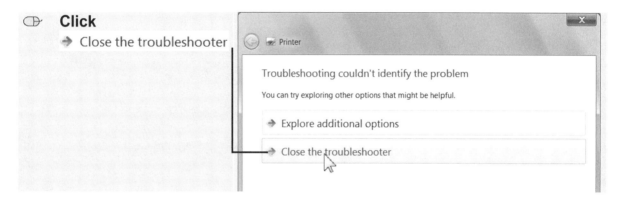

☞ **Click**
  ➡ Close the troubleshooter

9.11 System Restore Tool

It may also happen that *Windows 7* does not work properly anymore. For instance, after you have installed a new program that does not work well with *Windows 7*. If the troubleshooters cannot help you, you can also use the *System Restore* tool. This program will restore your computer to a *restore point*, that is, the state your computer was in at an earlier point in time. You can select a point in time at which *Windows* was still working properly. Such a restore point will reflect a certain state of all systems files on your computer.

 Please note!

The *System Restore* tool only records the changes in the operating system and in certain specific program files. If you restore the system to a previous state (restore point), this will not affect your personal data files. Your files, for example text files, e-mail messages, photos, etcetera, will not be modified.
This means you cannot use the *System Restore* tool to retrieve deleted documents, e-mail messages, or photos.

9.12 Creating Restore Points

Windows 7 creates restore points on a daily basis and also at important points in time, for example, when you install new programs or devices. If necessary, you can also create restore points for important operations yourself. This is how you do it:

In the *Find and fix problems* window:

☞ **Click** ⬅

Now you will see the *Control Panel* again:

☞ **Click**
System and Security

☞ **Click** System

☞ **Click**
🛡 System protection

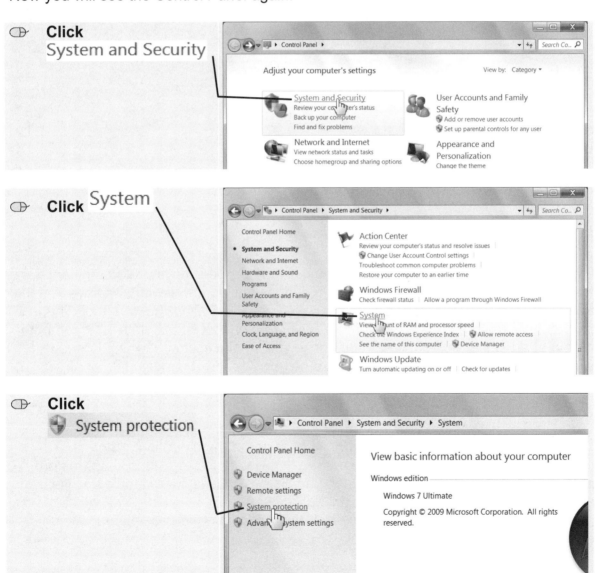

Now you will see the *System Protection* tab in the *System Properties* window:

☞ **Click drive C:**

In most cases, *Windows 7* will be installed to this drive.

☞ **Click**

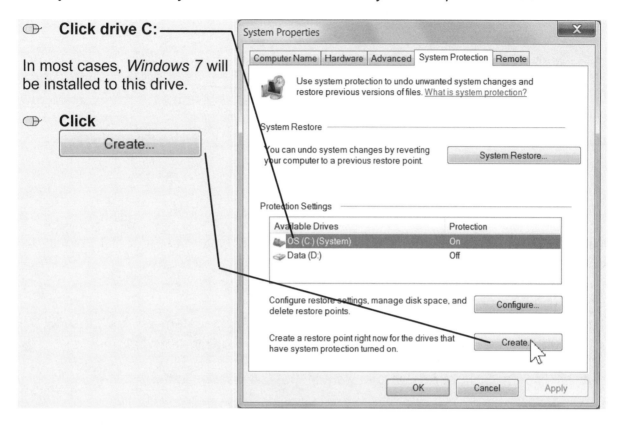

Now you can enter an easily identifiable name for the restore point:

⌨ **Type:** Practice
  restore point

☞ **Click** Create

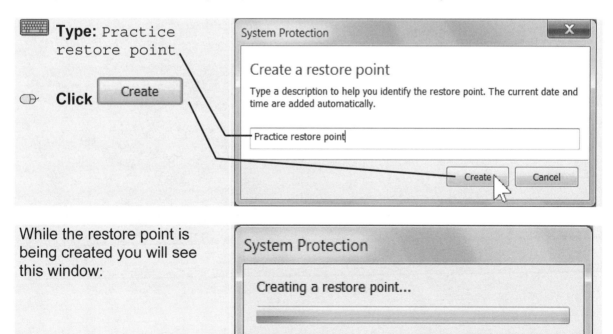

While the restore point is being created you will see this window:

After the restore point has
been created:

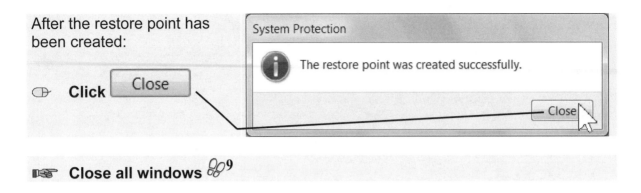

⊕ **Click** | Close |

☞ **Close all windows** 🐾⁹

9.13 Restoring the System

With the *System Restore* program you can restore the system to an earlier point in
time.

➦ Please note!

The *System Restore* program will cause your computer to restart. So, first close all
your programs and save all your files, before using the *System Restore* tool.

You will find the *System Restore* program in the *Accessories* folder:

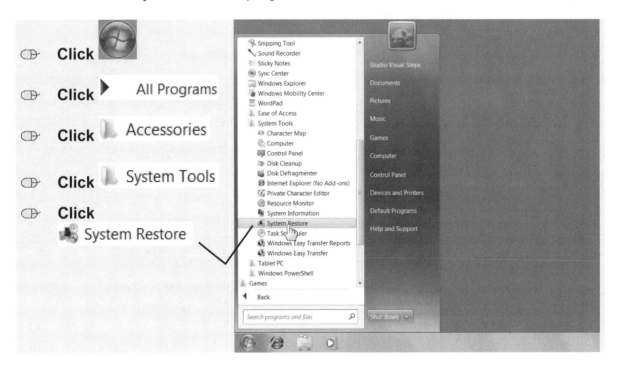

After a short while the *System Restore* program will open:

⊂⊃ **Click the radio button**
    ◉ next to
    Choose a different restore

⊂⊃ **Click** Next >

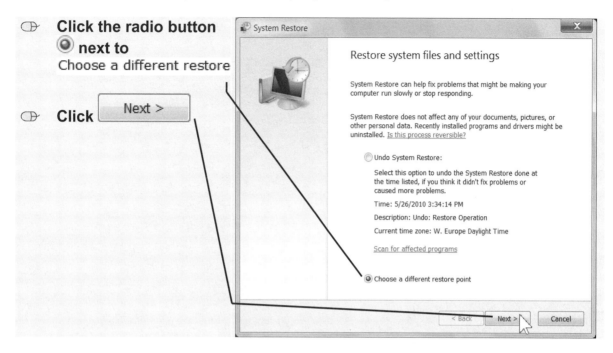

⊂⊃ **Click**
    Practice restore point

⊂⊃ **Click** Next >

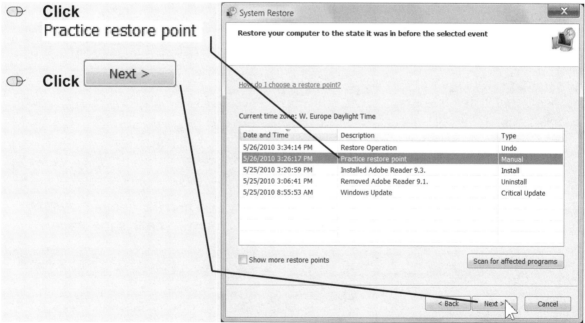

🢂 **Please note!**

By default, the program will only display the restore points of the previous five days.
If you have been experiencing problems for a longer period of time, for example,
since you installed a new printer a week ago, then you will need to click
Show more restore points to display older restore points.

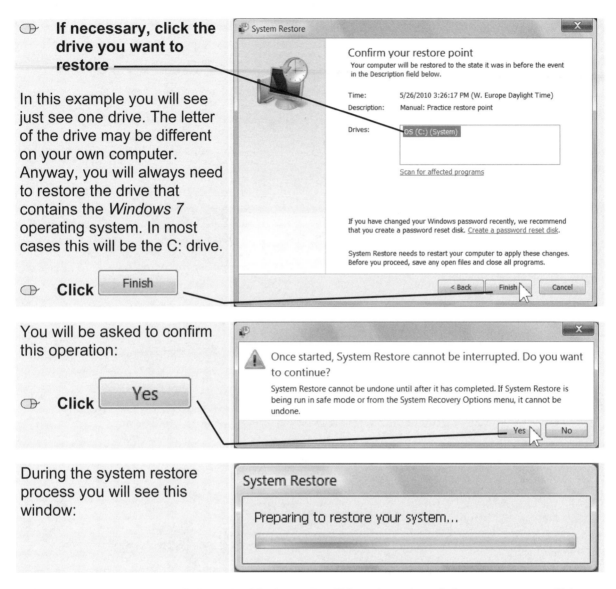

☞ **If necessary, click the drive you want to restore**

In this example you will see just see one drive. The letter of the drive may be different on your own computer. Anyway, you will always need to restore the drive that contains the *Windows 7* operating system. In most cases this will be the C: drive.

☞ **Click** Finish

You will be asked to confirm this operation:

☞ **Click** Yes

During the system restore process you will see this window:

After the operation has finished, *Windows 7* will be closed and the computer will be restarted. When you see your desktop appear again, you will see this message:

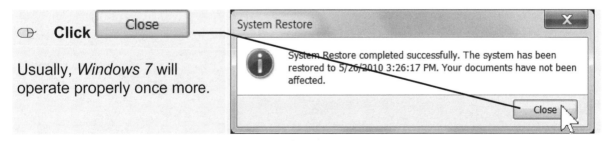

☞ **Click** Close

Usually, *Windows 7* will operate properly once more.

In this chapter you have learned how to maintain your computer. Also, you have practiced the use of troubleshooters and of the *System Restore* tool. In the following exercises you will be able to practice some of the operations you have learned.

9.14 Exercises

Have you forgotten how to do something? Then you can use the number next to the footsteps to look up the description in *Appendix B How Do I Do That Again?*

Exercise: Adobe Reader

In this exercise you can practice working with *Adobe Reader*.

☞ Open the *Adobe Reader* program. ϐϐ**105**

☞ Open the PDF file *Searching files in a folder* in the *pdf* folder. ϐϐ**106**

☞ Turn the printer on.

☞ Print the guide, if you want. ϐϐ**107**

☞ Close all windows. ϐϐ**9**

Exercise: Maintenance

In this exercise you will be running the *Disk Cleanup* and *Disk Defragmenter* programs once again.

☞ Open the *Computer* window. ϐϐ**56**

☞ Take a look at the properties of your hard drive. ϐϐ**108**

☞ Start *Disk Cleanup*. ϐϐ**109**

☞ Delete the files from the *Recycle Bin*. ϐϐ**110**

☞ Start the *Disk Defragmenter*. ϐϐ**111**

☞ Cancel the *Disk Defragmenter*. ϐϐ**112**

☞ Close all windows. ϐϐ**9**

9.15 Background Information

Dictionary	
Adobe Reader	Program you can use to view PDF files.
Disk Cleanup	Tool you can use to clean up unnecessary files on the hard drive and free up disk space.
Disk Defragmenter	Tool that rearranges the data on your hard drive and puts fragmented files back together so your computer can run more efficiently.
.EXE	File extension that indicates the file is a program.
Gadget	Miniature program that is displayed on the desktop.
Install	Copy a program to your computer's hard drive. All the files will be copied to the correct folder and the program will be included in the program list.
Installation program	Also called *setup program*. An auxiliary program that install's a software program in the correct way.
PDF file	The abbreviation PDF stands for *Portable Document File*. This file format is often used on business and institutional websites for information that you can download.
Restore point	A restore point is a representation of a stored state of your computer's system files. You can use a restore point to restore your computer's system files to an earlier point in time.
Setup program	Also called *Installation program*. Utility tool that correctly installs a software program on your computer.
System Restore	*Windows 7* tool that records changes in the operating system. Restore points will automatically be created; you can use these restore points to restore the system to an earlier state.
System tools	Collection of tools you can use to perform maintenance on your computer or to improve the performance of your computer.

Source: Windows Help and Support

10. Bonus Online Chapters and Extra Information

Now you have come to the last chapter of this book. However, on the website that goes with this book you can find a number of bonus chapters and appendices. In this chapter you will learn how to open these additional chapters and appendices.

Furthermore, you will take a look at the Visual Steps website. You will see that this website contains lots of useful, extra information.

In this chapter:

- you will learn how to open the Bonus Online Chapters;
- you will visit the Visual Steps website.

10.1 Opening the Bonus Online Chapters

The website that accompanies this book contains a number of bonus chapters, namely:

- *Bonus chapter 11 Word Processing with WordPad*
- *Bonus chapter 12 Special Editing Operations in Paint*

These chapters are provided as PDF files. These files can be opened with the free *Adobe Reader* software program. This is how you open these files on this book's website:

☞ **Open *Internet Explorer* ⬚⬚⁶⁶**

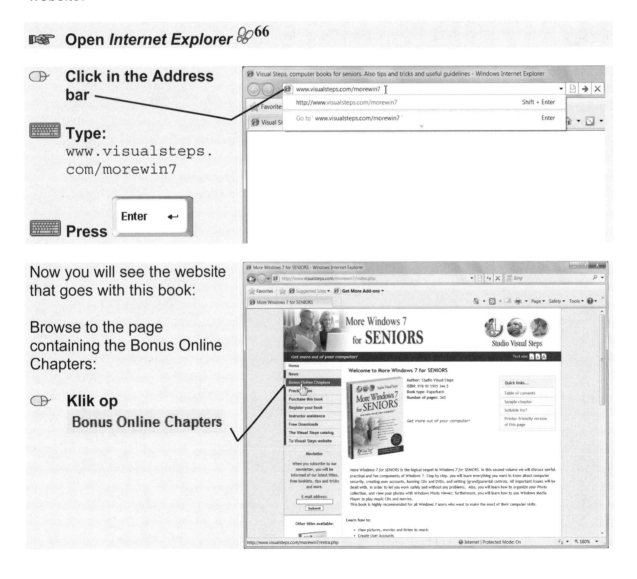

☞ **Click in the Address bar**

⌨ **Type:**
www.visualsteps.com/morewin7

⌨ **Press** Enter ↵

Now you will see the website that goes with this book:

Browse to the page containing the Bonus Online Chapters:

☞ **Klik op**
Bonus Online Chapters

Now you will see this webpage:

To open a chapter:

☞ **Click**
Start downloading »»

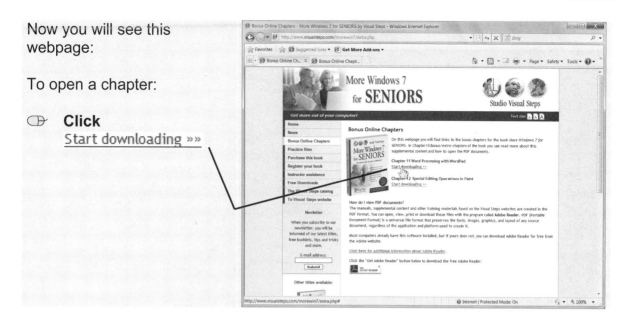

You can use the free *Adobe Reader* program to open these PDF files. This program allows you to view the files and even print them, if you wish.
The PDF files are secured by a password. To open the PDF files, you need to enter the password:

Type: 64019

☞ **Click** OK

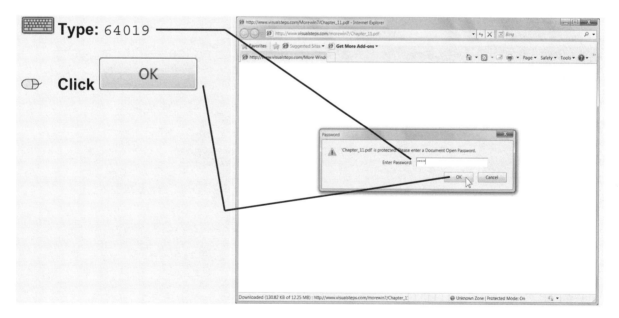

Now you will see the Bonus Online Chapter:

You can view this document by using the scroll bars:

You can print the document as well. Click the 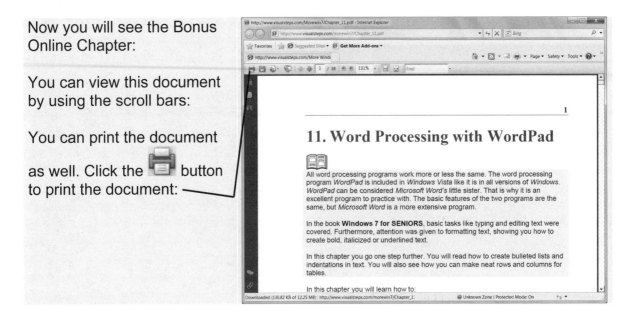 button to print the document:

You can work through this online chapter in the same way you have worked with the chapters in the book. After you have read or printed the chapter, you can close the window.

☞ **Close all windows** ✌⁹

The other chapters can be opened in a similar way, by using the same password:
`64019`

10.2 Visual Steps Website and Newsletter

So you have noticed that the Visual Steps-method is a great method to gather knowledge quickly and efficiently. All the books published by Visual Steps have been written according to this method. There are quite a lot of books available, on different subjects. For instance about *Windows*, photo editing, and about free programs, such as *Google Earth* and *Skype*.

Book + software
One of the Visual Steps books includes a CD with the program that is discussed. The full version of this high quality, easy-to-use software is included. You can recognize this Visual Steps book with enclosed CD by this logo on the book cover:

Website
Use the blue *Catalog* button on the **www.visualsteps.com** website to read an extensive description of all available Visual Steps titles, including the full table of contents and part of a chapter (as a PDF file). In this way you can find out if the book is what you expected.

This instructive website also contains:
- free computer booklets and informative guides (PDF files) on a range of subjects;
- free computer tips, described according to the Visual Steps method;
- a large number of frequently asked questions and their answers;
- information on the free Computer certificate you can obtain on the online test website **www.ccforseniors.com**;
- free 'Notify me' e-mail service: receive an e-mail when book of interest are published.

Visual Steps Newsletter
Do you want to keep yourself informed of all Visual Steps publications? Then subscribe (no strings attached) to the free Visual Steps Newsletter, which is sent by e-mail.

This Newsletter is issued once a month and provides you with information on:
- the latest titles, as well as older books;
- special offers and discounts;
- new, free computer booklets and guides.

As a subscriber to the Visual Steps Newsletter you have direct access to the free booklets and guides, at **www.visualsteps.com/info_downloads**

Appendix A. Download Practice Files

To be able to work through all the chapters you will need to download the practice files first. Here is how to do that:

☞ **Open *Internet Explorer*** 𝄞⁶⁶

☞ **Open the www.visualsteps.com/morewin7 web page** 𝄞⁶⁷

Now you will see the relevant website for this book. On the *Practice files* page you can download the practice files:

On the left-hand side of the window:

☞ **Click** Practice files

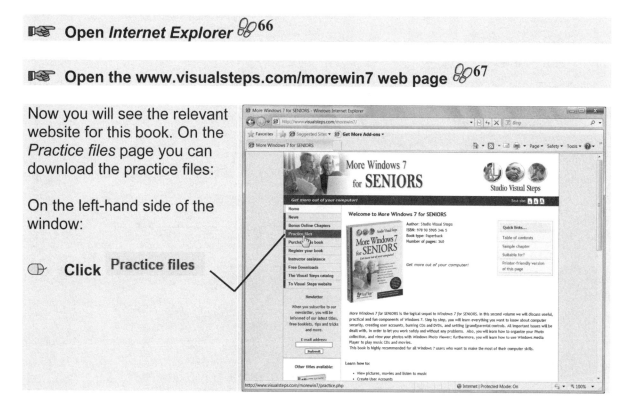

Now you will see a compressed folder containing the practice files. You need to copy this folder to the *My Documents* folder:

☞ **Right-click**
[Practice-files-MoreWin

Now you will see this menu:

☞ **Click** Save Target As...

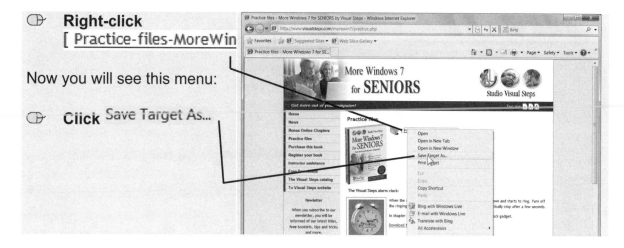

The *Practice-files-MoreWindows7* folder is a compressed folder. First, you need to save this folder to the *My Documents* folder.

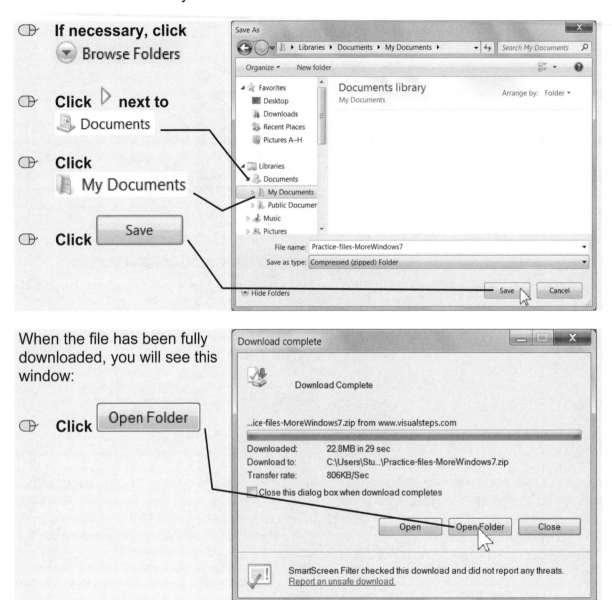

If necessary, click ⊙ Browse Folders

Click ▷ next to 🗎 Documents

Click 📁 My Documents

Click [Save]

When the file has been fully downloaded, you will see this window:

Click [Open Folder]

☞ **Right-click**

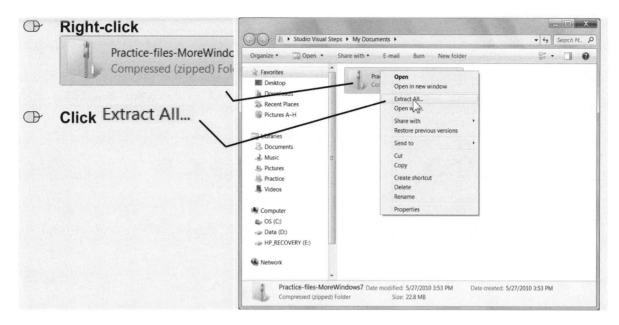

☞ **Click** Extract All...

Now the files will be extracted:

☞ **Uncheck the box** ☑
next to
Show extracted files wh

☞ **Click** Extract

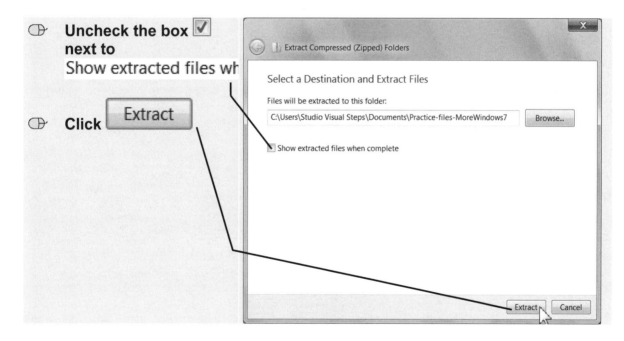

Now the files will be extracted and you will see this window:

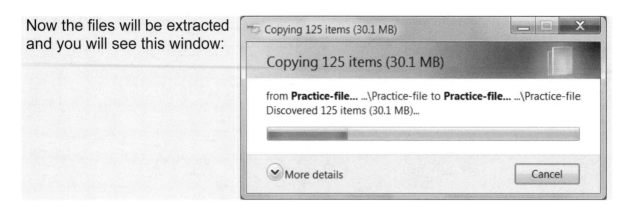

The *Practice-files-MoreWindows7* folder has been stored inside the *My Documents* folder.

You can delete the compressed folder:

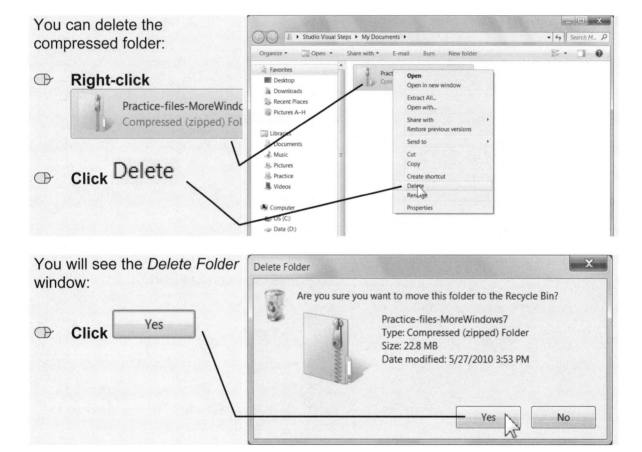

⊕ **Right-click**

Practice-files-MoreWindc
Compressed (zipped) Fol

⊕ **Click** Delete

You will see the *Delete Folder* window:

⊕ **Click** [Yes]

The compressed folder has been deleted:

☞ **Close all windows** 👣⁹

Appendix B. How Do I Do That Again?

In this book actions are marked with footsteps: 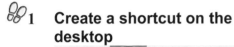1
Find the corresponding number in the appendix below to see how to execute a specific operation.

1 **Create a shortcut on the desktop**

- Click 🪟

- Right-click the program

- Click Send to

- Click 🖥 Desktop (create shortcut)

2 **Auto Arrange on/off**
- Right-click an empty area on the desktop

- Click View

- Click Auto arrange icons

3 **Pin a program to the taskbar**

- Click 🪟

- Right-click the program

- Click Pin to Taskbar

4 **Pin a program to Start menu**

- Click 🪟

- Right-click the program

- Click Pin to Start Menu

5 **Unpin a program from the taskbar**
- Right-click the button of the program

- Click
  📎 Unpin this program from taskbar

6 **Unpin a program from the Start menu**

- Click 🪟

- Right-click the program in the Start menu

- Click Unpin from Start Menu

7 **Remove a shortcut**
- Right-click the shortcut

- Click Delete

- Click [Yes]

8 **Add a gadget to the desktop**
- Right-click the desktop

- Click 🖥 Gadgets

- Double-click the gadget

9 **Close a window**
- Click [X]

10 Remove a gadget from the desktop
- Right-click the gadget
- Click Close gadget

11 Open *Windows Help and Support*
- Click
- Click Help and Support

12 Open *Default Programs* window
- Click
- Click Default Programs

13 Open *Set Associations* window
In the Default Programs window:
- Click Associate a file type or protocc with a program

14 Associate a file type with a program
- Click a file type, for example BMP File
- Click Change program...
- Click one of the recommended programs

Or:
- Click Browse... to select an alternative program

15 Set program as default program
In the Default Programs window:
- Click Set your default programs
- Click the program, for example Internet Explorer
- Click → Set this program as default

16 Check which extensions are opened
In the Default Programs window:
- Click → Choose defaults for this program

17 Open *Control Panel*
- Click
- Click Control Panel

18 Open the *Manage Accounts* window
In the Control Panel:
- Click Add or remove user accounts

When your screen goes dark:
- Click Yes

19 Open the *User Accounts* Window
In the Control Panel:
- Click User Accounts and Family Safety
- Click User Accounts

20 Create a standard user account
- Click Create a new account
- Type a name for the account
- Click ⊙ next to Standard user
- Click Create Account

21 Change account picture
- Click the user account you want to change
- Click Change the picture
- Click the picture you want to use
- Click Change Picture

22 Change account name
- Click the user account you want to change
- Click Change the account name
- Typ the new name
- Click Change Name

23 Remove a user account
- Click Delete the account
- Click Delete Files
- Click Delete Account

24 Add a tag to a photo
- Click a photo
- Click Add a tag or click the current tag
- Type a name for the tag
- Click Save

25 Close the message and do not save the changes
- Click X

Question:Save changes to this message?
- Click No

26 Open *Windows Media Player*
On the taskbar:
- Click

27 Exit full screen
- Right-click the window
- Click Exit full screen

28 Open library *Pictures*
- Click
- Click Pictures

29 Open *Sample Picture* folder
In library Pictures:

- Double-click Sample Pictures

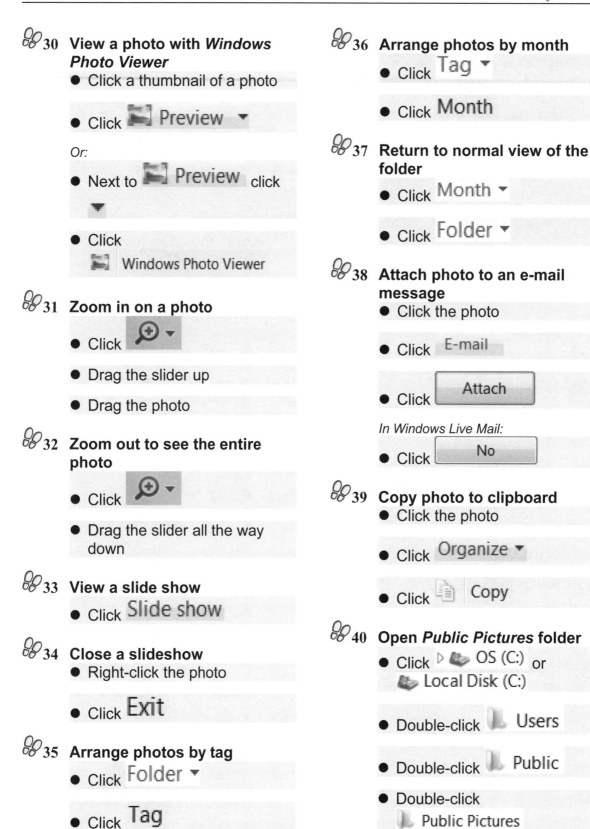

𝒪𝒪30 View a photo with *Windows Photo Viewer*
- Click a thumbnail of a photo
- Click ▦ Preview ▾

Or:
- Next to ▦ Preview click ▾
- Click ▦ Windows Photo Viewer

𝒪𝒪31 Zoom in on a photo
- Click ⊕▾
- Drag the slider up
- Drag the photo

𝒪𝒪32 Zoom out to see the entire photo
- Click ⊕▾
- Drag the slider all the way down

𝒪𝒪33 View a slide show
- Click Slide show

𝒪𝒪34 Close a slideshow
- Right-click the photo
- Click Exit

𝒪𝒪35 Arrange photos by tag
- Click Folder ▾
- Click Tag

𝒪𝒪36 Arrange photos by month
- Click Tag ▾
- Click Month

𝒪𝒪37 Return to normal view of the folder
- Click Month ▾
- Click Folder ▾

𝒪𝒪38 Attach photo to an e-mail message
- Click the photo
- Click E-mail
- Click Attach

In Windows Live Mail:
- Click No

𝒪𝒪39 Copy photo to clipboard
- Click the photo
- Click Organize ▾
- Click Copy

𝒪𝒪40 Open *Public Pictures* folder
- Click ▷ OS (C:) or Local Disk (C:)
- Double-click Users
- Double-click Public
- Double-click Public Pictures

41 Paste photo from clipboard in folder
- Click Organize ▼
- Click 📋 Paste

42 Print photo
- Click the photo
- Click Print
- Drag the scroll bar downwards

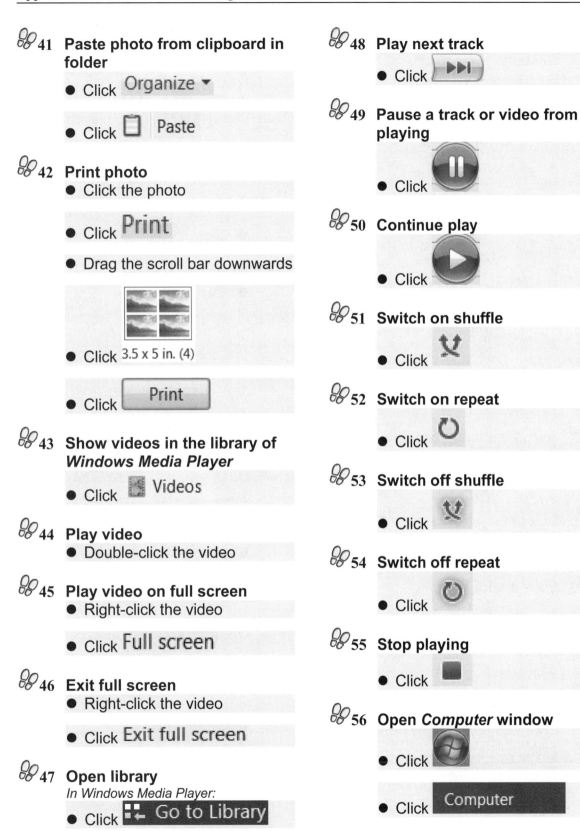

- Click 3.5 x 5 in. (4)
- Click Print

43 Show videos in the library of *Windows Media Player*
- Click 🎞 Videos

44 Play video
- Double-click the video

45 Play video on full screen
- Right-click the video
- Click Full screen

46 Exit full screen
- Right-click the video
- Click Exit full screen

47 Open library
In Windows Media Player:
- Click ⊞← Go to Library

48 Play next track
- Click ▶▶│

49 Pause a track or video from playing
- Click ⏸

50 Continue play
- Click ▶

51 Switch on shuffle
- Click ⤭

52 Switch on repeat
- Click ↻

53 Switch off shuffle
- Click ⤭

54 Switch off repeat
- Click ↻

55 Stop playing
- Click ■

56 Open *Computer* window
- Click ⊞
- Click Computer

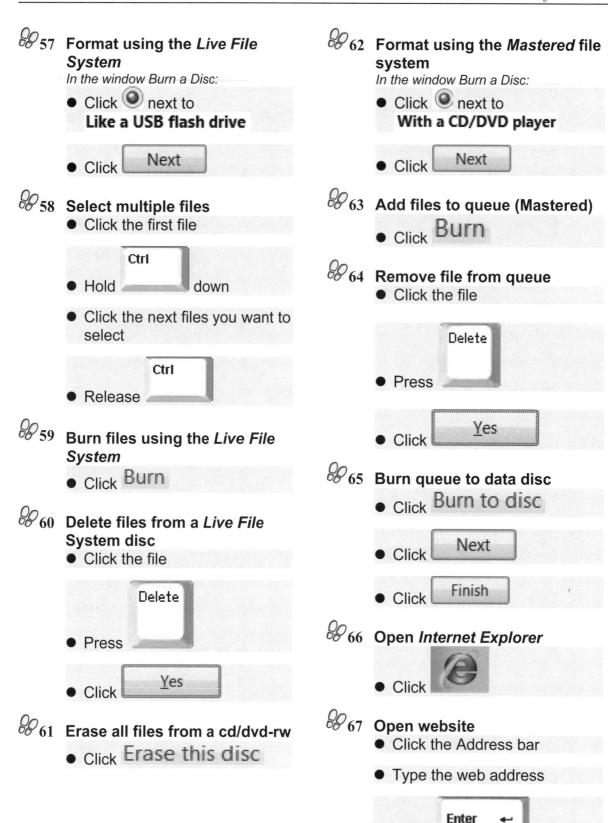

57 Format using the *Live File System*

In the window Burn a Disc:

● Click ◉ next to

Like a USB flash drive

● Click   Next

58 Select multiple files

● Click the first file

● Hold   Ctrl   down

● Click the next files you want to select

● Release   Ctrl

59 Burn files using the *Live File System*

● Click   Burn

60 Delete files from a *Live File System disc*

● Click the file

● Press   Delete

● Click   Yes

61 Erase all files from a cd/dvd-rw

● Click   Erase this disc

62 Format using the *Mastered* file system

In the window Burn a Disc:

● Click ◉ next to

With a CD/DVD player

● Click   Next

63 Add files to queue (Mastered)

● Click   Burn

64 Remove file from queue

● Click the file

● Press   Delete

● Click   Yes

65 Burn queue to data disc

● Click   Burn to disc

● Click   Next

● Click   Finish

66 Open *Internet Explorer*

● Click

67 Open website

● Click the Address bar

● Type the web address

● Press   Enter ⏎

68 Open *Calculator*

- Click

- Click ▶ All Programs

- Click 🗄 Accessories

- Click 🖩 Calculator

69 Open *Snipping Tool*

- Click

- Click ▶ All Programs

- Click 🗄 Accessories

- Click ✂ Snipping Tool

70 Select *Free-form Snip*

- By ✂ <u>N</u>ew click ▼

- Click Free-form Snip

71 Select *Window Snip*

- By ✂ <u>N</u>ew click ▼

- Click Window Snip

72 Select view *Unit conversion*

- Click View

- Click Unit conversion

73 Select View Scientific

- Click View

- Click Scientific

74 Close view *Unit conversion*

- Click View

- Click Basic

75 Select view *Standard*

- Click View

- Click Standard

76 Peek through open windows with *Aero Peek*
In the bottom right corner of your screen:

- Place the mouse pointer on ▐

77 Maximize window with *Aero Snap*
- Drag the window as far as possible tot the top of your screen

- Release the mouse button

78 View a preview window with *Aero Peek*
- Place the mouse pointer on the taskbar button of a program

- When the thumbnail appears, move the pointer onto it

79 Minimize window to its previous size
- Click and drag the windows down a bit

- Release the mouse button

80 Align windows with *Aero Snap*
- Drag one window as far to the right as possible

- Release the mouse button

- Drag the other window as far as possible to the left

- Release the mouse button

81 Open *Games* window
- Click

- Click Games

82 Start *Internet Checkers*
- Double-click

  Internet Checkers
  Microsoft Corporation

- Click Play

83 Rename a picture
- Click the picture's name twice

- Type the new name

- Press Enter ↵

84 Create a new folder
- Click New folder

85 Open *My Pictures* folder
- Click

- Click the button with your account name, for example

  Studio Visual Steps

In the folder window:

- Double-click My Pictures

86 Change the view of files and folders in a window
- By ▦ click ▼

- Click an option, for example Large Icons

87 Open *Holiday photos* folder
- Click Pictures

- Double-click  Holiday photos

88 Open *Windows Explorer*
- Click on the taskbar on

89 Create a new library

● Click New library

● Type the name

● Press Enter ←

90 Open *Sample Pictures* folder

● Click 🖳 Pictures

● Click Sample Pictures

91 Copy files to *Practice folder* folder

● Right-click a selected picture

● Click Copy

● Click 🖳 Pictures

● Double-click Practice folder

● Right-click on an empty area in the window

● Click Paste

92 Rename a file

● Click the files name twice

● Type the new name

● Press Enter ←

93 Add folder to library

● Right-click the folder

● Click Include in library

● Click the library where you want to add the folder

94 Delete text in the search box

● Click ✕

95 Use search filter *Type*

● Click the search box

● Click Type:

● Click a specific file type, for example .jpg

96 Filter search results with column header Name

● By Name click ▼

● Check the box ☑ by for example 📚 I – P

● Click the empty part under the search results

97 Open *Practice* library

● Click 🗔 Practice library

98 Delete file
- Click the file

- Press [Delete]

- Click [Yes]

99 Delete a folder from a library
- Click 1 location

- Click the folder

- Click [Remove]

- Click [OK]

100 Delete a library
- Click  Libraries

- Click the library

- Press [Delete]

- Click [Yes]

101 Delete folder
- Click the folder

- Press [Delete]

- Click [Yes]

102 Open the *My Documents* folder
- Click

- Click the button with your account name, for example

  Studio Visual Steps

In the folder window:

- Double-click My Documents

103 Open *Examples* folder
- Double-click

  Practice-files-MoreWindows7
  File folder

- Double-click

  Examples
  File folder

104 Open folder or file
- Double-click the folder or the file

105 Open *Adobe Reader*

- Double-click Adobe Reader 9

106 Open file
- Click File

- Click  Open...

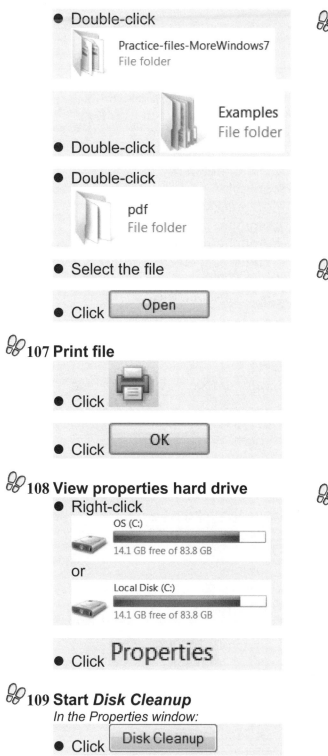

- Double-click

  Practice-files-MoreWindows7
  File folder

- Double-click

  Examples
  File folder

- Double-click

  pdf
  File folder

- Select the file

- Click **Open**

107 Print file

- Click 🖶

- Click **OK**

108 View properties hard drive

- Right-click

  OS (C:)
  14.1 GB free of 83.8 GB

  or

  Local Disk (C:)
  14.1 GB free of 83.8 GB

- Click Properties

109 Start *Disk Cleanup*

In the Properties window:

- Click **Disk Cleanup**

110 Remove files from the *Recycle Bin* using *Disk Cleanup*

- Drag the scroll bar down until you see the *Recycle Bin*

- Check the box ☑ next to 🗑 Recycle Bin

- Click **OK**

- Click **Delete Files**

111 Start the *Disk Defragmenter*

- Click the tab **Tools**

- Click **Defragment now...**

- Click the disk you want to defragment

- Click

  🛡 **Defragment disk**

112 Stop disk defragmentation

- Click 🛡 **Stop operation**

Appendix C. Index

A

Account
change name 72
create 77
delete 78
select different picture 75
Action Center 36
Activate *Parental Controls* 100
Adapting work environment 19
Add files to queue 208
Add folder to library 269
Administrator account 72, 98, 105
Adobe Reader 332
installing 299
open 302
Aero Flip 3D 254, 261
Aero Peek 247, 261
Aero Shake 249, 261
Aero Snap 251, 252, 261
Appearance taskbar 30
Associate file type with program 62
Auto Arrange icons
enable 25
disable 23
AutoPlay options 65
AVI 120

B

BMP 120
Bonus online chapters 334
Burn files 191
Burn speed 229
lower 231
Burner/writer 192, 225

C

Calculator 239
Cancel alarm 312

Change name user account 72
Change order taskbar buttons 51
Clean up hard drive 313
Codecs 189
Column headers 294
Computer 107, 127
Computer clock 69
Computer maintenance 295
Computer's components 108, 116
Connect digital camera to computer 157
Control Panel 54, 69
Create library 267

D

Data 225
add to *Live File System* disc 200
delete from *Live File System* disc 202
Data disc
burn 199
create 196
Data stream burner 230
Date and time 55
Default program 69
set 59
Default settings 128
modify 95
revert to 70
Defragment hard drive 317
Delete
file from account 79
file from disc 203
file from library 287
folder from library 289
Desktop 20, 49
select background 51
Disk Cleanup 332
Disk Defragmenter 332
Disk menu 225
modify 220

DOC/DOCX 120
Download practice files 339
Drag files to disc 233
Driver 187
DVD
   decoder 187, 189
   drive 111
   play 178

E

Ease of Access Center 56, 69
Empty *Recycle Bin* 316
Exe 332
Extension 61, 127
External hard disk 127

F

File(s)
   add to queue 208
   burn to CD, DVD or Blu-ray disc 191
   delete from account 79
   delete from disc 203
   delete from library 287
   drag to disc 233
   open 122
   pin to Jump List 245
   properties 121
   removing from queue 212
   select 198
File name extension 69
File properties 121
File systems 193
   choose 227
File type 61, 69
   associate with program 62
Filter options 285
Filter search results 283
Finalize disc 202, 225
Firewire 158, 187
Fit picture to frame 149
Folder *Windows* 263
Formatting 225
   disc 194

Free PDF guides 307
Frequently occurring problems 320

G

Gadget(s) 49, 332
   drag 46
   install *Visual Steps Alarm* gadget 308
   remove 47
   use 44
Games 255, 257
GIF 120
Gigabyte 110, 127
Guest account 72, 105
   use 92

H

Hard drive
   clean up 313
   defragment 317
Hidden icons 37
Hint 105
How does burner operate 226
HTM/HTML 120

I

Import 187
Indexing 294
Install 332
   Visual Steps Alarm gadget 308
Installation program 332

J

JPG/JPEG 120
Jump Lists 244, 262

K

Kilobyte 110, 127

L

Labels on taskbar buttons 32

Library   263, 294
    add folder   269
    create   267
    delete folder   289
    open   264
    Pictures   130, 265
    select properties   268
Live File System   193, 225
    erase rewritable disc   204

M

Mastered (file system)   193, 206, 225
Media library   187
Megabyte   110, 127
Memory card   114, 187
Messages *User Account Control*   97
MID/MIDI   120
Modify
    default settings   95
    system tray   36
MPG/MPEG   120
MP3   120
Mute   187

N

Newsletter   337
Next track   171

O

Open bonus online chapters   334
Open file(s)   122

P

Password   106, 335
    change   84
    delete   102
    set   80
Password reset disk   106
    create   85
    use   91
Parental Controls   99, 105

    activate   100
PDF file   120, 332
    open   303
Photos
    arrange   144
    filter   142
    import from digital camera   160
    print   148
    rate   143
    send by e-mail   151
    share with other users   154
    view in preview pane   132
Pin files to Jump List   245
Pixel(s)   151, 187
Play full screen   177
Playing
    a video file   174, 175
    DVD   178
    in random order   172
    music CD   167
    options DVD   219
    pause   171
    start   181
PPS/PPT   120
Practice files   118
Preview pane   187
Preview window   50, 249
previous track   171
Processor   116
Program
    install   298, 308
    pin to taskbar   34
    uninstall   296
    unpin from taskbar   36
Properties
    file   121
    hard disk   109
    library   269
Protocol   69
Public folders   188

Q

Queue   208, 226

burn to disc 212
Quick format 226

R

Ram memory 116
Rating 188
Read-only 127
Recordable CD/DVD 228
Recycle Bin 29, 316
Removable media 114, 127
Removing file from queue 212
Repeat 172
Restore point 332
   create 326
Restoring system 328
Rewritable CD/DVD 228

S

Save files between operations 222
Save search operation 285
Screen saver 105
Screenshot 262
Search box 294
   use 276
Search filter 188, 278, 294
   use 278
Search folder window 283
Search outside library 281
Select
   desktop background 51
   different picture account 75
   files 198
Set *AutoPlay* options 65
Set date and time 55
Setting(s)
   default programs 59
   taskbar 30
Setting up *Windows* 53
Setup program 332
Share documents 83
Shortcut(s) 21, 49
   change icon 27
   copy from desktop 35

create 21
delete 29
display 37
move 23
on taskbar 34
Shuffle 188
Sleep state 106
Slide show 188
   view 138, 139
Snip 262
Snipping tool 237, 262
Standard (user) account 72, 98, 106
Start menu 21
   modify 42
Sticky Note(s) 236, 262
Switch between users 93
System management 295
System Restore 325, 332
System tools 320, 332
System tray 49
   modify 36

T

Tags 188
   use 140, 145
Taskbar 49
   set 30
Taskbar button 31, 49
Thumbnail 188
TIF/TIFF 120
Time limits 106
Tracks 169, 188
Troubleshooters 323
Turn off volume 170
TXT 120
Types
   CD and DVD discs 112, 228
   files 120
   user accounts 72

U

Uninterruptible Power Supply (UPS) 230
Upgrade 127

USB   188
  port   106
  stick   87, 106, 127
User account   71, 105
  change name   72
  change password   84
  change picture   75, 76
  create   77
  delete   78
  select password   80
User Account Control   97, 105
  messages   97
  settings   98

V

Video DVD   225
View computer's performance   117
View contents disc with *Windows
Explorer*   214
Visual Steps website/Newsletter   337
Volume   171

W

WAV   120
WMA   120
WMV   120
Windows
  maximize with *Aero Snap*   251
  align with *Aero Snap*   252
Windows
  does not recognize camera   159
  setting up   53
Windows DVD Maker   215, 226
Windows Explorer   214, 226, 263, 294
Windows Help and Support   58
Windows Media Player   188
  maximize   175
  open   165
  view   169
*Windows Photo
Viewer*   133, 137, 139, 188
Windows 7 programs/features   235

X

XLS/XLSX   120

Z

Zoom in/out   135, 188

Picasa for SENIORS

Picasa for SENIORS
Get Acquainted with Picasa: Free, Easy-to-Use
Photo Editing Software

Author: Studio Visual Steps
ISBN: 978 90 5905 246 8
Book type: Paperback
Number of pages: 264
Accompanying website:
www.visualsteps.com/picasa

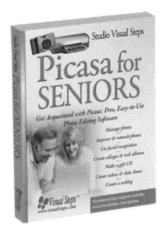

Are you looking for a handy and free photo management program? In that case the popular Picasa is an excellent choice! Picasa offers extended functionality for organizing and presenting your photo collection. It also offers several useful editing options. With just a few mouse clicks you can improve color quality and remove undesirable "red eyes". You can crop or straighten photos in a few seconds, print them or create a slide show. In order to safeguard your photos you can burn them to a CD or DVD. You can make internet web albums or publish your photos to your own blog. In other words, Picasa offers exactly what you are looking for: an easy way to manage, edit and present your photo collection.

Characteristics of this book:
- practical, useful topics
- geared towards the needs of the self-employed, independent contractor or freelancer
- clear instructions that anyone can follow
- handy, ready-made templates available on this website

You will learn how to:
- manage photos
- improve and retouch photos
- create collages and web albums
- make a gift CD
- create videos and slide shows
- create a blog

Google for SENIORS

Google for SENIORS
Get Acquainted with free Google applications

Author: Studio Visual Steps
ISBN: 978 90 5905 236 9
Book type: Paperback
Number of pages: 320
Accompanying website:
www.visualsteps.com/google

Google for SENIORS guides you through some of the most popular Google products. Google Search not only makes it easy to find something on the Internet, but you can also use it to search your own computer as well. With Google Earth you can check out your vacation destination in advance from a bird's eye view and with Google Maps you can plan your route to it.

Other topics explained in this book include learning how to create an agenda that can be managed and consulted online. Chat and make phone calls free of charge with Google Talk. Publish an online diary or a travel journal with Blogger and create a simple website with Google Sites.

Google also offers a simple word processor that allows you to save your documents online and lets you view and check them from any computer that is connected to the internet. For translating text you can get a good start with Google Translate. And last but not least this book will acquaint you with the popular photo editing program Picasa, a tool that allows you to manage your photos, create web albums and share them with other people.

You will learn how to:
- get more out of Google Search
- see the world or plan a trip with Google Maps and Google Earth
- send, receive and manage your e-mail with Gmail
- surf the web with Google Chrome
- create and manage an agenda or a discussion group
- call or chat with Google Talk
- create a blog
- work with Google Docs
- translate text with Google Translate
- upload your video to YouTube
- create a simple website
- manage and share your photos with Picasa